DATE DUE

JE 4 '95	MY 26 '99	MY 20 '03
	NO 17 '98	NO 11 03
JA 7 '94	AG 2 '99	JE 8 04
AP 1 '95	NO 1 '99	
JE 30 '94		DE 17 '04
JE 2 '94	DE 6 '99	JE 7 '05
AP 7 '95	JA 4 '00	NO 28 '05
MY 19 '95		NO 13 '07
AG 1 '96	JE 6 '00	AP 1 '9 10
	JA 3 '00	
	OC 18 '00	
NO 14 '96	DE 4 '00	
AP 10 '97		
	MY 15 '01	
MY 17 '97		
	AP 4 '02	
NO 25 '97	MY 28 '02	
DE 12 '98	DE 6 '02	
	AP 30 '03	

Literacy in the Television Age:

The Myth of the TV Effect

COMMUNICATION AND INFORMATION SCIENCE

Edited by
Brenda Dervin
The Ohio State University

Recent Titles

Laurien Alexandre • The Voice of America: From Detente to the Reagan Doctrine
Bruce Austin • Current Research in Film Volume 4
Barbara Bate & Anita Taylor • Women Communicating: Studies of Women's Talk
Donal Carbaugh • Talking American: Cultural Discourses on Donahue
Kathryn Carter & Carole Spitzack • Doing Research on Women's Communication: Perspectives on Theory and Method
Fred L. Casmir • Communication in Development
Gladys Ganley & Oswald Ganley • To Inform or to Control Revised Edition
Robert Goldman & Arvind Rajagopal • Mapping Hegemony: Television News Coverage of Industrial Conflict
Enrique Gonzalez-Manet • The Hidden War of Information
Karen Joy Greenberg • Conversations on Communications Ethics
Gary Gumpert & Sandra Fish • Talking to Strangers: Mediated Therapeutic Communication
Robert Jacobson • An "Open" Approach to Information Policymaking
Manfred Kochen • The Small World
John Lawrence and Bernard Timberg • Fair Use and Free Inquiry Second Edition
Sven B. Lundstedt • Telecommunications, Values, and the Public Interest
Thomas Mandeville • Understanding Novelty: Information Technological Changes and the Patent System
Richard Morris & Peter Ehrenhaus • Cultural Legacies of Vietnam: Uses of the Past in the Present
Susan B. Neuman • Literacy in the Television Age
Eli M. Noam & Joel C. Millonzi • The International Market in Film and Television Programs
Eli M. Noam & Gerald Pogorel • Asymmetric Deregulation: The Dynamics of Telecommunication Policy
Gerald M. Phillips • Teaching How to Work in Groups
Carl Erik Rosengren & Sven Windahl • Media Matter: TV Use in Childhood and Adolescence
Michael Rogers Rubin • Private Rights, Public Wrongs: The Computer and Personal Privacy
Ramona R. Rush & Donna Allen • Communications at the Crossroads. The Gender Gap Connection
Majid Tehranian • Technologies of Power: Information Machines and Democratic Processes
Sari Thomas • Studies in Mass Media and Technology, Volumes 1–4
J. M. Wober • Fission and Diffusion: The Possibility of Public Power Over and Through the Machine

Literacy in the Television Age:

The Myth of the TV Effect

Susan B. Neuman

Temple University

 ABLEX PUBLISHING CORPORATION
NORWOOD, NEW JERSEY

Cover design by Thomas Phon Graphics

Library of Congress Cataloging-in-Publication Data

Neuman, Susan B.
    Literacy in the television age / Susan B. Neuman.
        p.   cm. —(Communication and information science)
    Includes bibliographical references and index.
    ISBN 0-89391-485-1 (cloth)
    1. Television and children—United States.   2. Literacy—United
States.   I. Title.   II. Series.
HQ784.T4N42   1991
302.23'45'083—dc20   90-26123
                                                                        CIP

Ablex Publishing Corporation
355 Chestnut Street
Norwood, New Jersey 07648

To W.R.N.

Table of Contents

Acknowledgments

I wish to thank all the people who have helped and nourished my interest in children and television. From the very beginning of my research at the Yale University Family Television Research and Consultation Center, I have had the pleasure of working with so many fine teachers and children, making my efforts to learn about the relationship between television and literacy in classrooms and families, a truly worthwhile experience.

I am also indebted to the colleagues, and friends who reviewed drafts of chapters. They are Barbara Lee, Phil Harding, Gary Gaddy, Richard Clark, and Brenda Dervin. I especially thank Richard Anderson whose comments and suggestions improved the book immeasurably.

Special thanks are also given to Laura Lathrop, Barbara Neufeld, Dale Truman, Ann Marie Rowen, Anne and Brad Howe, and Jeannette and Hadley Reynolds for their help in collecting and analyzing data for the studies presented in the book. Thank you too, Samantha, Adam, Katie, Charlie, Willie, Heather, and Hannah.

Finally, I am grateful to my daughter, Sara, who in the best feminist spirit encouraged her mom on; to my son, David, who though reluctant at times, always came through for "just one more experimental treatment," and to my husband, Russell who got me into all this in the first place. Thank you all.

Introduction

The metaphor of television shaping and molding a generation of children reflects its uniqueness. No other medium is quite like television. The sheer amount of time for which it accounts alone distinguishes itself from others. Its ubiquitous presence in the home, its ability to absorb children into its imaginary world evokes both skepticism, fear, and uneasy acceptance from the public. It is acknowledged that television represents a potent social influence for today's children; whether it is a positive or negative force, however, continues to be hotly debated.

That television has the capacity to be a "great technology for great purposes" is widely accepted. Hailed by early media enthusiasts, television rekindled the hope of providing universal learning to a geographically and ethnically diverse public. But somehow these utopian possibilities of the medium have only rarely been realized. Like other media before it, the first wave of enthusiasm led to a far more mundane reality. Television, a potentially powerful educational force, has been used for the most part as an entertainment tool.

Perhaps it is this disjuncture between what television could have been and what it actually is that has caused such virulence among its critics. Known as the "boob tube," the "idiot box," television has been accused of promoting misinformation, twisted values, and dispensing dangerous ideas. Critics charge children's addiction to television for limiting the acquisition of reading skills, impairing social development, and lowering school performance.

The notion that television is eroding literacy is, of course, not new. Media activities have always been regarded rather suspiciously. In the 1930s movies were the target. The Payne Fund studies were designed to "definitively and scientifically" examine the potentially deleterious effects of movies on youth. By the mid-1930s radio, once praised as an "important cohesive force" in society, was criticized for becoming increasingly commercial, appealing to low level popular tastes. Even the emergence of paperback books in the 1950s caused a good deal of concern. At one point these books were described as a "revolutionary cultural technique" responsible for democratizing reading; at the other extreme, they were considered a threat, a "menace to morals," destroying independent thinking, producing "intellectual malaria."

Charges against other media, however, were short-lived compared to the embattled television industry. For over 25 years, television has been on the defensive. Research agendas, reflecting sociopolitical pressures of the times, typically centered on television as a likely target. Violence of the 1960s-1970s led to a broad research agenda focusing on television's effects on violence and aggression. Feminist and civil rights movements questioned television's effects on gender and racial stereotyping as well.

Television's influence on literacy and school learning reflects the current battlefield of concern. Calls for a return to basics mirror nostalgic images of times before television. Beginning with the decline in S.A.T. scores, followed by the alarming "Nation at Risk" report and other echoing similar findings, there is a general consensus that the schools are not providing the quality of education needed to survive in today's sophisticated society. It is maintained that the schools have relaxed their standards of excellence and that parents have relegated their traditional responsibilities to the communities and government agencies. Once again, television has emerged as a prime target. Reports Norman Cousins, "Neither parents nor teachers are any longer the principal shaper of children's minds in the United States. Television is."

Three major charges have been hurled against the television medium. The first focuses on displacement. Here it is assumed that television takes valuable time away from other leisure pursuits, particularly reading. The second is far more ominous. Followers of McLuhan suggest that television has influenced the very way people learn. "Television assaults the senses and conditions the brain to change" (Moody, 1980). The third reflects the public's concern that television affects school-related behaviors. Students' need for short-term gratification is considered a result of frequent viewing.

There are some voices, however, that have taken a more sanguine view of the medium's impact by suggesting that television may be stimulating children's interests and learning. Some educators maintain that television has opened up a window to the world for children, providing them with an extraordinary resource of information. Supporters claim that television has undoubtedly contributed to children's knowledge of current events and general understanding.

These four themes become the framework in this book for examining both argument and evidence for television's influence on literacy and school achievement. Together, they address the following issues: Has television contributed to a decline in literacy skills? Are the charges justified by existing evidence or by the results of current experimentation? Are there certain cultural biases toward television which narrowly define its uses as a learning tool? Can these issues be resolved to take advantage of new opportunities that the television medium presents?

This book takes a fresh look at these issues, starting with a review and synthesis of major studies to date which draws on literature from psychological and educational studies, and communications research. From here, it moves to new series of studies, analyzing the relationship between media and literacy using both quantitative and qualitative measures.

These studies argue that while television is clearly no panacea, the charges against the medium have been unfounded. Neither villain nor redeemer, television has certainly not replaced or diminished literacy. On the contrary, there is a synergy among media. Interests in one medium tend to be reflected in the other. Rather than compete, there is spirited interplay between print and video activities that may spark children's interests and enhance literacy opportunities.

Thus the notion that there is only one road to literacy is culturally derived. Television provides a wide variety of fare that when used appropriately, has the potential to complement and enliven literacy. The responsibility and the challenge of using television to expand children's learning and literacy, however, lies not in the technology, but in our hands.

1

Television and Literacy: The Central Issues

We remember the Egyptians for the pyramids, and the Greeks for their graceful stone temples. How shall we be remembered? As exporters of sensationalism and salaciousness? Or as builders of magical electronic tabernacles that can in an instant erase the limitations of time and geography, and make us into one people? (*A Public Trust*, 1979)

During the period from 1950 to 1960, the United States became a nation of television viewers. The rapid growth of set ownership dramatically reflected its instant popularity. In 1950, there were fewer than 100,000 television sets in the United States; one year later, a million sets were in American homes. Indeed, by 1959, more than 88% of U.S. households were the proud owners of this remarkable new box.

In less than a decade, television had become an integral part of the family. People arranged their eating schedules, their leisure time, even their living room furniture to accommodate the TV set. These changes appeared most striking in families with children, who were twice as likely to have a set than others. An early study by Maccoby (1954), for example, reported that children's bedtimes, meals, and free play were seriously affected by the 2½ to 3½ hours of viewing per night. For children, television had become a major socializing agent.

But the nature of its effects were unknown. Quite understandably, people began to question the impact of television on children's lives. What would be the effects of this massive exposure on the developing personality of the child? Did the new medium influence children's values, create passivity or aggression, enlarge or limit their intellectual capacity? Exactly what was happening to our children?

These concerns set in motion a great deal of research activity measuring the influence of television in the lives of children. This chapter gives a brief historical account of the major questions raised in the last 30 years of research, highlighting the ways in which prevailing social issues have guided the research questions asked. It describes the role of public opinion in helping to set the research agenda for studying the effects of television on schooling. From here, we examine four major themes which underlie the public's perception of television's impact on literacy and school achievement.

HISTORICAL OVERVIEW OF RESEARCH ON TELEVISION AND CHILDREN

By the mid-1950s, it was clear that television viewing had made inordinate inroads in patterns of lifestyles. Television had displaced radio as the major form of media use, occupying the vast majority of children's leisure time. Moviegoing and magazine reading had considerably decreased. Television had taken over the job of entertaining children, and had replaced playmates, babysitters, and comic books. Responding to increasing public concern, early research attempted to assess some of television's immediate effects, speculating, as well, on its potential impact for the future.

The early news was not good. The 1950s had produced a series of studies by the National Association of Educational Broadcasters reporting on the large number of crime and murder shows on television, and the growing problem of juvenile delinquency. Senate hearings in 1954 and 1961, followed by a Senate report in 1964, further supported these charges by concluding that there was a great deal of violence on television and that such content probably had a significant adverse effect on the young (see Liebert & Sprafkin, 1988, for an excellent review). From these initial reports, it was obvious that more substantive research on the nature and effects of television was clearly needed.

Attention in the 1960s, as a result, turned from general investigations concentrating on the role television played in the socialization processes of children to the more specific issue of violence. Determining the effects of television violence on aggressive behavior became the major research question of the decade. Given the potential seriousness of television's effects on the young, strong governmental funding support was forthcoming.

The Surgeon General's Report (1971) represented a massive research effort to probe the issue of televised violence. Led by Senator John Pastore, the Congress appropriated over $1,000,000 to the National Institute of Mental Health to solicit and fund 23 different research projects. Commissioned research from experts in the behavioral sciences and mental health disciplines were conducted using a wide range of methods, including content analyses, laboratory experiments, field experiments, observation studies, and opinion surveys. Five volumes of results plus a summary report, representing a consensus document, were published following the conclusion of these studies.

Despite the tremendous amount of data collected, the findings of the Surgeon General's Report (1971) were frustratingly indecisive. Summarizing its conclusions, the Committee reported:

> Thus the two sets of findings [laboratory and survey] converge in three respects: a preliminary and tentative indication of a causal relation between viewing violence on television and aggressive behavior; an indication that any such causal operation operates only on some children [who are predisposed to be aggressive]; and an indication that it operates only in some environmental contexts. (p. 11)

While this carefully phrased and qualified response in the summary report indicated marginal effects, there were indeed a good number of studies that suggested a causal relationship between televised violence and antisocial behavior. The Committee, composed of several members with a vested interest in commercial television, was said to choose the more tentative route due to the many mediating variables involved. Thus, the instigating effects of violence reportedly occurred primarily for children who were already somewhat aggressive and only in some environmental contexts.

The Report sparked a good deal of controversy especially regarding its interpretation of technical data. But even more important, it created a tremendous amount of interest in the issue itself: the potential causal relationship between television and violence. As a result, social scientists were actively encouraged through more grants from foundations and federal agencies to further explore the issue of violence for many different age levels and from different methodological approaches.

Two perspectives on the issue of television's effects tended to emerge. The first reflected a technocentric, or medium orientation. These investigations assumed that the overwhelming power of the television medium did "something" to the audience, particularly the vulnerable child audience. Children were typically seen as a homogeneous group, passively absorbing television's content. From this perspective, whether prosocial or antisocial, it was the television medium that influenced children's social behavior, albeit, in subtle more often than direct ways.

The second perspective focused on the issue from a child orientation. Here it was assumed that, rather than the medium per se, it was the child's use of television that determined its effects. Individual differences among children, their home environment, heredity, and values all played a significant role in determining television's impact. From this child-oriented approach, effects were seen as conditional, based on intervening variables. The oft-quoted conclusion of Schramm, Lyle, and Parker's *Television in the Lives of Our Children* (1961) was generally considered to reflect this basic perspective:

> For some children, under some conditions, some television is harmful. For other children under the same conditions, or for the same children under other conditions, it may be beneficial. For most children, under most conditions, most television is probably neither harmful nor beneficial. (p.1)

These orientations tended to polarize the field of television research. Study designs often reflected the researcher's perspective by either assuming deleterious effects of the medium or, on the other hand, conditional effects based on individual audience characteristics. Not surprisingly, network sponsored research following the conditional effects model, found little relationship between television and violence, while other research focusing on the medium's effects claimed that exposure to television violence "cultivated" the notion of the "mean and scary" world.

Despite this activity, little changed in terms of the content of commercial television programs. Following the court ruling against mandating 8:00–9:00 as family viewing hours, violence on television once again shot up to near record levels of over five violent acts per program during prime time (National Institute of Mental Health (NIMH), 1982). Recognizing the lack of responsiveness from the networks, researchers began to go on to more tractable fields of study.

The 1970s brought in a new set of topics from psychologists and specialists' groups on television research. A small number of investigators independently began to turn their attention from television's content to its form. Following in the McLuhan tradition (1964), the research thrust focused more specifically on the medium's symbol system—its mode of conveying information, and its potential influence on basic characteristics of thinking and cognitive processing. Emphasis shifted to a focus on the language and syntax of the medium and its relation to children's understanding of television. This line of inquiry reflected a paradigm shift, from an effects model to one based on individual's cognitive responses to media presentations.

But the technocentric orientation was still by far the most prevalent in research. The effects of advertising on the captive child audience became a major new concern. Citing such abuses as Fred Flintstone popping vitamin pills, toys which came unassembled, Soupy Sales asking children to take some money from "Mommy's purse," citizen's groups including Action for Children's Television and the Council on Children, Media, and Merchandising demanded intervention from the Federal Trade Commission. Despite a good deal of public attention, their successes were relatively short-lived. Counterattacked by the powerful advertising agencies, the FTC eventually buckled to pressures from Congress and dropped its case against unfair advertising.

At the same time women's and civil rights groups entered into the fray. Focusing on racial and sex stereotyping, political groups raised serious questions regarding the effects of such biased portrayals as *Amos and Andy* and *I Love Lucy*. Content analyses invariably showed few blacks in favorable roles. Women were rarely found in the world of work. Despite these concerns, however, research evidence failed to demonstrate any direct linkages between these stereotypic caricatures on children's developing attitudes. Faced once again with the intransigence of the broadcast industry, public interest and attention began to fade.

But the push to limit television's negative impact was also accompanied by a pull to harness its potential. A second trend was a major effort to capitalize on television's popularity to teach children basic skills. Begun in the late 1960s, *Sesame Street*, then followed by *Electric Company*, were designed to provide preschool experiences and beginning reading skills to a nation of children. Bringing together experts in the fields of learning theory, reading, and production, Joan Ganz Cooney and her team at Children's Television Workshop (CTW) provided a brilliant display of television's capability as an entertainment and intellectual tool. CTW's use of formative research to critique its own production efforts illustrated a unique and responsive collaboration among educators and broadcasters. Aided by a series of favorable Educational Testing Service (ETS) evaluations (Ball & Bogatz, 1970, 1972; Bogatz & Ball, 1971), *Sesame Street* and *Electric Company* were viewed as potential new vehicles to eliminate educational inequality.

Subsequent analysis of these summative evaluations, however, cast some doubt as to whether *Sesame Street*, in particular, was as effective as originally presumed. In 1975 reporting on a secondary analysis of the original Ball and Bogatz evaluations, Thomas Cook and his associates found that, contrary to narrowing the educational gap between advantaged and disadvantaged learners, *Sesame Street* had actually widened it (Cook et al., 1975). Thus, in contrast to original expectations, it was the children from advantaged homes that were more likely to watch *Sesame Street* than those from disadvantaged households. Further, once statistical controls for socioeconomic status were employed, learning gains, without parental intervention, proved to be quite small.

Though perhaps not the cure for educational inequality, *Sesame Street* did have a profound effect on young children's preparation for schooling (Minton, 1972). Preschool-kindergarten curricula were updated on the presumption that children already knew basic reading readiness principles taught on television. Yet despite these laudatory efforts, *Sesame Street* became open season to criticism from a number of educators and psychologists. Once again, television was embroiled in controversy.

It was the television medium itself that was the source of public skepticism. During the next several years, a number of mass market books were published, bringing the issue of television's effects to greater public attention. Among the most popular were *The Plug-In Drug* by Marie Winn (1977), *Remote Control* by Frank Mankiewicz and Joel Swerdlow (1978), *The Show and Tell Machine* by Rose Goldsen (1977), and *Four Arguments For the Elimination of Television*, by Jerry Mander (1978). All had a similar argument: Television was not only bad for our children, but dangerous.

These books relied heavily on anecdotal evidence, interspersed with research (often uncited) when needed to support its themes. Each attempted to present an interestingly persuasive case by weaving together selected scientific findings and good common sense. Winn, for example, writes:

> Reading is a two-way process: the reader can also write; television viewing is a one-way street, the viewer cannot create television images. Books are ever available, ever controllable. Television controls. (p. 64)

Mankiewicz and Swerdlow, purporting to provide a definitive analysis of research on television's effects, find the task too difficult:

> Television is too much with us, too much an irreplaceable part of our lives, too ingrained in our own thinking and too central to our verbal and cognitive pattern. It is impossible to provide totally unimpeachable scientific data because television has affected everyone, tester and test subject, as well as skeptic. (p. 240)

Even *Sesame Street* did not escape their wrath. "Sesame Street teaches them [children] to read not books but television" (p. 245) reports Rose Goldsen. What appeared to be most disturbing to these writers was its very success. Teachers reportedly felt in competition with the program. "Whenever I start a project or a lesson, I have the children's attention for about two minutes . . . Unless I arrange for some sort of film or slide show, I lose them" (Mankiewicz & Swerdlow, 1978, pp. 219-220). The novelty and lively action of *Sesame Street*, according to these critics, appeared to threaten the traditional structure and methods of teaching in the schools.

News magazines, as well, contributed to growing public concerns. Claiming that TV was "turning kids minds to mush, and their psyches toward mayhem," one *Newsweek* article argued that the "U.S. was spawning a generation of semi-literates" (February 21, 1977). Students spent their days not reading, but sitting catatonic before "the flicking blue parent." *U.S. News & World Report* (1981), in a similar vein, reported on "vidkid virus." Television was viewed as a uniform evil.

These publications all shared a common theme regarding television's effects on young children. There was a strong and unquestionable assumption that the content of television had a direct and undifferentiated impact on children. Reflecting this medium-orientation, it was assumed that all children were affected in similar ways regardless of their needs, prior knowledge, or background. No one was impervious to its effects.

These books sparked a public debate among parents, teachers, and Board of Education groups, many of whom demanded some form of action to control television's effects. Parent–teacher associations developed alternative curricula, a number of states mandated "visual literacy" instructional materials, school districts became involved in special programs which encouraged children not to view. Frustrated with the lack of governmental intervention regarding program or commercial content, "critical television viewing skills" curricula were developed to protect children from adverse TV influences. Common terms such as "TV- saturated environment," "Television Generation" (always capitalized), harnessing, controlling, avoiding all became part of the natural vocabulary used to describe television.

Continuing reports of the decline in S.A.T scores provided a frightening indicator of the potential effects of television on learning and school achievement. As reported in the NIMH report (1982), excessive viewing was named by 49% in a Gallup poll as the cause of the poor quality of education. A flurry of research activity began, examining television's impact on children's reading and school performance. Unlike the issue of televised violence, however, no particular research community formed to explore the issue in greater depth. Television's potential impact on school learning attracted no strong financial support from governmental agencies or private foundations. Rather, single studies based on small samples, conducted by teachers, educational researchers, advertising personnel, and librarians became the rule rather than the exception. Due to the timeliness of the issue, these reports were as likely to appear in the *Journal of Educational Research* as they were in *Family Circle, Psychology Today,* and *TV Guide.*

Furthermore, because few were truly versed in mass media research, study designs did not reflect sophisticated theories of media impact. Causal relationships were attributed to correlational studies. Case studies, involving either the researcher's child or selected classroom students, were reported. Quasiexperimental studies were often more closely related to action research. In addition, at times the issue of bias strongly flavored research designs. The question became not whether television influenced achievement; rather it was how to prove its devastating effects on the child.

By the 1980s, public interest in the question of television's influence had peaked. Only a smattering of articles were published in popular magazines or journals. Fewer conference presentations were given. Schools abandoned critical television viewing curricula. The 10-year update of the Surgeon General's Report, supported by NIMH (1982), served as a virtual finale to a concerted group effort to assess a broad spectrum of effects on behavior. Many researchers believed that, considering the constraints of conducting experimental research on television, the answers summarized in that research were probably as definitive as could be attained. In addition, interest in television began to wane with the rise of the new computer technology, and the promise of new available research dollars.

The decline in research interest, however, does not suggest that the issue of television's influence on school learning has been resolved. Rather, it has become quite clear that research results, no matter how definitive, would not effectively change deeply ingrained television habits, nor the character of network television. Even television's new evolutions, promising to adjust children's viewing habits in the form of cable television, MTV, and videotape recorders has not significantly reversed this trend; research activity in the last few years, with the exception of a few centers, has remained rather sparse.

In summary, the last 30 years produced a massive number of research studies on television's impact. Recognizing that television was a major socializing influence, research first focused on the question of televised violence, then turned to other potentially negative influences including advertising and social stereotyping. At the same time, the educational possibilities of using television to teach cognitive skills were also explored, most notably through *Sesame Street* and *Electric Company.* Their success signaled a brief respite for the embattled television industry. Research priorities shifted slightly from the antisocial to the more prosocial effects of television.

Renewed concerns for the quality of school education, however, made television once again the target. Short of doing away with the television set, schools rushed to develop curricula on television literacy and critical viewing skills. But the NIMH's prediction that "television would probably become more and more important in all educational systems" (p. 79) did not hold true. The momentum of research productivity achieved in the 1970s, was not to be continued in the 1980s. As national achievement test scores began to rise, interest in television effects on schooling declined. To date, there has been no systematic analysis of television's impact on schooling. While its role as a formidable educator whose effects are both pervasive and cumulative is widely believed, the magnitude of these effects is still unknown. Clearly it is time to answer these critical questions.

THE CENTRAL ISSUES

This section describes the central theories that relate television to literacy and school achievement. These theories reflect one commonality. None of them hypothesizes that viewing directly affects academic performance. Rather, each details a mechanism to describe how television might indirectly relate to achievement by affecting what children might bring to and take away from school.

One must approach this literature cautiously on several grounds. First, very little of the empirical research actually bears on a particular theory. Many studies have examined the number of television hours and school performance without concern for why such a relationship might occur. There might be an underlying assumption that television is displacing more academic pursuits, but these issues are neither specifically stated nor adequately measured. Second, a good deal of the literature, purporting at times to be qualitative research, is strictly anecdotal. Typical of this writing, for example, Moody (1980) bases her inferences of television effects on interviews from such experts as journalists, psychiatrists, and one hypnotist. Third, there is a common assumption that print is the intellectually superior medium. Television, in most of its guises, is thought to be antithetical to school learning. The literature, therefore, reflects a disproportionate emphasis on the negative impact of television. Few researchers or writers have focused their energies on examining its potentially constructive influences. Finally, television's effects on schooling have been narrowly defined and measured, focusing, for the most part, on reading achievement scores. Relationships between viewing and children's interests in reading or achievement in other subject matter, including science, social studies, and geography have not been explored.

Four major themes are found throughout the literature. This section will briefly describe each theory, summarizing the proposed linkage between television, literacy, and school learning. Evidence for the validity of these issues will be dealt with in subsequent chapters.

Television Takes Time Away From Other Leisure Pursuits: The Displacement Theory

Displacement—a common theme throughout the literature—refers to the reorganization of activities which occur as a result of the time spent watching television. Based on bench-mark studies by Schramm, Lyle, and Parker (1961) and Himmelweit, Oppenheim, and Vince (1958) of the introduction of television in a new community, the theory was originally formulated to account for the uneven substitution of other media activities as a result of television. This overall pattern of displacement led to the principle of functional similarity; children confronted with multiple leisure alternatives sacrificed those media activities appearing to satisfy the same needs as television, only less efficiently or effectively. Media, determined to be functionally different, however, remained unaffected by television. Thus, for example, television's cartoons clearly displaced comic books, but book reading serving a different function, remained unaffected.

Since then, the theory of displacement has been further extended to include other activities outside the realm of media. Studies reporting on displacement have looked at the relation between the time spent television viewing and many leisure activities, including free play, reading, and homework (Brown, Cramond, & Wilde, 1974; Furu, 1971; Hornik, 1978; Murray & Kippax, 1978; Williams, 1986). These studies reflect two major concerns: (a) that the sheer amount of time spent viewing means that children do not have time to be involved in other activities, and (b) that the amount of time spent on such a passive recreational activity means that other, more worthwhile pursuits are being forfeited or neglected. One issue, therefore, deals with the quantity of available time spent viewing; the other deals with the quality of that time.

These two concerns, however, are inextricably combined due to the nature of the medium. Once the decision has been made to view, a rather narrow range of content choices are available. Material on television is sequenced in a fixed pattern and rate over which children have no control. To examine both questions, therefore, studies must first account for the time spent viewing and the program content, and then ask the far more difficult question of whether these activities seriously impinge on the time and the quality of alternative activities.

Would children actively engage in more purposeful activities if not for viewing?

Based on what is known regarding children's viewing patterns and children's engagement in other out-of-school activities there are plausible reasons to suggest why television, unlike any other media, might significantly influence how children spend their leisure time.

The viewing of television. Television households, on the average, are reported to view an estimate of 7 hours and 7 minutes a day (Nielsen, 1987). This figure, of course, does not indicate the average viewing time for each person in the family. Sometimes television is watched only by adults, other times only by the children in the household, as well as other times when the television is on, but not being watched by anyone at all.

Still, Figure 1.1 shows that there is a good deal of actual television viewing. Most children have become purposeful viewers by the time they are age 3. Time spent watching steadily increases until just before elementary school when it tapers off slightly. Viewing increases again in early adolescence, then dips to its lowest level during the teen years, rising again in later adulthood.

Television's primary function for children is entertainment. Definite program preferences appear very early with preschoolers prefer-

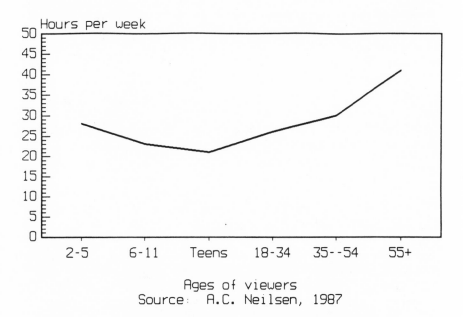

Figure 1.1.   Weekly Viewing Activity for children, teens, and adults.

ring cartoons, situation comedies, and noncartoon programs in that order. *Sesame Street* and *Mister Roger's Neighborhood* command large audiences, though for a relatively narrow age range. By the first and second grades, situation comedies dominate the list of preferred shows. The end of the elementary years tends to mark a period of transition, when, in addition to the popular situation comedies, children begin to watch a broader selection of shows including adult-oriented programming.

Preferences depend, however, on the program options available during a particular time of day. Like their parents, children tend to watch the least objectionable program, flipping the dial until they find an acceptable option. Rather than watch a particular program per se, they watch television. Thus the first, and by far, the most important question is when to watch; the second is what to watch. Since television time for children is often after school and before prime time, cartoons and reruns of familiar classic situation comedies are often the typical and thus the "favorite" television fare.

Parents apparently do try to supervise when and what children view. Bower reports that in 1980, over 50% of parents claimed to have definite rules for watching (1985). Supervision, however, tends to be one-sided; parents try not so much to positively guide viewing as much as to restrict it. For example in one study, parents reported that restrictions were made primarily to settle disputes among siblings over program choices, to limit viewing around bedtime, and to prevent children from watching some undesirable violent content. Reports from their own children, however, suggested that these restrictions tended to be kept rather infrequently (Streicher & Bonney, 1974).

Apart from family restrictions, the amount of time spent viewing is based on children's perception of available free time. A persistent theme throughout the literature is that most young people watch television when there is nothing better or more necessary to do (Comstock, 1978). Frequently, television is watched because it is easily accessible, when other attractive alternatives are not. As children grow older and the range of alternatives and school demands increase, time alloted for viewing declines. Teenagers who continue to be heavy viewers tend to perceive themselves as having fewer outside activities and thus fewer constraints on their free time.

Children, therefore, watch a good deal of television, most of which is lighthearted fare. There are no intentional learning goals, no primary objectives other than the passive pleasure of being entertained. While children clearly do learn information from television, it is incidental, like the young fourth grader who wrote an essay about why he enjoyed the *Bill Cosby Show*, "I like to see how the boys handel machuritey problems."

Other activities. Children are not heavily engaged in many other leisure pursuits. According to Figure 1.2, on weekdays, at least 75% of children's time is consumed by such nondiscretionary daily routines as sleeping, school, personal care, and eating. Weekends allow for more sleeping, church activities, chores, and television viewing for children.

It is clear from Figure 1.2 that viewing is a major free-time activity (Timmer, Eccles, & O'Brien, 1985). Only playing and visiting with friends, for the young children, consumes as much of their free time. Older children, while spending slightly more time on their studying, sports, and visiting with friends, still manage to spend a great deal of their available time on television viewing.

In contrast, time spent leisure reading is minimal. The estimates of less than 15 minutes per day have been replicated in a number of research findings for children ages 3–11 (Anderson, Hiebert, Scott, & Wilkinson 1985; Neuman, 1986a). Of even greater concern, however, are reports that the time spent reading actually declines at ages 12–17.

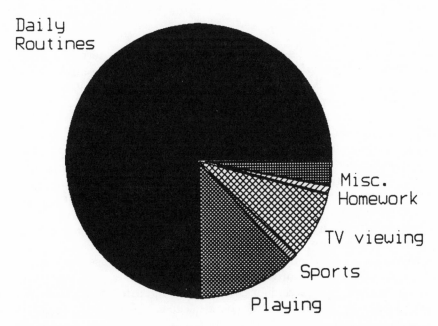

Figure 1.2a.   Percentage of time children ages 3-11 spend on activities: Weekdays.

Daily
Routines

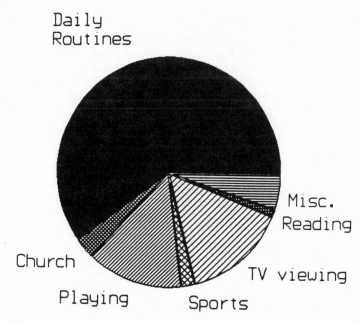

Misc.
Reading

Church

TV viewing

Playing   Sports

Figure 1.2b.   Percentage of time children ages 3-11 spend on activities: Weekends.

This decline seems to be related to children's lack of interest in reading. When children were asked in a recent Consumer Research Study whether reading a book was an activity they liked to do, 74% of those aged 8–10 answered yes, while only 59% of those in the 11–15 age ranges answered affirmatively (Book Industry Study Group, 1984). Reading, outside of the school setting, does not appear to be a major leisure activity for children at any age.

Neither is homework a primary activity outside of school. Children ages 3–11 reported studying approximately 15 minutes per day (National Assessment of Educational Progress, 1986). This amount of time generally reflects the standards set by schools for children grades 4 and below. It is more surprising, however, to see the minimal amount of time spent studying at the middle and high school levels. Less than one-fourth of the 13- and 17-year-old students in the assessment reported spending more than an hour per night on homework. Even more disturbing, over 33 percent of the students indicated that either no homework was assigned or they chose not to complete it. While there are many complex issues here at work, clearly homework does not represent a major portion of children's out-of-school activities.

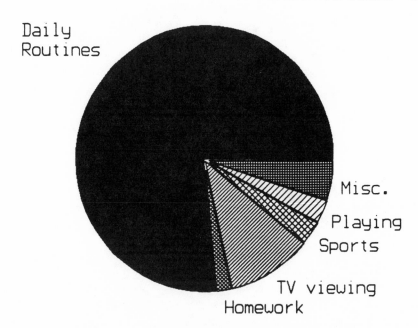

Daily
Routines

Misc.

Playing

Sports

TV viewing

Homework

Figure 1.2c.   Percentage of time children ages 12-17 spend on activities: Week-days.

The question then becomes: Does the time spent viewing television displace other activities or more worthwhile pursuits? Would children be involved in more active or academically oriented activities if not for television? Children exercise choice in how much they view, and the way they make time for viewing. They may drop a few activities completely, reduce some proportionately, or reduce some more than others. Are they reading less, ignoring their homework assignments more, not completing chores around the home because they simply do not have the time or energy to do so? Considering the inordinate amount of time spent viewing, it is not unreasonable to assume that other activities, far more critical to children's growth and development, have been displaced.

**Television Influences the Way People Think:
The Information-Processing Theory**

Television is a unique form of communication that requires viewers to extract meaning from auditory and visual symbols. These images are sent to the brain, coded, and stored to form abstract knowledge struc-

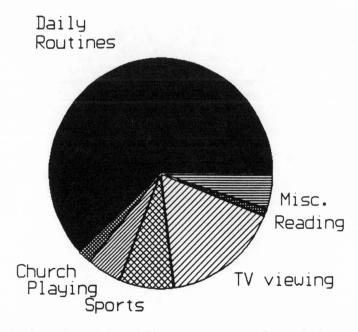

Figure 1.2d.   Percentage of time children ages 12-17 spend on activities: Weekends.

tures or schemata. Schemata provide an internal mechanism for organizing new, incoming information, generating inferences about that content, and recalling these experiences at some later point. A story schema, for example, is a set of stereotypic expectations of narratives which readers or viewers use to comprehend and predict story outcomes.

This information processing model is certainly not unique to television. All experiences contribute to the formation of increasingly refined schemata. What is distinct, however, is the characteristic symbol system television uses to carry its messages. The visual image can zoom, pan across a scene, fade, dissolve, and jump from one viewing angle to another. The auditory signal presents artificial noises, laughing, and dramatic sound effects. Further, television presents these symbols at a preestablished pace. The viewer has no more control over the medium than switching the channel or turning it on or off.

How these formal properties, working together, might influence basic modes of thinking and cognitive processing has become a major research thrust reflecting both the fear and the promise of television's ultimate capacity to influence learning. At one extreme there are the technological determinists who claim that television has had a profound effect on the information environment and the culture of society (McLuhan, 1964; Postman, 1982). Others argue that television exposure might actually improve cognitive skills, though not those typically rewarded in schools (Hornik, 1981). Both views, however, speculate that television may be training students to process information in a way that is far different from what traditional school-based learning requires.

Technological determinists. That "the medium is the message" has been one of the catch-phrases of the past two decades. It emphasizes that the medium of expression, independent of the content being transmitted, has a powerful constraining effect on the message one can convey. In his books, *The Gutenberg Galaxy* (1962) and *Understanding Media* (1964), Marshall McLuhan described every medium of communication as possessing a logic or grammar that constituted a set of devices for organizing experiences. Hot media are those which present sensory stimuli filled with data, requiring little work to complete them. Cool media are those which present little sensory stimuli, little information, and thus compel users to complete the sensory image. Print, for example, is a hot medium; television, a cool medium, eliciting high but passive audience participation. For McLuhan, television as a medium not only changed communication, it led to the devaluation of the word. Civilization based on print, from his view, was dead.

Strongly endorsing this thesis, Neil Postman argues that a draconian solution is necessary from the schools to counteract and balance the particular biases of the new information environment (1979). Postman's argument is based on a comparison of television and other media's symbol systems. Television, according to his view, communicates through analogical forms (direct images), while schools rely on the use of digital forms (words and numbers). The first form is regarded as concrete, and unambiguous; the second is conceptual, requiring knowledge of semantic codes and syntactical structures. It follows then, from his viewpoint, that digital symbols lead to complex cognitive processing, while analogical merely elicit emotional responses. Reading fosters rational idea-centered thinking, while television makes for irrational, concrete, unstructured processing.

What can the school do to counter this trend? Since patterns of communication are viewed by Postman to behave like genes which act invisibly and in mysterious ways, it is useless to try to improve television. Rather, schools must give more stress to language, tradition, and continuity to offset the volatility and novelty of television. Even with these efforts, however, nonlinguistic information in nonlogical patterns are moving too rapidly. Postman's message, like McLuhan's, ultimately spells doom for the printed word.

McLuhan and his followers have had a tremendous impact on society's sensitivity to media and its consequences. These writings, however, have provided more free-ranging speculations than scientifically grounded information. McLuhan, for example, often expressed his views in the form of pithy sayings, metaphors, and illustrations, permitting the reader to read and construct his/her own meaning. The more mundane world of scholarly research and theory building was left for others to further explore.

Cognitive aspects of media attributes. That television's unique symbol systems might influence the way children process information clearly hit a responsive chord among a number of media researchers (Clark & Salomon, 1986). No longer was the content as important as the symbol system used to convey it. Television, for example, calls upon people's understanding of production techniques, changes in visual perspectives, action, and music to interpret its messages. Print, on the other hand, requires the development of mental imagery, of sustained attention, of the recognition of subtle changes in character and plot. It stands to reason, therefore, that regular exposure to a particular medium might cultivate skills in manipulating that particular symbol system.

Salomon, in a series of intriguing experiments, explored whether some of these symbolic features could be internalized by learners (1974, 1979). In one study for example, students deficient in cue attending, were able to internalize with training the "zooming" feature on film, and thus increase their cuing skills. His research indicates that TV programs, making use of specific cinematic techniques, may facilitate the acquisition of certain cognitive skills as attention focusing and perspective-taking (1974).

But what if these newly-developed skills are at odds with reading and school performance? Television's appeal can be partly attributed to its pace, quick changes of content, and its use of a symbol system that aids comprehension. Its formulaic aspects make it a rather easy medium to use, requiring far less mental effort than the more difficult task of decoding in reading. Television presents ready-made images; reading, however, demands the construction of meaning from a more abstract symbol system. Under normal viewing conditions outside of school, children tend to exert little mental effort while viewing, allowing for shallow information processing.

Two consequences might follow. First, television's highly visual and entertaining format might lead children to an expectation that all information processing tasks require little mental effort, and to adopt television norms for undertaking new learning tasks. Second, television viewing may develop mental skills that differ from those required by the print-oriented school curricula. If skills developed by television are of a less logical, analytical, or abstract kind than those cultivated by reading, we can expect that the development of one might come at the expense of the other. It follows that television may negatively affect children's reading by developing skills that are otherwise not related to school performance.

Television Affects School-Related Behaviors: The Short-term Gratification Theory

Gratification patterns, broadly defined, reflect two basic dimensions (Schramm et al., 1961). People who defer gratification typically establish realistic goals in work and home, feel a moral obligation to save, to plan ahead, and to postpone a wide variety of gratifications and impulses. On the other hand, those who seek immediate gratification are characterized by impulse following, often prefer to enjoy life rather than to prepare for tomorrow, to spend freely rather than save, and to have little drive toward upward mobility.

These patterns were related to television viewing in a 1956 survey analyzing the social norms of TV fans (Geiger & Sokol, 1959). As a predominantly entertainment medium, these investigators found that television viewing tended to clash with people who valued traditional commitments and goal-directed concerns. Rather, television viewing as a basically passive, escapist activity, seemed to be more congruous with those who tended to seek immediate gratification. The excitement, drama, and action scenes appeared to cater to their needs to withdraw from social activity and responsibilities.

Since this survey, a generation of children have grown up with television. In a one half-hour show, children will see more excitement and adventure than an average person would see in a lifetime. By comparison, everyday life might seem dull, routine and slow. Mankiewicz and Swerdlow comment on the effects of children's changing expectations (1978):

Teachers who remember pre-television students talk emotionally about longer attention spans, greater imagination, more fantasies and creativity, less passivity and an infinitely greater tolerance for situations that are not immediately gratifying. The one-hour span of a typical television program, and the inevitable satisfactory resolution of all problems raised during that period, has contributed unquestionably to a decline in the willingness of a whole generation of Americans to postpone—however briefly—gratification. (p. 219)

Television exposure, therefore, may have deleterious effects on two grounds. First, it might lead children to the expectation that all activities have immediate benefits or rewards. Second, television's rapid pacing and fragmented presentation might induce shortened attention spans and cause hyperactive behavior. Both, of course, are antithetical to school learning.

Schools demand the practicing of learned behaviors and hard work. Classrooms tend to follow a rather routine schedule, where students are required to sit at their desks for long periods of time. Sustained periods of attention are required. In contrast, television provides no-effort entertainment, requires little attention, and offers many opportunities, if one is bored, to change the content. Considering that children watch more television than attend school, they might develop an increasing intolerance over time for the slower pace of schooling.

Indeed, some scholars, journalists, and educators believe that television, through the combination of sound effects, exciting music, and rapid-action images, may generate in children a generalized arousal and an inability to tolerate the long conversations or explanations, the necessary delays that characterize the nontelevision or school-related world (Larrick, 1975; Singer, Singer, & Rapaczynski, 1984; Winn, 1977). Halpern (1975) suspects that the effects of such fast-paced bombardment might "turn on" youngsters beyond anyone's expectations. "When children's nervous systems become overtaxed, they resort to diffuse tension discharge behaviors, exemplified by unfocused hyperactivity and irritability" (p. 69).

These behaviors, according to Halpern (1975), can be directly traceable to the television program, *Sesame Street*. The program's lively action leads children to "compulsively recite numbers and letters like restless, wound-up robots" (p. 68). In fact a number of critics, among them Winn (1977), Singer and Singer (1983), Lesser (1977) attribute children's motor restlessness and need for instant gratification to the popular television program.

The controversy centers primarily on the program's pacing. Singer and Singer (1983) argue that the short (usually no longer than three minutes) unrelated sequences produce high levels of arousal, an expectation about how the world really is, as teachers often complain, that leads to jumpiness or hyperactivity. Secondly, the speed of the dialogue on the program, the quick shifts of focus, hold young children's attention so well that information simply may never have the time to be processed. This rapid-fire presentation might lead to cognitive overload, and to the inability to think logically in a sustained manner. Children simply do not have the time to comprehend what is seen, compared to the slower, and more deliberately paced, *Misterogers' Neighborhood*. According to this view, *Sesame Street* might actually be detrimental to learning, by maximizing unreflective viewing patterns.

Sesame Street is not the only villain, however. These critics claim that all television viewing is an essentially passive, almost an addicting, experience. Children use the visual movements, music, and sound effects of programs as an "orienting reflex" which holds their attention. By using the forms and codes of the medium to enhance understanding, television minimizes opportunities for reflection, and thus for efficient encoding, storage, and retrieval of information. Because viewers watch so much, they rely more on their passive recognition memory rather than their more active processes of retrieval of stored information. Over time, skills that are not used simply atrophy. Children who do not engage actively in learning lose their zest to do so in the school setting.

They might also lose their interest in reading. In contrast to the remarkably cluttered fast-paced world of television, reading requires children to use concentration skills and mental imagery in developing meaning from text. It is a complex form of mental activity. While television viewing clearly does not prevent children from acquiring reading skills, it may draw those who are less adept away from it, by offering them a pleasurable, easy alternative. A 1978 study reported by Busch, for example, indicated that the majority of preschool and primary-school students felt that school books were a waste of time. Offered the same story on television or in book form, 69% of the second graders chose television; the figure jumped to 86% at the third grade level. Winn (1977) reported an increase in the use of "nonbooks," paperbacks designed to accommodate a new reading style. These books rely heavily on photographs, or pictures, without a consecutive storyline. Some even eliminate words all together because, as Winn argues, children seem no longer to have patience with print. Even informational print materials are unnecessary. Larrick (1975), for example, claims that textbooks cannot possibly keep up with the on-the-spot television coverage of news events, making every social studies book hopelessly out of date.

These critics argue that children's learning styles have become far too geared to television's "electronic sound and fury" to return to the quiet environment of the schoolhouse. Parents and teachers, as a result, cannot hope to compete with such exciting fare. Doerken (1983), for example, reports that children no longer appear to demonstrate school behaviors requiring in-depth thinking, skill development and practice, and self-initiated learning. Rather, they seem to desire immediate gratification, short-term goals, and try to "get by" with as little work as possible. These changes seem to suggest a dramatic, and perhaps permanent, shift away from the traditional goals of schooling and the perceived functions that literacy provides to children.

Television Enhances Learning:
The Interest Stimulation Theory

There have been a few optimists, however, who maintain that television may help to enhance children's learning. Here, it is argued that children who see a program on a given topic may be more likely to pursue these interests in school or during their leisure time. Even though practically all of children's early use of television is in pursuit of entertainment, some supporters suggest that children may indeed learn a good deal from television, albeit without directly seeking information from it (Comstock, 1980). Thus, the learning that takes place during home viewing is considered mostly incidental. In contrast to school instruction, television's teaching, for the most part, is unplanned, nonsequential, and informal in nature.

The amount of incidental learning that actually occurs among children, however, is difficult to gauge. Exposure to a particular program might trigger interest from one young individual, yet not another. Contrary to school learning, children are by no means a captive audience in front of the TV set; rather, they tend to show considerable variation in attention to programs, and program details based on their interests and their prior knowledge (Anderson & Lorch, 1983). Further, as J. Anderson has noted (1981), children's comprehension of television does not simply end when ideas are first received. Ideas are often mulled over, stored, and retrieved at some later point. For example, a child exclaiming "C'est ce bon!" when eating his favorite food may vaguely recall hearing the phrase from a favorite television show.

Proponents of the interest stimulation theory (Chamberlin & Chambers, 1976; Potter, 1976) argue that television opens up a whole new world for young children. Exposed to new vocabulary and information, television is thought to provide children with an environment that goes far beyond their direct observation and their immediate family.

Even commercials are said to furnish incidental information. Children recite jingles, learn to read key words like McDonalds, and dress in the latest "jazz hats." Examples of incidental information are many and seem related not only to new knowledge, but to even more subtle factors, including children's attitudes and values (Cook, Curtin, Ettema, Miller, & Van Camp, 1986).

However, due to its very fragmentary nature, and its relationship to the unique needs and interests of the individual child, many researchers have held back from studying incidental learning from television. Schramm and his colleagues (Schramm et al., 1981), for example, found that it was more fruitful to describe learning from the child's perspective. Their analysis indicated that children learn incidental information when ideas on television are new, real to them, and potentially useful.

Thus, the most that can be said of television at this time is that some learning under some conditions takes place. This appears to be especially, but not only, true for very young children who are just entering the world of media and school experiences (Collins, 1983). More recently, however, reports of significant positive correlations between learning achievement and viewing suggest that this relationship might also hold true for elementary and intermediate students. Moderate amounts of television viewing, ranging from 2–4 hours daily, appear to be positively correlated with achievement on the National Assessment of Educational Progress (1986).

In addition, there is some anecdotal evidence suggesting that the effects of incidental learning might be particularly significant for specific subgroups. The Gesell Institute, for example, found that popular TV shows were an excellent source for teaching story structure with those children diagnosed as having attentional deficient disorders (Ames, 1979). New immigrant populations for whom English is a second language also appear to benefit from television (Price, 1983). Though not systematically documented, some teachers claim that children seen to absorb the language and customs of their new country from watching popular television shows.

It may be that television enhances learning by directly stimulating new interests. A small body of literature has explored television's potential influence on involvement with other media activities. Himmelweit, Oppenheim, and Vince (1958), for example, found that patterns of media preferences were not haphazard and idiosyncratic; interests in one medium tended to be reflected in others. From these findings, it might be logical to assume that children who see a program on a given topic would be more likely to display greater interest, or encouraged to read a book to explore the topic in greater depth.

In fact, surveys have shown that the borrowing and selling of books related to television programs generally soar after their broadcast (Hornik, 1981). The most dramatic example of this cross-media connection, of course, was *Roots*, selling over a million hardback copies following its broadcast on television. Though far less spectacularly, many other TV adaptations, including *ABC Afterschool Specials* and *CBS Storybreak* productions have shown remarkable success in drawing children to bookstores and the library.

Based on these successes, a number of educators have explicitly used television as a motivator to stimulate reading among those students who have been traditionally reluctant to read. Hamilton (1976) conducting a survey of 253 seventh graders, reported that children overwhelmingly preferred books seen on television, or books about popular television heroes. At the very forefront of this effort, Rosemary Lee Potter, through her columns in teacher magazines and books, has strongly advocated the use of television-based interests to foster reading among her learning disabilities students. Not surprisingly, these activities have been actively encouraged by the networks. CBS television, for example, developed a "scripting" program which allowed students to view television programs in the classroom at the same time they read the script. *Prime Time School Television* and *Teachers Guides to Television* are only two of the organizations that have attempted to help teachers link commercial television with traditional school curricula.

Television, at its best, can go almost anywhere in the world to find its subject matter; it can provide inspired performers, speakers, and experts in all fields; it can use dramatic aides and music to intrigue its young audience. According to its proponents, there is every reason to believe that its lively presentations might stimulate new interests and provide new information. These advocates suggest that rather than discourage reading, television viewing might actually encourage more reading. Interests in specific subjects such as science or social studies, or particular careers including law, education, or medicine, might be introduced to children for the first time through the television medium. From this perspective, it seems reasonable to assume that television viewing could play a positive role in the development of literacy and school achievement by providing an accessible, highly enjoyable, unplanned educational learning experience for children.

SUMMARY

These four theories—displacement, information processing, short-term gratification, and interest stimulation—frame our discussion of television's effects on literacy and school achievement. There is legitimate controversy over each of them. Taken together, however, they reflect the common perception that television is indeed a powerful influence in children's lives.

We thus arrive at a paradox. Television is seductive, drawing huge young audiences which seem to thrive on pleasure and entertainment. But is it also a Pied Piper? Does its lively presentation drive children to distraction, to withdrawing from active participation in events and experiences? Does it hold children's attention so well that there is simply no time for other activities, particularly those associated with schooling? With its ability to evoke some senses such as sight and sound, does it destroy others? Have children lost their ability to learn, to interact with others in two-way exchanges, and to think in logical systematic ways? We will explore the evidence in the remaining chapters.

2

The Displacement Theory

The doom of the reading habit has been falsely prophesied ever since the invention of the pneumatic tire which spelled the end of the fireside reading circle by putting the whole family on bicycles. (Altick, 1957, p. 375)

Television came as an interloper into children's lives. Once acquired, it made tremendous demands of children's time, taking away at least two to three hours a day of lives which already seemed full. Such an intrusion required profound and far-reaching changes in time spent on other activities. With concern over its possible effects, time spent viewing became the subject of a great deal of public speculation and concern.

Early studies confirmed that television was certainly not replacing the fireside reading circles. Those activities had been long gone before television's arrival. Lyness (1952), for example, in a study of children mass media habits before television in the 1950s, found that radio dominated children's attention for as much as 2 to 3 hours a day. Children spent their leisure time seeing an average of one movie a week, playing cards, and reading comic books. Most were not active book readers at the time, reporting only an average of one book read per month.

But the exciting new world of television threatened to devour even more time and attention than these other mass media activities. These concerns led to one of the most plausible hypotheses regarding television's effects. Questions were raised about the consequences of viewing on children's leisure and academic activities. These questions all seemed related to whether the time spent viewing television displaced other more valuable pursuits, such as reading, homework, or active problem solving in the "real" world.

The displacement theory generally assumes a negative impact of television viewing on achievement by drawing children's attention away from activities thought to be critical for cognitive development. Its potential effects on literacy, therefore, are hypothesized to be indirectly related to reading achievement. Time spent viewing reduces reading ability by limiting the practicing of these skills outside of the school setting.

Beyond anecdotal evidence, however, it is difficult to build a strong case for displacement. To do so requires two sources of evidence. One is an indication that other activities are actually being displaced. For example, it must be demonstrated that children would be actively engaged in other activities if not for television. Second, it must be established that the quality of the activities being replaced are more beneficial for reading and school achievement than television viewing. Though some might speculate that any activity (including doing nothing at all) would be preferable to viewing, these sources of information are not easily attainable.

This chapter reviews these issues of displacement, focusing on the impact of time spent viewing on reading and school achievement. It begins by looking at the activities thought to be replaced by television, then turns to an analysis of the theoretical assumptions of the displacement theory. The final section of the chapter offers an alternative explanation for how the time spent viewing might relate to children's choices of leisure activities and reading achievement.

WHAT DID TELEVISION REPLACE?

One of the earliest research strategies for analyzing television's impact called for the comparison of children from homes or communities without television to those where TV was available. A study of this type was reported by Maccoby (1954) in her analysis of the consequences of television in Cambridge, Massachusetts. Comparing typical activities of television children with those of their nontelevision counterparts, she observed a number of disturbing trends. Television children were indeed adjusting their nonmedia activities to suit their viewing, often to the detriment of school-related activities. Children in TV homes went to bed about 25 minutes later on weekdays, were less likely to do any homework, and generally sacrificed about an hour and a half of active playtime to the new medium.

But it was difficult to generalize from these initial findings. After all, television was new, and children's behavior probably reflected its novelty. In addition, ownership at the time was a status symbol;

families who could ill afford to buy a set cut corners to become identified as a TV owner. Rather than measuring immediate effects, the more important issue was to determine which of these changes persisted over time. This required a massive research effort to detail comprehensively children's viewing and leisure habits on a more long-term basis.

Two major studies became benchmarks in the field: one conducted by Himmelweit, Oppenheim, and Vince studying British television viewing habits of over 4,000 children ages 10 to 11 and 13 to 14 (1958), and the other by Schramm, Lyle and Parker (1961), analyzing patterns of viewing from over 5,000 children, 2,000 parents, several hundred teachers, and officials from 10 communities with or without television in the United States and Canada.

Though conducted independently, their findings showed some striking similarities. Each study clearly detailed that television had indeed made major inroads into children's leisure time, causing a considerable rearrangement in outside activities.

As Table 2.1 from Schramm et al.'s study indicates, those activities most affected were the use of other media, including radio listening, cinema attendance, comic book reading, and to some extent, play time with other children. Interestingly, bedtimes and time devoted to homework were among those activities least influenced. Little time, as well, was apparently taken from newspaper or book reading. In slight contrast to the Schramm et al. study, the British researchers noted that children, when first beginning to view television, read significantly less than the controls. Like their American and Canadian counterparts, however, this pattern changed after a few years of viewing, with reading reverting to its pre-viewing pattern.

More recent research of this type, referred to as "ownership/ reception studies," have replicated these findings in other countries as well. (See Table 2.2.)

The pattern of displacement found in these studies appeared to follow those in earlier research: Typically, television tended to displace other entertainment activities, including radio, movies, and comic book reading for school-age children. Only minor displacement, at the very beginning of television's introduction in the community, was recorded in reading (e.g., Hornik, 1978; Williams, 1986) and homework activities (Furu, 1971), suggesting that the displacement theory was confined primarily to changes in leisure activities.

In particular, these studies emphasized that the portion of leisure time typically rearranged by television was that time already devoted to other mass media. Once the novelty of television wore off, bedtimes, homework, spending time with friends, and leisure reading did not appear to be permanently affected.

Table 2.1.   Average Leisure Time Activities for Children in Two Canadian Communities

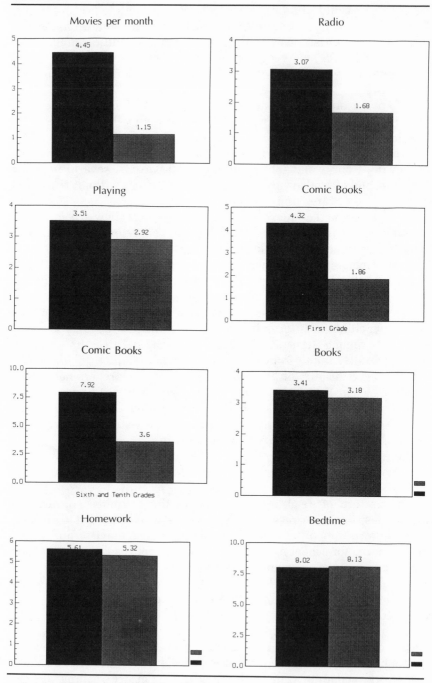

Source: Schramm, Lyle, & Parker (1961).

Table 2.2.   Ownership/Reception Studies

Study	Date	Country
Himmelweit, Oppenheim, & Vince	1958	England
Schramm, Lyle, & Parker	1961	U.S. and Canada
Furu	1971	Japan
Brown, Cramond, & Wilde	1974	Scotland
Murray & Kippax	1978	New South Wales and Queensland, Australia
Hornik	1978	El Salvador
Williams	1986	Canada

These conclusions, however, only led to a set of additional questions. Why was it that some media activities changed more than others? Which of these patterns would persist and which ones were only temporary? To understand this uneven pattern of displacement, these researchers derived a set of principles to predict television's effects on leisure behavior in the future.

Principles of Displacement

With television available, children found themselves in a conflict situation. Given the many alternative activities, they had to determine, consciously or unconsciously, how much to view, and how to make room for viewing. As shown in Table 2.3, the resulting compromise

Table 2.3.   Principles of Displacement

Principle	Definition
Functional Similarity	Children will sacrifice those activities appearing to satisfy the same needs as television only less effectively. ex.: Cartoons will replace comic book reading.
Marginal Fringe Activities	The more casual unstructured activities are more likely to be displaced than organized and structured activities. ex.: Free play will be displaced but homework will not.
Transformation	Established media will come to be used in a specialized way so as not to overlap with viewing. ex.: radio might narrowcast to meet specialized needs for specific audiences.
Physical and Psychological Proximity	Activities are more likely to be displaced if they share the same physical space, and provide more satisfaction to the child. ex.: Television might displace homework because it better fulfills children's needs.

seemed to be made on the basis of four principles: functional similarity, transformation, marginal fringe activities, and physical and psychological proximity.

Functional similarity. Given the known and available alternatives, the principle of functional similarity assumed that children were selective in their leisure activities, choosing among those activities the options that could most effectively satisfy their needs. Activities considered to serve similar functions, yet less efficiently, were naturally discarded in favor of the easier or more enjoyable alternatives.

Comic book reading, for example, clearly became a target for displacement on the basis of functional similarity. Television's arrival provided the deathblow for the previously lucrative comic book industry. In 1950, over 60 million comic books were sold every month. Five years after the introduction of television, the number of regularly issued comic books dropped to one-third of its prior circulation (Nye, 1970).

Television also had a shattering effect on the movie industry. In 1946, over 82 million were going to the movies each week; by 1955, only about 36 million; attendance declined from almost one movie per week to less than one movie per month. For young children, in particular, movies were regarded as relatively interchangeable with television, and thus, a primary candidate for displacement. But movies were not regarded as functionally similar to television for the teen market. Here, the decline in movie-going was not as dramatic due to their additional social function of spending time with friends away from their homes—a need that television clearly could not gratify.

Activities determined to be functionally different, however, were not affected by the introduction of television. Given a choice between viewing and playing with others, the majority of children still continued to prefer social interaction. Schramm and his colleagues also noted that newspaper and book reading were not affected because they served as a primary source of information, as opposed to the entertainment function of television.

Transformation. Rather than compete with television, the principle of transformation assumed that some media were forced to change in character in order to survive. As a result, these newly transformed media were used in more specialized ways that did not necessarily conflict or overlap with television.

Radio, for example, found television a formidable competitor. Following the first months of television, listening fell almost to zero. In order to stay alive, radio was forced to find new ways to satisfy its audience's needs that were not being met by television. From being a family institution in the evening prime time hours, it was consigned to places where it was not possible for television to go. Stations changed to music and news; traffic reports, weather, local talk shows developed a following. Radio shows also began to narrowcast more effectively, providing programs for specialized audiences like teenagers, specific ethnic groups, and serious music lovers.

In this transition, radio became a secondary medium, often to be used while engaging in other primary activities. Adults listened to news and music while driving. Children used radio chiefly for popular music or as background while doing homework. Radio also served a social function for teenagers who wanted to keep up with the current hits, concert dates, and popular stars.

Both the Himmelweit and Schramm studies noted some interesting trends in reading. Readership in nonfiction books increased, turning reading slightly away from the light, entertaining format of television. This trend in reading more nonfiction books, as noted by Parker, continued for several years following the reporting of their large-scale study (1963). Similarly, circulation figures for general interest magazines dropped, but not for specialized and nonfiction ones. Indeed, the special interest magazine market continued to flourish since television's introduction (cf. Compaine, 1980).

Marginal fringe activities. The principle of marginal fringe activities assumed that children made room for television at the expense of other unstructured activities. These casual activities tended to lack specific time boundaries, were generally of low priority in the first place, and often had an undefined character about them. Such activities included time spent at the local hangout, casual visiting, and taking a leisurely walk. Consequently, there was a reduction in pure leisure itself or the time spent relaxing, as children's lives inevitably became more crowded with other activities.

On the basis of the principle of marginal fringe activities, it was not surprising that studies comparing television and nontelevision communities did not find major reductions in free play, particularly after extensive experience with television. These activities, though unstructured, were of high priority to children. In fact, Murray and Kippax (1978) reported that television actually seemed to stimulate free play, by serving as a focal point for shared activities. Rather, what appeared to suffer most from the onset of television, were those activities seen as less purposeful to children. For example, Himmelweit reported that book reading was most severely reduced among those children who read with only marginal interest in them in the first place. Once children developed a specific function or purpose for reading (i.e., to read for information), book reading returned to its previous levels.

Physical and psychological proximity. Based on the principle of physical and psychological proximity, those activities which shared the same physical space, yet provided less satisfaction to children, were sacrificed in favor of viewing.

For example, Furu found slight disparities between students in the TV and non-TV groups for homework and household activities in his study. Children tended to do fewer chores and less homework in the television community than others in the sample. He explained this phenomenon in terms of two key variables: activities that shared the same physical space and psychological satisfaction. Given the option of household chores, homework, or television viewing, all of which were equally accessible, children tended to select television viewing as the more psychologically satisfying activity, and in doing so, neglected their other responsibilities.

These findings, however, were not entirely replicated in the other studies after television's arrival. Schramm, Lyle, and Parker, for example, found homework time was only slightly higher in Radiotown than Teletown, but no differences between viewers and controls on the time spent on homework were recorded in the British investigation. These disparities might reflect different school expectations in Japanese and Western cultures. Schools in the U.S., for example, have traditionally assigned students little homework.

In summary, television's arrival greatly rearranged children's leisure time. Comic book reading, considered to be functionally equivalent, dropped off dramatically, never to regain its popularity. Radio, forced to look for new talent and format, secured a following by transforming itself into a secondary medium to be enjoyed while doing other things. Movie-going, greatly diminished, carved its niche by being a better social experience than television. General interest magazines gave way to more specialized, nonfiction ones targeted to specific audiences. Once the novelty phase of television was over, books and newspapers alone appeared unscathed, and returned to their former time and prestige.

It is doubtful that television's replacement of other entertainment fare seriously affected children's developing cognitive abilities. Movies in the days before television were roughly equivalent to the content of many television shows. Topics of crime, violence, and love were favorites with the public. Along with Disney's *Snow White* and *Sleeping Beauty*, children watched such popular hits as *All Quiet on the Western Front*, *The Criminal Code*, and *Numbered Men*. In addition, the decline from three or four movies to one movie per month could hardly have been objectionable to the schools.

Some might argue that radio listening encouraged children to use their imagination, and memory skills more than television. With radio, listeners were equal participants, constructing their own mental images of the radio personalities and characters in the dramas. In fact, a recent study found a positive relation between radio listening and imaginative responses from a sample of first- through fourth-grade students (Greenfield & Beagles-Roos, 1988). However, these findings have not been reported in more carefully controlled media comparison studies (Clark & Salomon, 1986). Beagles-Roos and Gat (1983), in a previous study, comparing the impact of radio and television on children's story comprehension, reported superior gains for those in the televised condition in plot details and sequence than their counterparts listening to radio.

Comic book reading might be the most likely candidate of the displaced activities to have effects on reading and school achievement. Despite its controversial content (Wertham, 1954), it was the major source of leisure reading for most youngsters before television. Comics probably provided some practice in reading for those who might otherwise not read. But comics were not without their critics. Some argued at the time that comic book reading was actually detrimental to children's reading achievement, by fostering an overreliance on pictures. No evidence, however, has ever been found concerning this particular issue.

Why were books not replaced by television viewing? No consensus emerged from these studies. Schramm et al. argued that books and television performed very different functions. Books served children's need for information; television, for fantasy and entertainment. In contrast, Brown et al.'s (1974) study suggested that books served multifunctional needs; thus, while television did indeed replace some, it could not subsume all due to its lack of flexibility as a medium. Himmelweit et al. (1958), and Murray and Kippax (1978), on the other hand, argued against displacement, reporting that television actually stimulated book reading, particularly for the duller adolescents. The actual amount of stimulation, however, was rather modest; even at the very height of the "reading craze," children in the British investigation read an average of two to four hours a week.

Early investigations of book reading, however, suggest that even before the introduction of television, book reading was a relatively minor activity. Studies in the 1940s and early 1950s reported that children rarely read more than 15 minutes per day (Lyness, 1952; Witty, 1967). These figures are no different than today. Reports now indicate that children spend only 1% of their leisure time reading books, or approximately 15 minutes a day (Anderson, Hiebert, Scott, & Wilkinson, 1985; Neuman, 1986a, 1988). Even if television viewing had displaced book reading, it may have been difficult to notice due to the little time devoted to the activity. Unfortunately, children were not reading very much before television, and they are not reading very much today.

WHAT ARE TELEVISION'S EFFECTS ON READING ACHIEVEMENT?

Research on the introduction of television in the community contributed a wealth of information on children's viewing habits, leisure patterns, and cognitive skills. Further, they attempted to theoretically explain complex changes in children's behavior toward changes in their communications environment. But these studies all contained a critical theoretical drawback when considering the relation between television viewing and schooling today: It is impossible to simply assume that the principles of displacement reported of early television use can adequately predict current media behavior. Since its introduction, television has become an ubiquitous phenomenon in children's lives; no one escapes it.

Concerns about television's influence on reading and school achievement, therefore, led to a second type of displacement study. This research analyzed the effects of viewing in places where television has been well established as an entertainment medium. Generally, these studies compared the time spent viewing on measures of reading achievement by using test scores, grade point averages, or number of books read per month as indicators. Two general categories of research were conducted: correlational studies, which analyzed the simple relationship between television viewing and achievement, and multivariate studies, which attempted to sort out the causal connections.

Correlational Studies

Research in this category analyzed the direct relationship between the number of hours children spent viewing television and reading performance. The underlying theoretical principle in these studies, though at times not explicitly articulated, was one of displacement. Specifically, these studies attempted to measure whether the time spent watching television displaced other activities thought to be related to school learning.

Correlational studies of this type, however, are naturally limited by analyzing only two variables: television time and achievement. No other outside activities in these studies were measured. In this respect, it was impossible to analyze whether the children who were watching a good deal of television were necessarily neglecting their homework or leisure reading or other activities. The linkage, therefore, between the theoretical assumptions of displacement and these study designs was weak.

Table 2.4 lists 15 correlational studies relating TV viewing and reading performance. These small-scale studies usually involved non-random samples conducted with different age groups using diverse

Table 2.4. Correlational Studies of Television and Achievement

Study	Date	N	Grade Levels	Results
Adams & Harrison	1975	228	4, 5, 6	98% of sample thought television helped their reading skills
Anderson, Wilson, & Fielding	1988	155	5	No significant differences
Busch	1978	—	All grades	Younger students benefited most from viewing; older students did not.
Clark	1951	1,000	6, 7	No significant differences
Greenstein	1954	67	4, 5, 6	No significant differences
LaBlonde	1967	294	5	No significant differences except positive relationship between TV & study skills
Long & Henderson	1973	150	5	Time spent viewing negatively related to time spent reading but no figures given
Moldenhauer & Miller	1980	78	7	No significant differences
Quisenberry & Kasek	1976	341	4, 5, 6	No significant differences
Ridder	1963	2428	7, 8	No significant differences
Scott	1958	456	6, 7	Heavy viewers were less proficient in math and reading than those who viewed less
Slater	1965	500	3	A significant negative relationship
Starkey & Swinford	1974	226	5, 6	A "slight" relationship*
Telfer & Kann	1984	234	4, 8, 11	Lower scores—more time with television—for 4th graders only
Witty	1967	—	Elem.	No significant differences

*Only frequencies used

methodological strategies. Busch (1978), for example, based her analysis of the viewing-achievement relationship using informal interviews with teachers and students. Starkey and Swinford (1974) employed teacher assessments of children's reading achievement levels. Greenstein (1954) compared the amount of television watched with grade point averages.

Of these studies, only three (Long & Henderson, 1973; Scott, 1958; Slater, 1965) reported significant negative correlations between viewing and achievement. Scott's early investigation, however, must be viewed with some reservation. While inferior achievement scores were clearly linked with high viewing in his study, television receivership in the community was still a relatively new phenomenon (the study was actually conducted in 1954). Probably reflecting the public's great initial interest in television viewing, high-viewing children in the study watched between 22¾ to 69½ per week! Long and Henderson reported a negative relationship between television viewing time and leisure reading; however, no correlations indicating the actual size of the relationship, nor any significance figures are given. Slater's study, alone, found unequivocal negative correlations for all groups.

The great majority of these studies, however, reported nonsignificant or inconsistent findings. Witty, for example, conducted a series of studies from 1949 to 1965 analyzing children's leisure reading activities, achievement, and television viewing. He found that in the beginning of his studies, some parents and teachers reported that children read less than they did before television. Once television became well established, however, this pattern changed.

> Our most recent studies show that relatively few pupils now believe that TV has influenced their reading adversely. Many point out that television has led to an increase in reading. In fact, in 1958, 45% of the elementary school pupils believed that they read more now; 29% less, and 26% the same amount.

Starkey and Swinford's study (1974), on the other hand, did find a "slight but distinct" negative relationship between viewing and reading level, indicating that the better readers watched less TV than the poor readers (though they base their argument on frequency tables, not correlations.) But then in another section of the paper, they claim that "television is a real boon to the dull child (or the poor reader)" (p. 6). As a result, they concluded that not all television viewing is really a bad influence on children. Telfer and Kann, replicating a study by Neuman and Prowda (1982) of fourth, eighth, and eleventh graders, reported a negative correlation for the fourth graders, but no relationships at the upper grade levels.

It is difficult to make specific recommendations on the basis of these series of studies due to their serious methodological flaws. Adams and Harrison (1975), for example, asked students for their own subjective judgments of how television affected their reading habits. The low reading groups (80%) thought that television helped their silent reading just fine. Such data hardly provide convincing evidence of television's effects.

The fact that so few of these studies found significant relationships, however, did not eliminate a growing concern over television's potential influence on schooling. Instead, it invited further inquiry. New questions were raised, focusing on whether the small correlations actually reflected the relationship between television viewing and reading achievement. For example, might these small correlations be masking a nonlinear association? Could television viewing indirectly relate to achievement in school by affecting such school-related behaviors as the amount of time spent on homework? Could these small overall correlations have obscured larger effects for specific subgroups?

It would have been wrong, therefore, to extrapolate from this research that there were no other potential linkages between television viewing and achievement. These studies examined only rather crude measures of the time spent viewing with overall achievement. The relationship between the two media seemed to require far more sophisticated measures of both viewing and reading in order to accurately detail television's effects.

Sorting Out Causal Connections

Central to any argument for television's effects is the issue of causality. Correlations merely indicate the relationship between two variables; they cannot provide a basis for causal inference. Recognizing the limitations of these initial studies, a number of researchers began to probe the television-reading relationship in greater depth by introducing control variables in their research designs.

Chief among those controls were IQ and social class (SES). Based on the early displacement studies, there was reason to believe that television viewing and reading achievement were negatively associated with IQ for students beyond the elementary school years; similarly, socioeconomic status (SES) was also inversely related to the amount of time spent viewing and reading. Several researchers attempted to measure a number of factors related to these control variables. Morgan (1982), for example, analyzed parental viewing habits, and their educational aspirations for their children. Potter (1987) used a measure of "locus of control" to analyze children's perceptions of their own ability

Table 2.5.   Multivariate Studies of Television and Achievement

Study	Date	Control Variables	Viewing Measure
Angle	1981	IQ	How many hours watched on the average
Childers & Ross	1973	IQ	How many hours watched on average weekday
Lu & Tweeten	1973	SES	How much time spent generally on watching TV
Morgan	1980	IQ, Ed. aspiration parents viewing, other media habits	How much time spent watching TV on an average day, including morning, afternoon, evening (asked 2 × a year for 3 years)
Neuman	1980a	IQ; SES	Logs, measuring quantity and specific programs viewed
Neuman	1981	IQ; SES; grade	Logs, measuring quantity and specific programs viewed, and specific reading selections
Peirce	1983	No. of books read; parent interest	Hours per day viewed Favorite type Restricted or not
Potter	1987	IQ; SES; Locus of control	Log of one week's TV viewing
Ridley-Johnson, Cooper, & Chance	1983	IQ	Logs, measuring quantity and specific programs viewed Types of shows preferred Parent rules Viewing environment
Ritchie, Price, & Roberts	1987	SES; IQ	Time spent viewing
Roberts, Bachen, Hornby, & Hernandez-Ramos	1984	SES; IQ	Home environ. for TV and reading; Orientation toward TV and print Time estimates of viewing and reading
Smyser	1981	IQ	Logs measuring the amount and type of programs watched over 1 week
Thompson	1964	IQ	Amount of time spent viewing; favorite programs
Zuckerman, Singer, and Singer	1980	IQ; SES	Logs, measuring quantity and specific programs viewed

to learn. Roberts, Bachen, Hornby, and Hernanadez-Ramos (1984), and the more recent Ritchie, Price, and Roberts (1987) studies analyzed television and reading within a conceptual framework of constructs including media availability, parental media behavior, and children's uses and attitudes toward print and television.

Achievement Measure	No. of Subjects	Grade Level	Relationship
Reading attitudes; Amount of book reading; achievement	143	5	Insignificant achievement; negative relationship between reading attitudes & TV
Iowa Test of Basic Skills; G.P.A.	100	4, 5	Insignificant relationship between TV and reading
S.R.A. (4th & 8th) I.T.B.S. (11th)	1,073	4, 8, 11	Significant negative 4th; insignificant 8th & 11th
California Achievement Test	650	6th–10th	Insignificant for total group; significant for specific subgroups
Circus Test (ETS)	200	Preschool	Insignificant relationship between viewing and listening
Metropolitan Achievement Test	124	4, 5, 6	Insignificant relationship between viewing and achievement; negative relationship between adventure and achievement
National Assessment of Educational Progress (NAEP) Paragraphs in Writing	102	5, 7, 8, 9	Writing ability correlated negatively with amount of TV viewed
McGraw-Hill Comprehensive Test of Basic Skills	543	8–12	Insignificant relationship between TV & reading
C.A.T.	322	5–8	Insignificant relationship between TV & reading
C.T.B.S. or S.A.T. or S.R.A.	270	2–8	Insignificant relationship between TV & reading
C.T.B.S.	539	2, 3, 6	Insignificant relationship between amount of TV and reading achievement
S.R.A.	80	1	Insignificant relationship between TV & reading achievement
(not specified)	100	3	Insignificant relationship between TV & reading
McGraw-Hill Reading Test	282	3, 4, 5	Insignificant relationship between TV & achievement

Table 2.5 lists the characteristics of these multivariate studies. It is clear from the pattern that emerges in this review that intelligence appeared to be a significant factor in explaining the association between viewing and achievement. Studies by Childers and Ross (1973), Morgan and Gross (1980), Neuman (1980), Potter (1987), Thompson

Table 2.6.   Secondary Analyses of Television and Achievement

Study	Date	Data Source	Control Variables	Grade
Clemens	1983	Pennsylvania Assessment Test	SES Ethnicity Type of Community	5, 8, 11
Fetler	1984	California Assessment	Parents Occupation Home environ. measures	6
Gaddy	1986	High school and Beyond		12
Goodwin	1983	High school and Beyond	SES Ethnicity Gender	12
Keith, Reimers, Fehrmann, Pottebaum, & Aubey	1986	High school and Beyond	SES Ethnicity Gender Ability	12
Neuman	1988	National Assessment of Educational Progress California Connecticut Illinois Maine Michigan Pennsylvania Rhode Island Texas	SES Gender	Elementary Intermediate Secondary
Neuman & Prowda	1982	Connecticut Assessment	Home environ. measures Gender	4, 8, 11
Searls, Mead, & Ward	1985	National Assessment of Educational Progress	Community types	Ages 9, 13, 17
Williams, Haertel, Haertel, & Walberg	1982	Meta-analysis of 23 Studies	(If available) SES Gender IQ	K–12

(1964), Zuckerman, Singer and Singer (1980) all report that when IQ was controlled, the ability to predict achievement from television viewing was substantially reduced to nonsignificant levels. These studies indicated that the less intelligent, poorer achievers were more likely to be heavy viewers than others.

Using large-scale data sets from national or state samples, a second pattern emerged from secondary analyses found in Table 2.6 (Clemens,

Viewing Measure	Relationship
Hours of TV watched from after school until bedtime	Significant but small absolute difference
How much TV watched on a typical day	Correlations of achievement with the amount of viewing were modest ($-.09$)
How many hours watched per day	Small negative effects of television on achievement reported.
How many hours watched per day	Significant but small absolute difference (only 2% of variance accounted for) between television and achievement.
How many hours watched per day	Significant but small absolute difference.
TV questions asked in many different forms	Modest positive relationship between TV and reading for elementary and intermediate students, a negative relationship for secondary students.
Hours of TV watched per day	Significant but small absolute difference ($-.07$).
Average amount of TV viewed per day	Modest positive relationship between TV and reading for 9 and 13 years old; for 17 years old, a modest negative relationship.
TV questions asked in many different forms	Small negative correlation between TV and achievement ($-.05$).

1983; Fetler, 1984; Gaddy, 1986; Goodwin, 1983; Neuman & Prowda, 1982). These studies benefited from large multi-age samples and tapped a broad array of reading performance skills. Together, they describe a consistent and dramatic account of the relationship between television and achievement: when students beyond the elementary levels were tested, hours of viewing were *uniformly* negatively associated with reading performance.

These results, however, must be carefully interpreted. The relationships, while consistent, were rather small. Neuman and Prowda, for example, reported partial correlations (controlling for gender and SES) of −.18 and −.17 for eighth and eleventh graders respectively. The size of the correlations reported in the other secondary studies tended to be even smaller. In addition, IQ information was not available in these large surveys of reading performance. Given its substantial contribution in explaining the reading-viewing relationship, it must be assumed that if available, some or all of the apparent association might have disappeared. Finally, all the SES control variables in these studies, based on self-reported data, were particularly weak. For example, in the Connecticut and Pennsylvania assessment, SES was determined by asking children to check off whether their home contained such educational resources as a newspaper, typewriter, encyclopedia, and sewing machine.

A status report on television's effects on reading achievement, therefore, is complex because it is highly dependent on the interpreter's definition of what determines conclusive evidence. Williams, Haertel, Haertel, and Walberg's (1982) meta-analysis is an excellent case in point. Synthesizing the results of 23 studies of television and learning, they reported 277 correlations between measures of viewing and achievement. For all the correlations, the median association was −.06. Analyzing the time spent viewing in greater depth, they noted significant curvilinear effects. For those students watching from 1 to 10 hours per week, the correlation was positive indicating that a moderate amount of viewing was associated with higher achievement than no viewing at all. From 11 to 35 hours, there were negative relationships (−.09), showing that within this level, as viewing increased, achievement declined slightly. Their conclusion: "Televiewing accounts for little variance in achievement: It is neither the villain nor redeemer some have claimed" (p. 35).

But Gerbner, Gross, Morgan, and Signorelli (1984), reporting on this same study, interpret these findings very differently:

In the synthesis [Williams et al.], the authors find a preponderance of negative associations and conclude that there is a small but overwhelmingly consistent negative association between viewing and achievement. (1984, p. 11)

Both views, of course, are correct. One focused more on the size of the relationship; the other, on the consistency of the relationship. Each conclusion, however, called for a very different research strategy. Cook and his colleagues (1986), reviewing the evidence, concluded that further work on the television-achievement relationship was not advisable—rather, television might influence achievement slightly but not enough to be worthy of consideration. Hornik (1981), on the other hand, noting the consistency of the findings, recommended further work using more highly sophisticated methodological designs which measure the viewing-achievement relationship of specific subgroups.

At the very minimum then, there appears to be a negative, though modest, relationship between television and reading achievement which is influenced by such independent factors as intelligence and motivation, as well as contextual factors including home environment and parental restrictions. About 10 weekly hours of television time seems optimal for learning; more hours than this relates to consistently lower achievement scores, particularly for older students in school.

On the basis of these results, can we assume that television is displacing reading? Unfortunately not. To a large extent, the linkage between theory and hypothesis is lacking in many of these multivariate analyses. Peirce's (1983) study of viewing and writing achievement is one example. This study indicated that viewing was negatively related to writing skills of children in grades 5, 7, 8, and 9. However, on the basis of the research design, it is impossible to explain the particular causal mechanism. For example, is it that a child would be writing at home, if not for watching television? This appears far-fetched. Is it that children's eyes are being affected, not allowing them to focus accurately on a piece of paper? Again, this seems unlikely. Or, could it be that a child's interest in writing is probably related to other active interests in schooling? Probably so. But without a distinct theoretical foundation, conclusions remained problematic.

A study by Ridley-Johnson, Cooper, and Chance (1982) is another example. In their case, the hypothesis clearly reflected an analysis of the displacement theory:

> Because of the lack of clarity concerning the relationship between television viewing and academics, the present study was undertaken. Television viewing was expected to be negatively related to school achievement, because children may choose television as a preferred activity over others, such as reading, thereby adversely affecting basic skills development.

Yet despite interest in the potential relationship between television viewing and other outside activities, only reading and math achievement are measured. It is impossible, however, without looking at any leisure behaviors to assume that poor achievement was a direct result of the lack of leisure reading in the home. Studies prior to the introduction of television should warn researchers to be wary of these over-generalizations.

In summary, television and achievement studies have attempted to narrowly examine the displacement theory by focusing on the time spent viewing and its impact on reading scores. Even when more control variables have been added, this research still reflects an analysis of the relationship in a relatively narrow framework; rarely have any of children's other activities been measured. Further research should seek a more comprehensive picture of children's school and leisure behaviors.

But even with these efforts, it is doubtful that studies in this tradition will be able to capture the subtleties of television's influence on literacy and school achievement. The causal path may be just too difficult to chart. Children presumably choose television viewing in preference to a number of other possible activities. But indeed, are we certain that other viable alternatives exist for all children? As one inner city parent once asked, "Is it better for my kid to be hanging out at a street corner bar or to be home watching television." It is also risky to assume that some activities are more cognitively valuable than watching television. Gadberry (1980), for example, attempted to argue that the time spent coloring by first graders, rather than television viewing, significantly influenced performance IQ scores. No other study, however, has ever verified such a claim. Similarly, movies, talking on the telephone, and radio have certainly not established themselves as superior to television viewing.

In addition, it is impossible to determine with any certainty the direction of effects. For example, are children neglecting their homework in favor of viewing, or are teachers not assigning homework? These issues warrant further analysis which goes beyond the notion of television viewing as simply replacing reading or other cognitive activities. Perhaps it is time to rethink the displacement theory.

CHALLENGING THE DISPLACEMENT THEORY

According to the theory of displacement, television tends to replace other activities thought to serve similar needs but are less readily available or require more effort. As we have seen, four basic principles of displacement emerged from early studies of the introduction of television in a community, most of which were derived from Himmelweit et al. (1958) and implicit in the interpretation by Schramm et al. (1961) of their similar findings.

In practice, however, the weight of the interpretation fell on the principle of functional similarity. This view regarded children as ac-

Table 2.7. Challenging the Displacement Effect: The First Challenge

Assumption	Challenge
Media content serves a limited set of functions, and thus may be treated as unifunctional	Uses and gratifications research suggests that most media serve multi-functional needs (see Katz, Gurevitch, & Haas, 1973).
Media satisfactions suit certain needs at all times	Media-related needs and uses evolve at different stages of development (see Brown, Cramond, & Wilde, 1974; Greaney & Neuman, 1983).

tively seeking media on the basis of their needs; television was thought to displace certain activities because it better satisfied those needs than other leisure pursuits. Schramm et al., for example, broadly dichotomized these functions, arguing that television provided for entertainment needs, and therefore was functionally equivalent to most media activities, whereas newspapers and reading books catered to children's reality needs, and hence were not affected by television viewing. From this perspective, literacy activities were not competing with other entertainment media for the time and attention of children.

This functionalist explanation, however, tended to drop out of the correlational and multivariate studies of displacement. These studies essentially used a reductionist approach by measuring displacement by the time spent viewing, not the functions or needs that the medium served. In doing so, they relied on the general argument that watching television instead of anything else—either academically beneficial or not—constituted a negative effect in its own right.

Both arguments rest on a set of assumptions that are neither necessarily self-evident nor verified in other studies of actual viewing or reading behavior. Once challenged, it becomes evident that alternative mechanisms other than the concept of functional equivalence or the more general approach to displacement may be at work.

The First Challenge

An implicit assumption underlying the principle of functional similarity is its reliance on categorically defining media as serving a limited set of functions. Television, for example, is thought to provide distraction, wish-fulfillment, and an opportunity for vicarious problem solving, thus serving the escapist function and displacing other functionally similar media. Print media (newspapers, magazines, and books), however, are considered to remain outside this cycle of displacement because they serve a different set of needs than typical entertainment fare. The functional similarity principle, therefore posits that: (a) satisfactions from media are primarily unifunctional, (b) interests in leisure activities are relatively permanent and not episodic in nature.

Do media serve unifunctional needs? Numerous studies in the "uses and gratifications" tradition have undermined the basic assumption that each medium provides only a limited set of functions. This research has attempted to explain some of the ways in which individuals use media among other resources in their environment to satisfy their needs. Katz, Gurevitch, and Haas (1973) analyzing the uses and gratifications of media for Israeli adults, found that cinema and books were more helpful as a means of "escape" than television. Von Feilitzen (1976), in a study of Swedish children, reported that television met informative needs with almost equal frequency as its entertainment functions. Children regarded books as more escapist than television, radio, and magazines.

The basic premise that television viewing or book reading has a singular, linear effect on an individual disregards the multifunctional uses of the media for children. In Von Feilitzen's study for example, over 30 functions of mass media were reported by students ages 7 through 15. A recent study of reading uses and gratifications in 18 countries indicated over 10 functions for books alone. Books provided opportunities for wish fulfillment and vicarious problem solving, only in a different form than television (Greaney & Neuman, 1990). Thus, the notion that media serve a set of circumscribed needs has not been supported by more recent research.

Are media uses developmentally stable? In contrast to the notion that media served a fixed set of needs, research suggests that children's media preferences interact and change with their growing interests. Brown, Cramond, and Wilde's (1974) study indicated dramatic shifts in media-related needs at different phases of development. While television was clearly reported to be the most important source of excitement for children at age 7, it begins to decline at age 9 until the mid-teens when it became undifferentiated from other media, including records and books. At the same time, there is a striking increase in the extent to which children regard their peers as a primary source of excitement. Brown and his colleagues argued that rather than functional similarity, these changes indicate a "functional reorganization" of media patterns, subject to changes in the communications environment and developments in the audience member's specialized needs.

These conceptual distinctions—the multifunctional uses of the media and age differentiation of needs—suggest several important implications in the argument for displacement. First, by emphasizing television's escapist functions over other motivations, researchers have presented an unbalanced picture of the gratifications derived from

Table 2.8.   Age Trends for 3 Satisfactions for Television and Book Reading

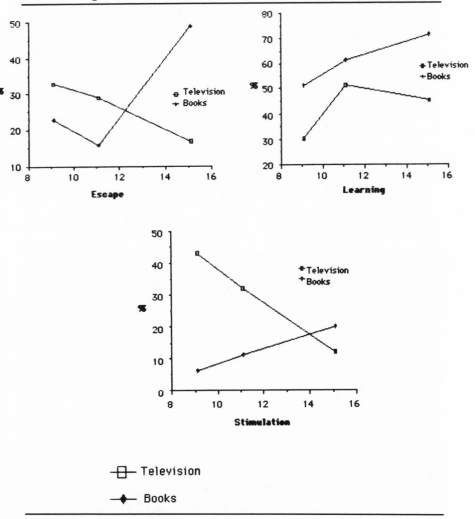

Escape

Learning

Stimulation

—☐— Television

—◆— Books

*Television Data Based on Brown et al. (1974)
**Book Reading Data Based on Neuman (1980b)

television. In contrast, children acquire information as they watch entertaining programs. This information, differing from typical school learning, tends to be in a form of "reality orientation," relating to current events, values, and concepts concerning occupations, status, and people's roles outside the home and the schools.

Second, rather than merely substituting one functionally equivalent activity for another, media habits change as children grow older,

Table 2.9.   Challenging the Displacement Effect: The Second Challenge

Assumption	Challenge
Children watch 30 hours per week	Discrepant estimates of how much time children spend with television; national rating services overestimate; academic researchers report viewing approximately 12 hours Children also watch while engaged in concurrent activities (see Anderson, Field, Collins, Lorch, & Nathan, 1985).
Television affects achievement	It is impossible to determine whether television causally affects achievement or whether aspects of school experiences have an effect on the way children use television (see Jonsson, 1986). Poor achievers may use TV as escape (see Dweck & Bempechat, 1983).

reflecting how well the particular medium serves children's needs. Television and book reading do indeed serve similar functions, but often at different stages of development. Table 2.8 identifies some of these functions and describes age-related trends for three of the common gratifications. While television clearly appears to provide greater stimulation to young children than book reading, it cannot compete with books in serving learning and escapist needs for older students.

As children grow older however, both media tend to become subsumed by more social activities including radio, records, and spending time with friends. Television viewing time is at its lowest ebb during the teenage years. Similarly, age trends for book reading are characterized by a gradual decline in overall time and functional uses for teenagers. These trends together suggest a far more comprehensive restructuring of media patterns than is assumed by the principle of functional similarity. Instead of provoking irrevocable changes in the communications environment, there seems to be an ongoing process of changing media patterns reflecting changing needs. Mass media do not compel certain behaviors; rather the control lies within the individual to use mass media in specialized ways to gratify their needs.

The Second Challenge

Recent research on viewing and reading patterns have elicited new questions regarding the utility of the displacement theory in describing the television-reading association. These questions challenge such basic assumptions of displacement as (a) the amount of time children spend viewing television, and (b) the direction of the causal path for television and achievement.

Do most children spend an inordinate amount of time watching TV?: How much time do American children actually spend watching television? The answer, surprisingly, is not clear-cut. Even at the most general level, there are substantial discrepancies in the reports of how much time is spent watching. Nielsen (1987) estimates, based on a sampling of announced "sweeps" measurement periods, indicate an average of more than 30 hours per week for youngsters. These figures, however, have been shown to be heavily biased by the use of special programs designed to maximize audiences, allowing broadcasters to raise advertising fees to their sponsors. In contrast, viewing diaries from a study by Anderson and his colleagues of 99 families in the Springfield, Massachusetts area indicated figures that were only about 60 percent of those reported by the rating services (Anderson, Field, Collins, Lorch, & Nathan, 1985). Other studies measuring television time use diaries, as well, report significantly lower viewing figures (see, for example, Zuckerman, Singer, & Singer, 1980; Timmer, Eccles, & O'Brien, 1985).

These family diary estimates are probably better indicators of children's time spent watching television than other techniques including self-reported measures (although as Cook et al., 1986, indicate, little research has examined the validity of these television viewing measures). But even these accounts fail to measure how children actually spend their time before the television set. Viewing rooms in Anderson's time-lapse videotape study, for example, contained no people 15% of the time the set was on. Children frequently exited and entered the room, restlessly played with changing the channel all during viewing sessions.

Certainly, even these lower estimates of time spent with television may exert some influence on other activities, though hardly as dramatic as previous figures have suggested. Still another problem with interpreting displacement, however, is that some activities are not mutually exclusive with viewing. Children are commonly engaged in other overlapping activities including conversation, reading, and homework. In their study of time-shared activities during homework, Patton, Stinard, and Routh (1983) reported that 22% of the elementary students reading with television as a background noise; 37% completed math with the television set on. Viewing incorporates many interacting and competing activities and events. Some of these activities serve as a point of departure from viewing; others occur concurrently while viewing.

The inference that television replaces other valuable activities also fails to account for the time when most children spend viewing television. Heaviest viewing occurs during prime time, from 8:00–9:00 at night. Other heavy periods include before dinner, and early Saturday and Sunday morning programs. Most of this time might be appropriately regarded as "down-time," when few outside activities are ongoing. Television is often watched during these time periods precisely due to the lack of alternative attractions.

In sum, the popular notion of the "zombie viewer," sitting catatonic before the set, is not confirmed in real observations of children spending time with television. Not only do children seem to spend less time than popular rating services have reported, they use television as a secondary activity about a third of the time they are watching. Based on these considerations, an estimate of time spent actually viewing television for elementary students might be closer to 12 hours per week, and 10 hours for teenagers.

Average estimates, however, mask the range of viewing hours. Clearly some children do watch excessive amounts of television. In Zuckerman, Singer, and Singer's (1980) diary study for example, mean hours of viewing was 15, with a range between 1 and 40 hours a week (1980) for students in the third, fourth, and fifth grades. For the small percentage of students consuming an immoderate number of hours, television is obviously taking time away from other activities. But can we assume displacement?

Determining the causal path. Unfortunately not. Since almost all studies in the field have been correlational and cross-sectional, it is impossible to determine with any certainty the direction of the causal path. Studies of viewing and achievement have assumed that television is the predictor causally linked to reading scores as the response variable. However, there are two important rival hypotheses. One possibility is that the effects might flow in the other direction: Aspects of school experience might effect how much and in what way television is watched. The second possibility that is that both causal paths are occurring simultaneously in a reciprocal form.

There are several reasons why low achievement in school might relate to the amount of television watched. One such influence is mental ability (Morgan & Gross, 1980; Schramm et al., 1961). Less intelligent students tend to watch more television as they grow older than their brighter counterparts who are finding satisfaction in other competing media and activities. Intelligence alone, however, cannot account for heavy viewing. Lyle and Hoffman (1972) in their study, for example, report that brighter tenth graders also tend to view a good deal of television and engage in more competing activities.

Motivational factors appear to be at least equally important. Both high television viewers and low achievers tend to share a number of personality characteristics apart from native ability. For example, Himmelweit et al. found that television addicts often showed less initiative than others, were insecure and afraid of striking out for themselves. They hypothesized that these characteristics were more likely to be the cause than the result of heavy viewing. Dweck and Bempechat's (1983) studies of underachieving students showed similar personality traits. Underachievers demonstrated "learned helplessness," avoiding challenges, questioning their ability to solve problems, perceiving future effort in school to be futile. To date, however, only one study by Potter (1987) has explored the potential linkage between the characteristics of underachievers and excessive viewing. This naturally might lead to the following question: Could it be that extreme television watching, compulsive reading, extended video game play are forms of avoidance strategies which allow children to withdraw from real-world responsibilities?

Another possibility is that the relationship between schooling and television viewing is not unidirectional. A study by Jonsson (1986) in Sweden explored this alternative hypothesis. Linking children's uses and gratifications of television with school achievement, she found that low and high achievers used television differently. High achievers tended to use television instrumentally while low achievers used television more as an entertainer or pastime. Measuring the home television environment, Jonsson found that those children who grew up in a more cognizant television environment, that is, who were encouraged to watch appropriate programs for their age group, to learn from television, and to ask questions regarding the content of programs also coped better with the cognitive requirements of school. They also showed more inclination to use television as a complement to school, viewing programs purposefully. These results suggest circular effects of viewing and achievement, probably rooted in parents intentions to guide their children, and their expectations for school success.

Displacement is conspicuously absent in Jonsson's study. Rather, viewing and achievement are reflections of priorities and values set by families. Bryce's (1987) ethnographic study of three families further articulates this theme by describing the coherent nature of family behavior that applies equally to organizing family trips, family dinners, exposure to television and schooling. Unwritten rules govern family activities which provide the basis for both exposure and interpretation of experiences. In one home, for example, where television was viewed as one of several concurrent activities, attention to programs was sporadic and comprehension minimal. In another highly organized family, television viewing was considered purposive, requiring children's attention and understanding. From this perspective, time and attention to viewing, homework, books—among other activities—are hardly independent of one another, but instead, tend to reflect the microculture established by the family. In that sense, the care and attention awarded to children's various activities, both leisure and academic, reveal the construct of family values.

A REASSESSMENT

The displacement theory, originally formulated in the late 1950s, continues to be the major explanation for describing the supposed negative effects of television on reading and school achievement. Time spent viewing is thought to replace opportunities for "skill practice, contingent reinforcement, and active exploration" (Gadberry, 1980, p. 46), inhibiting cognitive growth over time.

But as shown in these previous sections, the theory of displacement has not gone unchallenged in the past 30 years. Its original formulation failed to take into account the obvious multiplicity of functions which a single medium will perform, as well as the redistribution of functions among the media for various age groups. More recent research argues that rating services have vastly overestimated the actual time spent with television, and that the case for assuming a causal relationship from television to achievement has not been adequately established. Other concerns raised throughout the review note that studies of displacement have rarely analyzed differential effects of content exposure and achievement or if, as assumed, children really do have a variety of alternative attractions available to them outside of viewing.

The displacement theory at the time of its conceptualization was a useful model to describe broad changes in the communications environment as a result of new media. However, it is an inadequate model to analyze the more subtle and complex relationship of television, reading, and school achievement today. Even with better measurement techniques, it is extremely questionable whether specific causal factors can be isolated from the broader social context of the home and school environment. Similarly, Cook et al. (1986), in their review of television and achievement, argue that the relationship might closely mirror patterns found in Jonsson and Bryce's research:

> If television influences life in schools, it is likely to be in ways that relate more directly to values than to achievement, and to values in a contextual relationship from which school, home and peer values cannot be removed, for the possibility exists that in some respects all these agencies of socialization are pulling towards the same ends while in other respects their aims and influences may be countervailing.

Rather than the theory of displacement, it has become obvious that any discussion of children's television viewing and reading development must reflect the primacy of the home environment on attitudes and expectations toward literacy and school achievement. Children's developing interests in schooling simply do not occur in isolation, but are part of the influences, behaviors, and values that are esteemed at home.

The most recent working hypothesis of research on this topic holds that the pattern of parent–child interactions in the home environment relates significantly to reading achievement and how much time they perceive to have available to read or view television during their leisure time (Bloom, 1981; Dave, 1963; Greaney & Hegarty, 1987; Neuman, 1986a; Wolf, 1964). This research further extends investigations by Jonsson and Bryce, by detailing specific types of behaviors in homes that relate to positive schooling outcomes.

In these studies, home environment is defined in terms of process variables: dynamic characteristics in the home that emphasize what parents do in interacting with their children (in contrast to such static characteristics as SES). Six of these process characteristics have been investigated:

- *Work habits:* the degree of routine and participation by children in household management and the priority given to homework over other activities.
- *Parental academic guidance:* the availability and quality of help parents give their children with school work and the conditions they provide at home to support school activities.
- *Diverse leisure activities:* the number of family opportunities to become involved in activities outside the home and to explore the larger environment.
- *Parental expectations:* parents' expectations for their child's general educational performance and the standards they set for school achievement.
- *Independence and responsibility:* the degree of independence given to the child to develop responsibility in social and work related tasks.
- *Parental encouragement of reading:* the availability of reading materials in the home, parents' reading behavior, and how often they read to their child.

These home variables not only shape children's expectations of school achievement, but also their uses of leisure time. Studies by Bloom (1981) and his colleagues, for example, have reported correla-

Table 2.10.   Correlations between Home Environmental Process
Variables and the Amount of Time Children Devote to Reading

Process Variables	Correlation
Work habits	−.16
Parental guidance	.18
Diverse leisure activities	.37***
Parental expectations	.10
Independence and responsibility	.30**
Parental encouragement of reading	.53***
Television viewing	−.14

*p < .05
**p < .01
***p < .001
Source: From Neuman (1986a). The home environment and fifth-grade students'
leisure reading. The Elementary School Journal, 335–343.

tions of +. 80 between these process variables and school achievement, indicating the important linkages between parents interactions with their children at home and behaviors associated with school success (p. 75). Similarly, in more recent studies, these home environmental process variables have been used to analyze how much time children devote to leisure reading and television viewing. An examination of these measures has shown some of these process variables to be better predictors of the amount of time children devote to book reading and television viewing than any intellectual or SES demographic factors.

These studies have found that in families where there is a greater emphasis on reading with children, strong encouragement to become involved in diverse leisure activities, and ongoing parental efforts to foster independence and responsibility, children tend to spend more of their available free time on leisure reading and less time on television viewing.

But in homes where there is less parent interaction, and where fewer alternative activities are either available or encouraged, perceptions of available free-time are greater, and television viewing is one of fewer options to fill the vacuum of time. Thus, children who view excessively may tend to do so not only because there is "nothing else to do" but because of the lack of structure and general interaction that occurs in the family environment. This is particularly true for young children where viewing is one of the least dependent free time activities available and where book reading still requires the assistance and time of an older companion.

This type of research is promising because it emphasizes ongoing processes in the home that are considered to be alterable as opposed to the more static characteristics of social class. The evidence so far supports the hypothesis that some of these communications patterns, in particular, are associated with strategies that influence the children's perceptions of free time and their behaviors and attitudes toward schooling.

Television's influence on achievement, therefore, may depend to a very large extent on a more complex set of interactive patterns in the home environment than has been previously researched. When television is awarded greater space due to the lack of attractive options, it will naturally have greater opportunity to influence achievement. In this respect, television may not displace activities as much as exert a more primary influence when there are fewer other factors that do so.

SUMMARY

From the earliest studies of television's introduction in a community to today's complex multivariate analyses, there has been a propensity to focus on the issue of displacement. The recurrent explanation for television's influence on reading skills has been that it displaces out-of-school reading, and thus negatively affects overall achievement.

What is truly intriguing however, is that television has never been shown to displace reading. Even during its novelty phase, studies by Himmelweit, Schramm, and others did not report changes in leisure reading. Indeed, these studies indicated that there was little reading time for television to displace in the first place. Time spent leisure reading has remained surprisingly stable over the years: There was not much reading before television, and there is not much reading today.

Perhaps the very endurance of the displacement theory lies in its elegant simplicity. Conceivably, if we can account for children's lack of leisure reading and poor achievement as a result of viewing, then its curtailment will naturally lead to greater interest in reading along with higher achievement levels in schools. But simple explanations in this case cannot account for complex phenomena. Both television and home-based reading defy easy manipulation. More likely, the amount, type, and attention to television viewing and book reading are factors of a much larger, more difficult-to-separate set of expectations related to children's home environment. In this respect, viewing and reading are not so independent, but tied to a nexus of family influences (see Chapter 7 for a descriptive analysis of these factors). The displacement theory typically portrays various media as battling against each other, vying for the time and attention of children. Once freed from this substitution model, we can begin to view the media from a different perspective, one that focuses on the notion of complementarity. Going beyond the displacement model then, the next chapters will further explore the powerful interconnections between the two media.

3

The Information
Processing Theory

We have confused reason with literacy and rationalism with a single
technology. (McLuhan, 1964, p. 15)

Marshall McLuhan's elliptical phrase, "the medium is the message," created a revolutionary change in the way people viewed media.
Television as a medium, from this perspective, was now seen as having
certain characteristics that transcended content and thus defined it as
a particular information-processing environment. These attributes
were thought to describe a medium that, regardless of the content
being presented, offered particular cognitive tasks and opportunities to
children.

It was during this same period that a major paradigm shift was
occurring in psychology with the stimulus-response models of learning
giving way to the more cognitive orientation which predominates
today. As a result of these forces, a new research tradition in media
emerged—one that focused on individual differences in how children
perceived television and the ways in which the medium itself might
modify those perceptions.

Print and television, from this view, could be differentiated by the
degree of involvement necessary to extract meaning from the medium
(McLuhan, 1964). Print, according to McLuhan, being a "hot" medium,
presents sensory stimuli filled with data and therefore requires little
or no work from the child to complete its signals. Television, on the
other hand, is a "cool" medium, demanding viewers participation in
order to integrate television's lines of dots in order to form a complete
image. Based on the type of physical stimuli media transmit,

McLuhan's analysis suggests that users must adjust their information processing skills to encode these messages. Reading, for example, involves no direct sensory experience, only that of interpreting abstract symbols. Television, however closely approximating real life, requires viewers to virtually become part of the event itself. This participational quality distinguishes it from other media which involve the mental processing of symbols representing the experience of others.

McLuhan's legacy persists and challenges researchers to confirm or reject his free-ranging speculations. From his fascinating conjectures, systematic research on media symbol systems has evolved, focusing on how information is conveyed and learned in different media. This chapter first reviews this research, and then offers a countervailing model of media and learning. In contrast to McLuhan's thesis, this model posits that the information processing demands from television and reading, although they rely on different codes, are equivalent and serve a similar role in knowledge acquisition.

THE THEORIES

McLuhan's style of writing—which relies heavily on proverbs, slang, and illustrations—allowed for multiple interpretations. Many have attempted—from philosopher Susan Sontag to colorful essayist, Tom Wolfe— to restate in some type of logical form what McLuhan "really" meant. McLuhan (1967), however, was never to cast his ideas into a more systematic form, arguing that "I don't explain, I explore."

Others, therefore, were left to develop a systematic body of knowledge reflecting McLuhan's sensitivity to media and its consequences. This could only be done by first creating an explicit theory along with a methodology for testing the theory. Several researchers took on this ambitious task.

A Theory of Instructional Means

Capitalizing on the intriguing insights of McLuhan, David Olson and Jerome Bruner (1974) proposed a model of instruction which clearly differentiated knowledge and skills. Each medium, they argued, employs a symbol system: "a set of symbols which forms a system of interrelated options that are correlated with a field of reference" (p.12), such as language, music, and numbers. Various symbol systems, tied to the media, produce a unique pattern of skills for dealing with or thinking about the world. These symbols have certain inherent characteristics that tend to constrain what kind of messages are transmitted and how these messages are attended to, understood, and acted upon, overtly and covertly.

According to their argument, it is naive to assume that the information potential of all media is the same. Media might converge on the information they convey but they diverge on the skills they assume and develop. For example, the skill of obtaining information through visual images on television is a radically different skill from that of extracting the same information from language. The critical issue, then, becomes one of deciding which skill one wishes to cultivate.

Extending this work, Olson (1976) proposed a theory of instructional means. The theory classifies any experience as having both a content and a means. The content of the medium relates to the knowledge acquired, while the means, or the code in which the knowledge is presented, is related to "the skills, strategies and heuristics that are called on and developed" (p. 26). Unlike knowledge, skills are not directly teachable. They are implicit, developed through repeated attempts of performance with "feedback from a master" (p. 19).

Studies have typically concentrated on knowledge acquisition and transfer rather than the skills developed during that period, according to Olson. However, skills are potentially transferable as well. He illustrates this point by describing a series of studies on discovery learning versus the traditional expository means of teaching and learning. In this research, the discovery method showed disappointingly little advantage in the application of learned principles to new tasks. Yet, he points out, the discovery group did show some superiority on a transfer test of problem-solving skills, suggesting that while the content acquired was similar, different intellectual skills were employed and transferred.

The theory of instructional means suggests that a medium's symbol system or code not only conveys knowledge but rather cultivates new skills for exploration and internal representation (Clark & Salomon, 1986). In the school setting, the skills acquired are based on the medium of text. As a result, Olson reports "when children are taught to read, they are learning both to read and to treat language as text" (1977, p. 103). Television, employing its unique symbol system, will yield a different set of skills in acquiring new knowledge.

Olson does not specify what the particular skills inherent in each medium actually are. We can surmise, however from his general argument, that practice in reading, regardless of the content, leads to greater skill in reading. Time spent viewing television, again, apart from the content watched, leads to greater sophistication in how children watch television.

The Theory of Media Attributes

Extending the work of Olson and Bruner, Gavriel Salomon (1979) proposed that by activating mental skills, cognition—the very way people think—may be influenced by the symbol systems employed by media. Not only can a medium implicitly teach a symbol system, as Olson and Bruner assumed, but it has the capacity to arouse certain general attentional processes and become internalized, serving as a "scheme of thought." While media are complex entities, it is the symbol system employed in each medium that constitutes its most important attribute or essential mode of representation.

In a series of studies measuring children's ability to internalize filmic codes, Salomon (1974) reported that students deficient in cue attending were able to internalize the "zooming" of a camera lens into a stimulus field, increasing their cue-attending skills. A more recent study, using computers to stimulate metacognitive skills in reading, demonstrated that students were able to transfer these metacognitive modes of representation when given a new condition (Salomon, 1987). While Salomon acknowledges that these features may merely activate already established skills, he contends that these data show evidence that media codes were internalized, schematized, and then applied to new circumstances (Salomon, 1986).

Mental processes are not activated automatically, however. Children learn on the basis of what is meaningful to them. Preschoolers, with their limited schemata, tend only to pick up highly salient, and fragmentary units of information from any medium. But around ages 6–7, children's mastery of a specific mental skill can be affected to the extent that they find the information useful. For example, Salomon's (1979) study of *Sesame Street* in Israel indicated that as the amount of viewing increased, children's mastery of skills (such as relating parts to a whole) improved, along with better knowledge acquisition.

Others, however, have suggested a rival hypothesis (Clark, 1983; Rumulhart, 1980). They argue that symbol systems themselves might not directly influence learning. Rather, learning is reflected in how closely the particular attribute mirrors the task to be learned. For example, the outstanding feature in the cue-attending study by Salomon was probably the filmic presentation's capacity to isolate the relevant cues for the learner. Therefore, when a symbol system is shaped to represent the specific learning objectives inherent in the task, learning will occur.

The Dual-Coding Theory

Are pictures and words encoded and stored in a single, underlying representational system or in separate systems? Paivio (1978) likens the dual coding theoretical approach to an audiovisual metaphor. The theory proposes that two systems are actually at work, a verbal system specializing in processing linguistic information in various modalities, and a separate nonverbal system for spatial information and mental imagery. Each of these systems are thought to differ in the nature of their representation-cognitive units, the way these units are organized and transformed, and in their function as mediators of performance in perceptual memory, language, and cognitive tasks (Paivio & Begg, 1981).

They are, however, also partly interconnected. For example, a child looking at a picture might also engage in covert verbalization. When a concept is registered in both memory systems, it is said to be dual-coded. Paivio argues that dual coding is more likely to occur with the image than with the verbal system. Since two memory traces are better than one, the dual-coding theory suggests that memory for visual imagery may be superior than memory for words. In a review of the theory, Paivio (1983) provides 10 types of research evidence and 60 empirical findings ranging from imagery-concreteness effects of language, picture versus word effects to neuropsychological evidence and subjective report data that may be interpreted in favor of the dual-code model.

He argues that pictures are easier to remember than words especially when they serve as a source of retrieving information rather than simply a response. However, the dual systems have an additive effect on free recall. For example, in one experiment, subjects were required to compare the sizes of angles formed by the hands of two clocks when the clock times were presented in either digital or analog, or mixed (one of both) forms. The comparisons were naturally faster for the two analog than the two digital times, because the former simply required a perceptual judgement. Interestingly, however, the reaction time was intermediate for the mixed case time in which one clock was analog and the other digital. These data, according to Paivio, describe the additive effect that one system may have on the other.

The dual-coding theory bears some resemblance to the media attribute theories in that it proposes that two symbol systems are at work in encoding and storing information. Salomon's (1979) theory of the internalization of the symbolic forms of television, as well as Olson and Bruner's (1974) claim that particular strategies may be implicitly taught through the audio-visual medium, seem to be related to the dual-coding argument.

The Formal Features of Television

Symbol system theorists proposed a compelling argument for analyzing a medium's form rather than its content. What was now needed was a method for systematically characterizing a medium's form, identifying how its attributes might influence children's learning. Following this research tradition, a number of psychologists became interested in television's "formal features," the unique forms by which television producers encode information for communication (Huston & Wright, 1983; Krull, 1983; Watkins, Huston-Stein, & Wright, 1981; Watt & Welch, 1983). In addition to the theoretical interests generated by McLuhan's proposals, these researchers had some practical goals in mind. Specifically, if one could identify the formal properties that were effective in attracting children's attention, perhaps these same features could be used to enhance television's educational effectiveness without detracting from its entertainment functions.

Foremost has been the work by Aletha Huston and John Wright and colleagues at the Center for Research on the Influences of Television on Children (CRITC) who analyzed these forms with an approach similar to that used by linguists, carefully defining the formal rules or syntax of television's code (Huston-Stein & Wright, 1979). Formal features, from their theoretical model, serve in structuring and giving meaning to the sensory images emerging from the screen. Salient features can enhance children's comprehension of content by emphasizing or spotlighting plot elements or themes. Music, a loud crash, can announce an event or a certain component of a program critical for viewers to comprehend. In one study, for example, kindergarten children were tested for recall of television content that was presented with highly salient formal features compared to a group seeing similar content with low salience techniques. They found that enhanced comprehension was associated with familiar formal features which focus children's attention on central story content (Calvert, Huston, Watkins, & Wright, 1982).

Huston and Wright identified three clusters of formal features, constituting a taxonomy of television forms. The first includes perceptually salient events, including sound effects, loud music, and rapid cuts. The second, often used in educational children's programs, involves reflection, including such features as long zooms, singing, and moderate levels of physical activity. The third cluster consists of character dialogue or speech. The researchers hypothesized that with age and increasing exposure, children's attention gradually habituates from salient stimuli to those features that are more informative or relevant to the understanding of stories.

Contrary to expectations, their data suggest that children continue to attend to perceptually salient features across a wide age range. Uses of other formal features, indicative of higher levels of processing, are dependent upon a much more complex set of interactions, which take into account not only the children's developing cognitive and linguistic skills but their goals, purposes, and intentions for viewing.

Huston and Wright's major contribution has been to set forth a model for defining the language of television. Like other symbol systems, television's code has a logic or grammar that, when used along with children's growing cognitive skills, and linguistic competence, may help us understand how children learn from television.

COMPARING MEDIA

Common to these symbol system theories is the belief that the most profound and enduring differences between media are related to its form, rather than its content. Each medium uses specific symbols to tell a story and structure how individuals process and acquire information. Over time, children accumulate experiences and know-how with those symbol systems used most consistently. One might expect, then, that differences in the way children cognitively process information would occur on the basis of their media preferences. Could it be that those children who view television with its concrete representations develop more visual skills, while those who rely on more abstract symbols like print, more verbal or expressive language abilities?

Investigating the distinctive cognitive consequences of media was a direct outgrowth of the symbol system theories and, in part, reflected a growing concern on the potential negative influences of television. It was thought that with the activation and repeated utilization of certain mental skills that were closely allied with television viewing, children might limit their opportunities to practice and cultivate other skills more specific to school learning.

Media Comparison Studies

Laurene Meringoff (1980) and her colleagues at Project Zero were among the first to investigate the distinctive features of learning from television and other media. One study, for example, analyzed children's apprehension of an African folktale presented in either an animated televised film or read aloud from a picture storybook. Verbal retellings indicated that children in the television group used character actions and visual cues to describe the story content, while the read-aloud group responded to aural cues or information not given in the story at all. These findings indicated that the specific details of content, and the more subtle skills of drawing on one's prior knowledge, may vary according to the medium.

But are they medium-specific? Beagles-Roos and Gat (1983), using similar instruments and methodology as in Meringoff's study, analyzed cross-media comparisons of television and radio on first and fourth grader's story comprehension. Children retold the story equivalently with radio and television presentations. However, there were striking differences across media in the way they told the story. Here, it was the radio version that induced children to go beyond explicit and implicit story content to substantiate their inferences, much like the storybook treatment in Meringoff's study. Students, viewing the televised presentation, once again based their inferences on story actions. These results, substantiating Clark's thesis (1983), suggest that many different media (in this case radio and print) may be shaped in a form that can enhance children's learning. Attributes of symbol systems, therefore, are not necessarily medium-specific; there is considerable overlap between media.

Evidence of this overlap was reported by Pezdek, Lehrer, and Simon (1984). Their study of media differences between radio, television, and print indicated significant correlations on children's comprehension from radio and storybook presentations. Children who read a story aloud with understanding were also likely to comprehend material heard on the radio, suggesting an overlap between the information-processing skills used in both media. In contrast, performance in the television and reading conditions was not significantly correlated, indicating that the skills in extracting and remembering information from these two media were relatively independent of each other. The probable reason for these findings, according to Greenfield (1984), is that print and radio are exclusively verbal media and thus have considerable overlap, whereas the visual medium of television contrasts more sharply with print.

Other media comparison studies, however, have not substantiated these claims that specific media enhance specific skills. Table 3.1 summarizes a number of these studies.

While most report distinctive differences between media presentations in their own investigations, there is no consistency across studies regarding the specific information processing skills a particular medium elicits. Beagles-Roos and Gat's study, for example, reported greater expressive language in oral retelling from the radio condition, whereas Char and Meringoff (1982) found that children used fewer words, and showed less story comprehension when listening to a story from radio. Banker and Meringoff (1982) reported that children's inferences from a film story were more varied than those from the same story delivered by a storyteller, yet children's inferences from television in Meringoff's first study (1980) were found to be more narrowly tied to story actions.

Therefore, while indicating that different media presentations of similar stories might elicit slightly different interpretations of that

Table 3.1.   Comparing Media

Study	Media Compared	Results
Banker & Meringoff (1982)	Film	Used various bases for substantiating inferences Conveyed appropriate character affect
	Silent film	Made comments of how film was made
	Descriptive aural version of film	Used more words in retellings Conveyed appropriate character affect
	Recorded story	Used more words in retelling Rarely used inferences other than those provided.
Beagles-Roos & Gat (1983)	TV	Students scored higher in picture sorting. More uses of vague references in retellings Cited more details Justifications in references tied to story actions
	Radio	More expressive language Inferences drawn from verbal content and prior knowledge
Char & Meringoff (1982)	TV	Produced most complete narratives Higher comprehension of vocabulary
	Storybook reading	Higher vocabulary
	Radio	Showed less comprehension of story Less comprehension of vocabulary
Hayes, Kelly, & Mandel (1986)	TV	Children's retention of action sequences greater Better comprehension
	Radio	More errors in summarizing Retention of dialogue not critical to story
Hoffner, Cantor, & Thorson (1988)	Audio only Visual only Audio-visual	Younger children had more difficulty understanding a narrative presented in an exclusively visual form than either audio only or audio-visual.
Meringoff (1980)	TV	Cited more character actions More physical gesturing Relied on visual content for inferences
	Storybook	Recalled more figurative lang. Based Inferences on textual content and outside story information.
Neuman (1989)	TV	No significant differences in expressive language, retellings of story events and inferences
	Storybook	

story, these studies do not provide convincing evidence that a medium's symbolic attributes activate specific cognitive processing skills. Of course, there are some important limitations in these studies. Media comparison studies are naturally constrained by having to achieve adequate comparability of content across media. To do this requires more conservative uses of the actual media being compared. For example, with the exception of Banker and Meringoff, these studies used animated films (usually supplied from Weston Woods) which employed the same graphic pictures as the book for their televised condition. This type of presentation, and the attributes they exploit, differ dramatically from typical television fare, therefore compromising the ecological validity of the study findings.

Further, unlike Salomon's media attribute studies (1974, 1979), these investigations have not clearly delineated the distinctive features of each presentation prior to the experimental treatment. Without doing so, it is impossible to link differential interpretations of stories to particular attributes of media. The symbol systems employed by each medium are simply too diverse to automatically assume that a televised version relies more heavily on visual information than an illustrated storybook without first analyzing the differences between treatments.

Finally, findings from a recent study by Gibbons, Anderson, Smith, Field, and Fischer (1986) indicate that media difference studies might be confounding information conveyed by the medium and cognitive skills. In their study of different media presentations (audio vs. audiovisual), these researchers experimentally controlled for redundancy of audiovisual information by providing narrated actions in the audio version. Analyzing young children's reconstruction of stories, they reported that all children, regardless of the particular medium, recalled more story actions than utterances. Their findings suggest that previous studies reporting media differences may have inadvertently confounded these differences with the type of information actually presented. Similarly, when Baggett (1979) experimentally measured structurally equivalent stories in movies and text on student recall, no differences were reported.

In sum, our knowledge of the potential linkage between exposure to a medium's symbol system and the development of specific cognitive abilities is limited. While Salomon's studies suggest that different media, making use of specific techniques, may facilitate the acquisition of such cognitive skills as attention focusing, and perspective taking, there is no evidence that such effects occur under normal conditions without direct instruction. To a great extent, these qualifications undercut the assumption that skill cultivation through symbol systems is implicit, occurring naturally as children attend to the media.

But this reservation is hardly as serious as more recent criticisms. Indeed, the very assumptions underlying symbol system theories have been challenged by critics (Clark, 1983; Rumelhart, 1980). Clark, in his synthesis of research on learning from media, finds no evidence to suggest that symbol systems serve any unique function at all in cognition and learning, arguing that "media are mere vehicles that deliver instruction but do not influence student achievement any more than the truck that delivers our groceries cause changes in our nutrition" (p. 445). According to Clark, it is not the symbolic element itself that influences learning. Rather, it is how well the symbol system is shaped to represent the critical features of a cognitive task. From this perspective, a variety of symbol systems may be used to achieve the same performance, implying that the choice of media may be less important for learning than the symbol system theories had assumed.

Differences in Processing Media

Symbol systems are but one aspect of the differences among media. Other media attributes such as the psychological energy needed to process its information, the pacing of information, and level of interactivity might relate to the specific information-processing activities which children engage in while using media, and these activities might relate to children's subsequent knowledge and skills.

Based partly on the perceived demand characteristics of the media as well as its modes of representation, Salomon (1983) introduced the construct of the amount of invested mental effort (AIME) to conceptualize differences in learning from media. According to Salomon's model, AIME reflects the level of processing or mental energy needed to be expended in order to comprehend a medium. Television, with its format and pictures, is regarded by most as an easy medium, requiring little effort expenditure. As a result, children tend to view mindlessly, missing valuable opportunities to learn from it. Print, on the other hand, is perceived as a more demanding medium, requiring greater AIME, which can lead to greater in-depth processing.

Initial findings from several studies support his thesis (Salomon, 1983, 1984). Reporting on the invested mental effort in reading a narrative story or a televised version, Salomon (1984) found that sixth graders invested more effort in reading, and made more correct inferences, than from seeing the televised version. Further, children in both versions made more correct inferences the more effort they reported investing.

While the notion of AIME is intriguing, further empirical evidence is needed to substantiate processing differences for print or television. Other studies, for example, have failed to link AIME with children's comprehension of the central content in television programs (Beentjes, 1989). In addition to instrumentation problems, AIME needs to be measured across a broader array of formats and contexts. The notion of "sameness" that is sometimes attributed to television's different programs and multiple formats does not apply in the case of print. Here, effort expenditure may vary widely across context (home vs. school), purposes (reading to do, reading for pleasure) as well different levels of skill mastery (expert readers vs. novice).

Few would argue, however, that most children tend to view television as relatively undemanding. But others lay blame on the medium's delivery system. Singer (1980), for example, argues that television's pacing, its constant sensory bombardment, leaves little time for mental elaboration. Its emphasis on visual images involving mainly the brain's right hemisphere, allows only holistic recognition, but hardly deeper analysis. Without the time necessary for efficient memory retrieval, television becomes a passive cognitive activity.

Singer's conception of television reflects the widely held view, promoted by mass market publications, that television is an extremely passive, almost addicting experience (Mander, 1978; Mankiewicz & Swerdlow, 1978; Winn, 1977). Television's compelling features are thought to "control" children. As a result according to Mander, the viewer shows, "no cognition, no discernment, no notations upon the experience one is having" (p. 204).

The very process of reading, according to these critics, contrasts sharply with viewing television. Aside from its supposedly more complicated symbol system, the slower-paced activity, by its very deliberation, provides the opportunity for greater integration of the material with patterns of memory, wishes, and intentions.

> Reading involves a complex form of mental activity, trains the mind in concentration skills, develops the powers of imagination and inner visualization, the flexibility of its pace, lends itself to a better and deeper comprehension of the materials communicated. Reading engrosses but does not hypnotize or seduce the reader from his human responsibilities. (Winn, 1977, p. 57)

While these differences have been noted and popularly adopted by a large number of critical groups, there is no evidence to suggest that differences in pacing alone affect levels of information processing and learning from media. Despite its acceptance by a number of intellectual communities, no research agenda has been formulated to actually test these hypotheses.

But it is not only the pacing that "dulls" the senses according to Marie Winn in *The Plug-in Drug*. Rather, it is that television, representing a one-way mode of communication, draws children away from actively experiencing their environment. From a Piagetian theory of child development, interactive sensory experiences with physical objects around them and active relationships with other people, are critical to their development. Yet with television, according to Winn, children develop a style of learning based on observation and imitation, an unacceptable substitute for real experience. The most pernicious aspect of television, therefore, lies not in its content or pacing, but in the deadness of the one-way experience.

Reading by its very nature, on the other hand, is interactive. It involves the construction of meaning from text. Here, the author and the reader are sharing in the process of making meaning, allowing for multiple interpretations of a story. "This aspect of reading, which might be called creative in the narrow sense of the word, is present during all reading experiences regardless of what is being read" (Winn, p. 50). Reading is a participatory activity; television, a passive, one-dimensional activity.

Winn's argument, once again, reflects the common perception of television as a passive, nonthinking activity, where children sit like "zombies," absorbing content without reflection or interaction. Differences in processing television and reading therefore, are seen as dramatic. Television is thought to be reactive; reading, however, challenges children to become a participant in their own learning.

Table 3.2 gives an overview of the hypothesized differences in processing television and reading.

Table 3.2.   Hypothesized Differences in Processing Television and Reading

Differences Relate to:	Proposed by	Perceived Relationship
AIME	Salomon (1984)	Television requires little effort expenditure Reading perceived as a more demanding medium, leading to greater in-depth processing
Pacing	Singer (1980) Mander (1978) H. Lesser (1977)	Television's pacing creates passivity Reading allows for greater attention and reflection
Interactivity	Winn (1977)	Television, a one-way medium, trains children to learn by observing and imitating Reading is constructive and interactive

Very apparent are the striking contrasts in the perceived information processing demands of the two media. Salomon's AIME model argues that while viewing television is an information-processing activity, children devote little energy based on their conception of the amount of effort such an activity requires to be understood. But there are those who argue that it is the technology—specifically, television's pacing and lack of interactivity— that is detrimental to how children comprehend the media. From this view, television's exceptionally powerful influence turns the active learner into a reactive learner—one who responds mechanistically to images provided on the screen.

THE SCHEMA-THEORETIC MODEL: A COUNTER THESIS

Symbol system theories and others based on media technology have focused on the different information processing demands of television and reading. The outcome of this work has been to emphasize differences in the ways in which information is conveyed by various media and how, in turn, these forms affect how knowledge is processed and used by children.

But there is an alternative view. Contrary to those who claim processing differences, media's symbolic systems may not call upon and cultivate different skills. Rather, processing of television and print materials may share a large number of important procedural and strategic components. Taking this viewpoint, it may be argued that the similarities in children's reasoning about television and print far outweigh its differences.

To further explicate this thesis, the following section will present a schema-driven model of television and reading, and present evidence for four specific aspects of the model. This is followed by a brief example, illustrating how a child uses his information to acquire new information from television and print. Finally, the implications of the model are described, returning once again to the important question— does the symbol system employed by the medium significantly affect the manner in which children process information?

The Child As Active

In contrast to the notion of "tabula rasa," cognitive theorists today regard children as playing an active and selective role in their own learning. To each environment, children bring pre-established schemata, or preparatory scripts, acquired and modified by induction from previous and ongoing experiences. Schemata are active processes which guide the comprehender in interpreting data, retrieving information from memory, and constructing expectations as to what information will occur next (Rumelhart, 1980). These cognitive structures consist of an organized set of concepts, both general and specific. For example, a child's cognitive structure may contain the schema ICE CREAM. More general concepts might include food, dessert, or things that are cold; more particular, vanilla or chocolate flavors, jimmies, and ice cream cones. When parts of one's schema become activated, these slots are instantiated with particular information.

Schema theory has had a tremendous impact on our understanding of the reading process. Foremost has been the work of Richard Anderson and his colleagues at the Center for the Study of Reading, who have dramatically reshaped theoretical interpretations of reading comprehension. In sharp contrast with prior notions of reading as a linear process consisting of aggregating the meanings of words to form the meaning of clauses, and then sentences, comprehension is seen as a matter of activating or constructing schema that provide a coherent explanation of objects and events mentioned in discourse (Anderson, 1984).

Readers are said to comprehend a text when they are able to activate a schema that gives a good account of the events described. "Goodness of fit" occurs when all the textual information can be fitted into slots in the schema, and when all major slots of the schema contain information from the text. Schemata, therefore, act as an executive editor, screening, directing, helping the reader to assimilate new information into existing knowledge structures.

As a theory of knowledge, it is natural to assume that schemata operate in a similar fashion for other incoming information as well. In keeping with this theoretical orientation, it is conceivable that the ongoing cognitive processing of television is, like reading, schema-driven. Anderson and Lorch (1983) propose such a model, theorizing that through experience with television and general world knowledge, children develop schemata about the temporal and conceptual flow of normal television programs. These schemata help monitor their attention to television, by directing their focus to the more salient parts of a program necessary to adequately comprehend its meaning.

A criterion of consistency is demanded in schema theory, even in the fictional world of television. If characters are expected to turn green and ominously stalk evil doers, then these expectations must be fulfilled. When such conventions are violated, knowledgeable viewers become unsettled; less knowledgeable viewers, confused (Anderson &

Table 3.3.   Four Aspects of Schema Theory

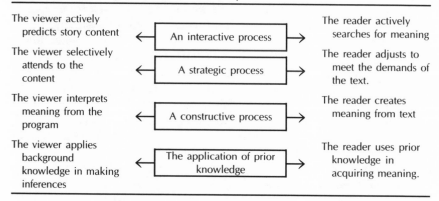

The viewer actively predicts story content	← An interactive process →	The reader actively searches for meaning
The viewer selectively attends to the content	← A strategic process →	The reader adjusts to meet the demands of the text.
The viewer interprets meaning from the program	← A constructive process →	The reader creates meaning from text
The viewer applies background knowledge in making inferences	← The application of prior knowledge →	The reader uses prior knowledge in acquiring meaning.

Lorch, 1983). When over the course of a program, incoming information can no longer be fit in existing slots, children's attention will naturally become diverted to other, more comprehensible activities.

Schema Theory and Reading and Television Viewing

Table 3.3 describes four aspects of the processes involved in reading and television viewing from the perspective of schema theory.[1] They highlight the active nature of learning from media, where individuals are approaching each new situation, anticipating certain consequences, and searching for information that will meet with previous plans and expectations. Each aspect is described below.

An interactive process. According to schema theory, reading is conceived of as an interactive process. This means that understanding does not progress in a strict order from the visual information in letters to the overall interpretation of text. Rather, reading involves a more or less simultaneous analysis at many different levels—graphophonemic, semantic, syntactic, and interpretive. This point is well illustrated by an example from the work of Bransford and McCarrell (1974):

The notes were sour because the seam split.

While all the words in the sentence are familiar, the sentence does not make sense. Yet, when the additional clue of "bagpipes" is provided, it becomes understandable because we are able to activate a

---

[1] Several aspects of the reading process are adapted from Mason and Au (1986).

schema that includes music, notes, material, interrelating these elements into a satisfying interpretation (R. Anderson, 1984).

This illustration suggests that comprehension of reading involves both the analysis of print and the schema one brings to the text. These two sources of data correspond to what Bobrow and Norman (1975) have called "data-driven" or bottom-up processes referring to information from print, and "conceptually driven" or top-down, from expectations or hypotheses based on prior knowledge.

Similar to reading, the process of television viewing is also interactive. Attention to programs reflects viewers moment-to-moment understanding of the television content (bottom-up processing) as well as the schema they bring to the program (top-down processing). D. Anderson and colleagues, for example, found that when segments of *Sesame Street* had their comprehensibility experimentally reduced by using backward speech or foreign language, visual attention greatly diminished (Anderson, Lorch, Field, & Sanders, 1981). These findings are interpreted as evidence that comprehension tends to guide children's attention to programs.

Television's repetitive formats, the constancy of its character actions contribute to the development of certain expectations, which facilitate children's ability to predict story content (Schramm, Lyle, & Parker, 1961). This predictability is one of television's central attractions because it frees viewers from having to maintain attention throughout the program (Comstock, Chaffee, Katzman, McCombs, & Roberts, 1978).

Schemata direct viewers to attend to specific parts of a show. As children watch a typical *Tom and Jerry* cartoon, for example, they fill in slots with information based on confrontation, cat and mouse tricks, and the inevitable chase scene. Details conforming to these parts of the cartoon will best be remembered. However, when a schema cannot be applied to a program, interest in viewing will decline (Anderson & Lorch, 1983). For example, a young child viewing a football game on television might be able to instantiate or activate an elementary schema involving "ball games" but be unable to comprehend any of the subtleties of the play by play. Since the incoming information cannot be organized into any available slots, attention will fall off, as the child becomes engaged in alternative activities if available. Comprehending television as an interactive process then, requires mental elaboration, including perceiving information, drawing inferences, and generating hypotheses about what comes next.

A strategic process. Good readers are strategic, adjusting their reading to meet the demands of the criterion task and text. These strategies include self-monitoring devices such as evaluating the task before reading, checking one's understanding, rereading parts, and summarizing the main points when finished reading (Paris, 1986). These cognitive monitoring processes tend to be experienced subconsciously, triggered only when a comprehension problem is detected. Take, for example, these sentences from Collins, Brown, and Larkin (1980):

> He plunked down $5 at the window. She tried to give him $2.50, but he refused to take it. So when they got inside, she bought him a large bag of popcorn.

Upon reading the second sentence, good readers might become aware of a "breakdown" in comprehension. Why would he possibly refuse the money? Aware of the ambiguity of the text, they might first guess that the woman was a cashier. As they move thoughtfully to the third sentence, they might reject their hypothesis, then reread and conclude that the "she" was more likely to be a girlfriend, trying to repay her date (Mason & Au, 1986).

Strategic readers tend to allocate their attention to text selectively. According to R. Anderson and Pearson's theory (1984), text elements are first processed to a minimal level, then graded for importance. Extra attention is devoted to elements that exceed some criterion of importance. Due to the extra attention received, these elements are categorized in existing schemata, learned and remembered better than others. This would explain why skilled readers seem better able to recall important elements and draw connecting inferences from text.

Recent research indicates that television viewing, as well, is highly strategic (Gibbons, Anderson, Smith, Field, & Fischer, 1986; Lorch, Bellack, & Augsbach, 1987; Pezdek & Hartman, 1983; Pingree, 1986). Studies confirm that children's attentional engagement varies considerably during television (about 100–200 variations per hour). These variations, however, appear to be selective, suggesting that children apply a rational, self-monitoring process appropriate to the content of the television program. Contrary to prior research on television comprehension (cf. Collins, 1983), these new studies suggest that attention is directed to content considered to be essential to understanding the program. Meadowcroft and Reeves (1985), for example, using secondary reaction time task procedures, measured children's attention to a cartoon consisting of scenes including central or incidental information. Reaction times during the central scenes were substantially slower than those during incidental scenes, indicating that children were more intensely engaged during the points in the story most critical to comprehension.

Formal features may also serve as signaling devices in structuring children's attention to the content of the program. Constellations of formal features unique to particular series or program genres, can suggest the presence of particular kinds of content worthy of attention (Huston & Wright, 1983). Planners of *Sesame Street* used these features liberally, arguing that such formats created a mental set, or called forth the appropriate schema for interpreting new information (Lesser, 1974).

The strategic nature of both television and reading, according to R. Anderson, and D. Anderson and Lorch, will naturally vary according to different task demands and context. Readers or viewers may apply different strategies depending on the purpose of the activity (entertainment vs. information), its overall value to the individual, and the social setting in which it takes place.

A constructive process. Schema theory highlights the constructive nature of the reading process. Text, from this perspective, merely provides a skeleton, a blueprint for the creation of meaning (Spiro, 1980). Such representations are enriched and embellished so that they conform with the understander's preexisting world views and the operative purposes of understanding at a given time. In this respect, Iser (1974) refers to the act of reading as a "sense-making activity."

Reading as a constructive process implies that there is no one "correct" meaning of a text. Rather, it is the convergence of the text and the reader, that brings a literary work into existence (Rosenblatt, 1978). The interpretation of text, therefore, is unique, reflecting one's own "identity theme" (Holland, 1975). Given a similar text, "the moralist will find a reinforcement of his ethical views; the scientifically minded man will see verifiable reality" (p. 125).

The television stimulus, like text, offers a panoply of social actions, events, and situations. Viewers must select and transform these experiences into synthesis or interpretation which is integrative and satisfying. For young children, in particular, responses to television may vary widely according to their own unique set of past experiences, information processing tools, and interpretive abilities. Such variance is indicative of "ill-structured problems," which characterize the cognitive tasks presented by television, requiring considerable attentional, organizational and inferential activity by the viewer (Collins, 1983).

The constructivist perspective affirms the individual's role in the transaction of meaning (Dorr, 1986). Viewers' interpretations become the medium's messages. Various problems can arise, however, for young children when schemata tend to be insufficiently or overly tied to personal experience. In one study for example, second graders' comprehension failures resulted from their stereotypical or inflexible application of common world knowledge to a particular scene (Collins & Wellman, 1982).

Klapper's (1960) principle of selective attention, selective perception, and selective retention reflects the constructivist position. His model suggests that from a multiplicity of available content, individuals will selectively attend to media, particularly if they are related to their attitudes and interests. In the event of being exposed to unsympathetic material, viewers tend not to perceive it, or to recast it in an interpretation that fits their existing views, or to simply forget it. From similar content, these mediating factors might lead to differing responses.

Television viewing as a constructive process emphasizes the active role of the viewer in interpreting program content. It also suggests that the individual viewer's plans and expectations may strongly influence the medium's message.

The application of prior knowledge. Readers acquire meaning from text against a backdrop of their own personal knowledge and experiences of the world. Perhaps no other aspect of the schema-theoretic model has been as experimentally investigated as the role of prior knowledge on comprehension (Anderson, Reynolds, Schallert, & Goetz, 1977; Pichert & Anderson, 1977; Reynolds, Taylor, Steffensen, Shirey, & Anderson, 1982). A good deal of evidence for its impact on interpretation comes from investigations which present students with ambiguous texts. A study of this type was conducted by Anderson, Reynolds, Schallert, and Goetz (1977), who gave a similar passage to female music majors and male wrestlers. A portion of the passage illustrates the two possible interpretations readers could generate:

> Rocky slowly got up from the mat, planning his escape. He hesitated a moment and thought. Things were not going well. What bothered him most was being held, especially since the charge against him had been weak.

Recall of the text showed strong differential patterns as a function of the group's prior knowledge and interests. Physical education majors gave a wrestling interpretation; music majors, a prison break explanation.

Background knowledge strongly influences comprehension of implied information from text. Readers must first make inferences to determine what schema, among many, should be called into play, what associations to make, what values to assign for missing information, and what perspective to bring to bear on the reading task. Pearson, Hansen, and Gordon (1979), for example, found that differences in prior knowledge of a topic accounted for large differences in children's ability to answer inferential questions.

Children's capacity to inference appears to be age-related (Omanson, Warren, & Trabasso, 1978; Paris & Upton, 1976). Young children seem to have some difficulty drawing inferences spontaneously from stories than older elementary students. But the reasons for these developmental differences remain unclear. Omanson et al. theorize that it is available prior knowledge, not differences in memory capacity, that accounts for distinctions in the quantity of inferences.

Prior knowledge also accounts for differences in children's comprehension of television.Perhaps the most extensive series of studies have been conducted by Collins (1983), analyzing the role of world knowledge and social expectations. One study, for example, examined the effects of children's social class background on their understanding of the intentions of lower or middle class television characters. Comprehension differed as a function of thè match between student's background and the characters portrayed in the program; lower-class children better understood the lower-class family plots, middle-class children, the middle-class plots (Collins, 1979). Differences were not found, however, for the fifth and eighth graders in the study. Presumably, the older children's greater sophistication with television, along with their more extensive background knowledge, allowed them to understand the shows equally well.

A small controversy has arisen over whether very young children are actually capable of inferencing from television content. Collins, for example, argues that much of children's comprehension failures may be due to their inability to make relevant inferences. Limited background knowledge, he suggests, may prevent children from understanding important plot-relevant information from televised stories. More recent studies, however, contradict these earlier claims. Pingree, et al. (1984), using a reconstruction procedure where preschool children reenacted a story, found surprisingly complete and connected comprehension and inferences of a televised family situation comedy. Lorch et al. (1987) and Gibbons et al. (1986) similarly reported that preschoolers were able to draw a variety of inferences and form coherent representations from television.

Anderson and Collins (1988) suggest several possible explanations for the discrepancies in findings. Beyond general instrumentation concerns, they propose that the differences in findings might relate to children's lack of a rich knowledge base for making relevant inferences in the adult dramas used in Collins' studies. When preschoolers view programs more characteristic of their age level, comprehension of implicit content contrasts dramatically with Collins' findings.

These studies indicate that children's media knowledge and general world knowledge clearly play a major role in comprehending television content. As children's background knowledge increases, so too does their ability to draw inferences from material, a central component of the overall comprehension process. Not surprisingly, this process appears to hold true for both television and text.

A New Perspective on Viewing: Summary

To some degree, regarding television viewing as a schema-driven process, is not new. Earliest explorations of television in the lives of young children held that viewing was an active cognitive experience. Schramm, Lyle, and Parker (1961), as well as Himmelweit, Oppenheim, and Vince (1958), for example, all subscribed to the theory that children were the central actors; that television was merely the vehicle to be acted upon. However, while their studies provided preliminary evidence supporting their views, neither study could fully articulate what it meant to be actively engaged in television viewing.

Schema theory provides such a definition. It suggests that viewers do not respond reflexively or automatically to the images on the screen; rather, like reading, individuals relate new incoming information to preexisting schemata based on prior experiences with the medium and general world knowledge. Viewing strategically, content is filtered to meet the perceived demands of the situation as well as the individual reasons for watching television. In this respect, interpretation of content varies among viewers depending on their abilities, needs, and inferential capacities.

While there is some empirical support for the theory, particularly on fluctuations of visual attention to television (Anderson & Lorch, 1983), it is clear that further development is required to tap children's understanding of television content. If, however, the processes of television viewing and reading are as similar as the following illustration suggests, schema theory represents an important new perspective on the perceived relationship between television viewing and reading.

An Illustration

To demonstrate the relevance of these four aspects of schema theory, the following illustration presents two examples from my son David, a fifth grader, as he reads a selection and as he views a segment from a television program. The mystery genre was used in both cases to analyze schema-selection inferences: The written story came from a chapter in *Encyclopedia Brown*, by Daniel Sobol, involving the adventures of an amateur detective; and the televised story, a segment of the "Bloodhound Gang" from *3-2-1 Contact*. David reads on a 5th-grade reading level and watches approximately 18 hours of television a week.

Each story was presented to David in seven episodes. He was first asked to read a portion of text, then report on his thinking processes. A similar procedure was used with the televised segment. Immediately after each episode, David was asked to report on what he was thinking and to answer any other relevant questions. Tables 3.4 and 3.5 present these protocols episode by episode as he works through the selections. To simulate the task, each episode is shown on the left, with David's responses on the right. Experimenter questions are in parentheses.

As shown in Table 3.4, inferencing is apparent at the very beginning of David's reading as he combines information from sentence 1 and 2 to explain why money was given. He also infers that the use of "Bugs Meany" is designed to inform him of the character's intentions. He uses his background knowledge to infer in episode 3 that the rubber pillow is one often used in camping trips.

It is clear by episode 4 and 5 that David does not question who actually stole the rubber pillow. Rather, he is tentatively predicting how Encyclopedia might catch Bugs Meany off guard. His inferences are most likely constructed on the basis of information from the text and other stories previously read with such nefarious characters.

By episode 6, David is pretty certain how the robbery actually took place. Now he attempts to fit all the textual information into his constructed schema by reviewing details from other episodes. Strategically he looks for clues to confirm his suspicions. As the experimentor tries to elicit his interpretation of events, David backs off, afraid that he might be wrong. While not providing any additional clues, his conclusions are confirmed with certainty in episode 7. Having accomplished his overall goal, he now is able to freely explain the chain of events which led to Bugs' capture.

David's interpretation conforms to the schema-theoretic model. Reading strategically, he constructs meaning from the text by applying his background knowledge to the events in the story. In this respect, his inferences, and predictions, have a unique character, reflecting how he might choose to solve the crime. His reading style is interactive, involving the simultaneous analysis of text at several different levels: He hypothesizes relationships which lead to his overall conclusion; at the same time, he analyzes specific words for their potential meaning in the story.

We see a similar iterative process in Table 3.5. While David is not

Table 3.4.   The Case of the Rubber Pillow

Episode	David's Responses
Episode 1 One day Danny Landis hurried into the Brown Detective Agency. He laid a quarter on the gasoline can beside Encyclopedia. "I want you to find my rubber pillow."	(Any questions) Nope. (What do you think is happening here?) A kid, Danny Lattice or something like that came in and placed a quarter on the gasoline tank and said my rubber pillow is missing. (Why did he lay a quarter?) Cause that must have been the detective's pay.
Episode 2 "I think Bugs Meany stole it," said Danny. "Bugs?" Immediately Encyclopedia became serious.	(Any questions?) Nope. (Why was his name Bugs Meany?) Probably cause he bugs people and he's mean.
Episode 3 "Tell me the facts," said Encyclopedia. "Early this morning," said Danny, "Dad and I were painting the wood on the front of our house—the three front steps, the porch railing and posts, and the front door. We painted everything white." "Where was the rubber pillow?" asked Encyclopedia.	(Any questions?) Nope. (What's the rubber pillow?) Maybe a blow-up pillow for camping trips.
Episode 4 "It was hanging on the clothesline at the side of the house," said Danny. "After we finished painting, I saw Bugs running away carrying my pillow." "Did your father see him too?" "No worse luck," said Danny. It will be my word against Bugs's."	(What are you thinking?) I think they're going to have to catch him in the act again or like maybe get bait or something. (What do you mean by bait?) Like something he wants again, like get a better rubber pillow and put it on the clothesline again.
Episode 5 Encyclopedia and Danny went to Bugs's house. Danny said to Bugs, "You stole my pillow." Bugs said, "I did not. I've been right here all morning." "Then you wouldn't mind going with us to Danny's house," said Encyclopedia. "Well OK, but you lead the way. Remember, I don't even know where he lives."	(What are you thinking?) I think Bugs wants to get them off his tail. I think that he stole it and that's why he said that cause he wanted to get them off his back.
Episode 6 "Go up and ring the doorbell," Encyclopedia dared Bugs.	Oh my gosh. Could I see the first page. I think I know it. (He

Table 3.4.   Continued

Episode	David's Responses
Episode 6 "Watch my style," said Bugs. He ran across the lawn and leaped over the three white wood steps. His heel struck the slate floor of the porch. He skidded but got back up without having to grab the railing. He looked back at Encyclopedia and Danny and smiled.	searches for sentences) Oh yeh, yup. See I knew it—he jumped three front steps, see? (No, tell me). He knew that the. . . . no, that's not right.
Episode 7 "Your plan to trap him didn't work," said Danny. "Oh yes it did!" said Encyclopedia.	Oh it did! It must have been it. He did jump over the three steps. (Why?) Cause they were painted. They knew he was there when they were painted. That's how he trapped him!

familiar with "The Bloodhound Gang" format, he is pretty certain that the needle and magnet are to be used to make a compass. His background knowledge clearly leads to a well-defined hypothesis of why it may be used. In episode 2, David recognizes that there is insufficient information to explain the rental cars, but identifies "1-2-3" as potential clues to be used for later reference.

David connects events in episodes 3 and 4 to make a tentative prediction of the outcome of the story. He does not question whether a swindle is in the making or not; rather, he focuses on how it is about to occur, backing up his inference with a specific event from the story. Episode 5 fits in neatly with his evolving interpretation.

Episode 6 catches David a bit by surprise when Ricardo runs downstairs. He modifies his understanding of the magnet used by quickly adjusting to this new information, adding "Oh, it's probably an electrical magnet." He draws a conclusion at the end of this episode, which is confirmed in episode 7.

David's considerable background knowledge clearly supports his inferencing of events in the story. He does not return to the "1-2-3" clue probably because he views it as unnecessary. Fairly sure of his interpretation by episode 4, he seems to anticipate the outcome of the story with relative confidence, fitting each new piece of information in his constructed framework.

David's interpretations in both stories were guided by schemata. In the first case, he is probably directed by a ROBBER schema; in the second, a MAGNET schema. Each contains elements which aid in

Table 3.5. The Bloodhound Gang*

Episodes	David's Responses
Scene: Detective Office. Cuff, Vikki, and Ricardo.	

Episode 1

(The phone rings) Bloodhound Detective Agency. "White Dwarf" from outer space? Yes, we'll be discrete.	(Any questions?) Nope. (What are you thinking about?) I think they're going to make a
Vikki to Ricardo: Here, look up Dwarf. They're stars. Someone's trying to see a piece of one and I smell a swindle.	compass out of the magnet and the pin and I don't know what they're going to do with it, but
Ricardo: It says here the white dwarfs are dead stars collapsed, shrunk, pressed by their own gravity. The stuff is so heavy you couldn't lift a teaspoon of it. No one knows how much it weighs because nothing that dense could exist on earth. It's got to be fake.	. . . Maybe they're going to find the direction where the magnetic force is.
Vikki: Fake? How?	
Ricardo: I don't know, but I've got a hunch. Cuff, run home and borrow a needle and if you have a magnet, bring that too.	

Episode 2

Scene: Outside of a large estate where the white dwarf will be auctioned.	(Any questions?) Nope. (Why do you think there were so many
Ricardo: Look at all the rental cars.	rental cars?) I don't know
Vikki: How do you know they're rented.	actually. But 1-2-3—I bet that
Cuff: The license plates are practically the same. EGI 1-2-3. They must come from the same garage.	was a clue.

Episode 3

Scene: Outside of auction	
Client talking to Vikki	
Client: I don't like to interfere with Mr. Oliver's hobbies but he's so easily swindled and I'm suspicious.	(What is happening?) I think the girl is going to make a compass.
Vikki: This whole thing's a hoax. But we can't prove it.	
Client: I hope you can	
Scene: At the Auction	
Vikki (to waiter): I'll have some water and can I also have the cork?	

Episode 4

Scene: At the auction. The Bloodhound gang makes a compass.	(What do you think is happening?) Well, I bet that it's
Vikki: The compass should point north.	probably a very strong magnet
Cuff: That's not north. The compass doesn't work.	in there and there's probably a
Ricardo: Sure it does. The compass is directed to a very strong magnetic force. There—	magnet in the box under it and I bet he can't move it. I think
(The compass points directly to the white dwarf)	
New Scene: The auction begins	

Table 3.5.   Continued

Episodes	David's Responses
Auctioneer: Millions of dollars are about to change hands today. Feast your eyes on the rarest rock on earth—a fragment of a white dwarf. Do we know the unique character of a white dwarf? Matter is condensed beyond the wildest imagination. Observe. Mr. Atlas can lift a car with his feet. But can he lift that bauble from outer space.	that's it. Cause when they had that compass, they found that there must be a strong magnet.
Episode 5 (Mr. Atlas can't move the white dwarf) Auctioneer: Would anyone else like to try?	(Why do you think he is willing to let someone else try?) Because there's probably a magnet under there and they wouldn't be able to move it.
Episode 6 Ricardo: You keep everyone busy. I'm going to run downstairs. Vikki: I'll keep them as long as I can.	Oh, its probably an electrical magnet under there.
Auctioneer: Shall we start the bidding at $500,000? Vikki: Mr. Butterfield, will you accept bids in silver? My client who has empowered me to bid, bids $.10. Auctioneer: Who is your client? Vikki: Mr. Oliver, and he is of the opinion that this whole auction is a joke, a swindle. That hunk of rock is a fake. I can lift it with one hand. Auctioneer: Nonsense.	Oh, I bet the guy's going to pull the plug on the electric magnet under it, so she can pull it up.
Episode 7 Vikki: So you think this is a white dwarf? Auctioneer: No question about it. (All of a sudden the room goes dark. The boy has turned off the electricity.) Vikki: (She picks it up with ease) See, it was just a hunk of iron held down by electromagnetic force.	I was right!

*From "The Case of the One Ton Jewel"

processing information and inferencing from the story. For example, the MAGNET schema might include such elements as fields of force, power, electric current. These elements are activated by incoming information either explicitly found in or derived from the stories.

These protocols describe an interesting progression in how schemata are selected. Using his background knowledge, David tentatively selects a schema based on limited cues. Following this initial selection, each new bit of information is measured or tested for "goodness of fit."

In both cases here, we have seen that the particular schema selected places David in good position to match elements with incoming information. His tentativeness, however, suggests that he is open to alternative interpretations, if new information refutes his major expectations. In a sense, he is hypothesis testing. Only when enough confirmatory information is provided does he definitively settle on a particular schema. Finally, he refines his understanding of events to seek a coherent interpretation of each story.

David's processing approach appears strikingly similar for both the print and televised stories. In each, he is actively engaged in searching for meaning. As an experienced reader and viewer, he tends to be drawn to creating an interpretive framework for each story; individual symbolic elements of each medium are not mentioned. While the means of conveying information are different, the skills and knowledge needed to interpret each medium appear to be the same.

Whether these processes actually occur during children's everyday television viewing and leisure reading is, of course, an open question. But these qualitative impressions clearly suggest that television viewing, as well as reading, is a thought-provoking, often complex processing task, involving the interaction in and about the "text," the individual's background knowledge, and individual responses.

IMPLICATIONS OF A SCHEMA-DRIVEN MODEL OF TELEVISION VIEWING

This notion of the child as actively engaged in processing television content contrasts sharply from prior conceptions of the viewer staring blankly at the screen, controlled by its formal features, invulnerable to outside influences. Such active engagement carries a number of important implications for understanding how and what children learn from the media. Our discussion focuses on three issues in particular: the role of symbol systems in information processing, the effects of television's content, and the possible synergy between television and reading in the development of literacy.

The Role of Symbol Systems

Symbol system theories contend that it is the means by which content is conveyed that greatly influences cognition (Olson & Bruner, 1974; Salomon, 1979). Symbolic codes of a message are converted and transformed to internal modes of representation. Consequently, they argue that with the acquisition of differential communicational coding systems (television, computers, videotext), individuals, using different mental tools, become able to think in new ways.

The problem of this argument, from a schema-based perspective, lies in the relative importance of symbol systems in the cultivation of mental skills. In contrast to Salomon's claims, Rumulhart (1980) argues that all kinds of incoming information, regardless of their symbol system, become transformed into "internal propositions." Symbolic codes are merely the carriers of information delivered by various media and experiences. Similarly, Pylyshyn (1981) argues that images are not a fundamentally different form of cognition, but merely a species of a single form used in all cognitive processing. Rather than the actual features perceived, images, as well, are governed by propositions.

Indeed, if information is converted into propositional structures, then the issue of symbol systems and medium diversity may not be as important in learning as was initially assumed. Clark and Salomon (1986) recently proposed an interesting compromise between these seemingly incompatible positions. They argue that symbol systems might affect only initial stages of decoding, but not higher levels of thinking. Inference generation and problem-solving skills might be symbol system independent. This might suggest that deeper levels of processing television and print are quite similar after all.

The role of television's formal features in explaining children's comprehension of content, therefore, becomes less consequential than some researchers have indicated. Formal features may serve important functions only at an initial stage, when children are just beginning to watch television. But like practiced readers, automaticity in decoding these forms are known to result with increased experience (Huston & Wright, 1983). Since television's forms are easier to decode than print, it follows that children's use of these features as a mechanism for defining central story content, might be relatively brief. While salient formal features such as music and motion might continue to trigger the orienting reflex, returning children's eyes to the screen, this information would not be passively incorporated in an involuntary manner. Rather, schema theory suggests that this new information would be evaluated, slotted into an existing organizational framework, and then interpreted.

From a schematic perspective, symbol systems, as conveyors of content, play a supporting role in processing information. Each system of codes, particularly at the decoding stage, do require a different set of activities. But the role they play is probably far more limited than symbol system theories have implied. Viewers, not media, are the major stars.

Content, Not Form

Inordinate attention on the forms of the television medium placed content in a secondary position. However, viewing children as active processors suggests that we reverse this trend. Conceivably if children do process television actively, then it is important to provide content worthy of their time and effort. Moreover, it is equally important to monitor and screen out content judged unsuitable for young children's understanding. With limited background and general world knowledge, preschoolers and young school age children cannot possibly activate appropriate schemata when viewing sophisticated adult programming. At best, such efforts on their part might lead to boredom and involvement in other activities; at worst, confusion and fear.

As noted in Chapter 1, initial forays in attempting to change the content of commercial television programs met with frustratingly few results. At that time, concerns about the harmful effects of television led to demands by citizen's action groups for major regulatory changes in the FCC. However, it may be time to refocus our attention on television's content in perhaps a more instructive way. Children's Television Workshop's use of formative research offers a model of how to assess children's understanding of television content. Similar to "think-aloud" strategies, they have attempted to analyze the process of interpreting content in very practical ways, by asking such questions as: Do children like the content? Do they attend to the content? Do they understand the intended messages? Do they construct unintended messages? (Dorr, 1986). In this way, we can begin to move beyond the stimulus-response model, indicative of much of the content research in the 1960s-1970s, to a more schema-based perspective focusing on the transactions between children's prior knowledge and television's content.

Assessing how children process program content might provide new opportunities for collaboration between program creators and experts in child development, concerned with creating content that will be both attractive and understandable for children. Such collaborative efforts might be beneficial to both sides, developing new formats for attracting audiences who might choose to view if only the right content were provided. *Sesame Street*, and other programs from CTW, of course, are exemplars of this approach. But collaboration need not only be designed for instructional programming. The work of Trabasso and Sperry (1985), Stein and Glenn (1979), and van den Broek and Trabasso (1986), studying causal chain networks on the comprehension of narratives, could vastly affect how entertaining stories might be shaped for the television medium to enable higher levels of inferencing. Their work suggests that children's understanding of stories are enhanced when they are well-structured, with a minimal number of incidental episodes. Recent research on previewing (Neuman, Burden, & Holden, 1990), using video advanced organizers as a mediation technique is another example. In two separate studies, children who received a 1 ½ minute preview of the central events, story characters, and vocabulary of an uncoming televised story were better able to remember specific details and recall plot-essential information.

Like good books, good television content is capable of providing opportunities for children to interact, to develop expectations, to inference beyond the "text." We must make continuing efforts to see that it does so.

The Synergism of Learning from Media

There is no doubt that television's effects on reading ability has been assumed to be largely negative. The gist of the argument, according to some critics, may be summarized as: "reading activates; television passivates" (Jonsson, 1986), suggesting that active processing is inherent in children's involvement with print, while television's pacing leaves little time for such elaboration and reflective thinking (Singer & Singer, 1983).

We have seen that schema theorists challenge this assumption. Recent studies on television comprehension have revealed no major discontinuities with research on the comprehension of text. While the mastery of symbolic codes for television and reading clearly differ with young children mastering television at a far earlier age than reading, comprehension in both media appear to develop in a strikingly similar pattern. As children's prior knowledge increases, so too does their ability to apply increasingly discriminating schema for making inferences beyond the content of the text or program.

Clearly there are important differences in the depth of processing media. These differences, however, relate more to the social contexts in which these activities tend to reside than the medium itself. Without any intended goals or formal learning objectives, television in the home is likely to be processed more casually than reading in the schools, with planned instructional objectives and established criteria for successful performance. When the context shifts, however, depth of processing also shifts. For example, little cognitive capacity is probably expended when curling up with a novel at night or flipping through the sports pages.

Rather than a threat to the development of reading, television might be seen as a complementary medium, engaging children in experiences that require similar processing tools. Though clearly different in style, children make judgements about the comprehensibility in both media, generate inferences, interpret content in terms of their own past experiences, and selectively edit content differentiating central from incidental events. Each of these component skills become increasingly refined with greater experience. Thus, the theories of comprehension for each medium correspond, forming a convergent model of the overall comprehension process.

But a theory of synergy goes one step beyond complementarity. Synergy implies not only a cooperative relationship, but one in which the total effect is greater than the sum of its parts. Operationally defined, this suggests that when used appropriately, television might enliven and even enhance literacy. The entertaining format of television, therefore, might belie its function as an informational resource, a cognitive processing tool, particularly for young children. Such a bold proposal will be further explored in the chapters that follow.

4

The Short-Term Gratifications Theory

School is shortened, discipline relaxed, philosophies, histories, languages dropped, English and spelling gradually ignored. Life is immediate, the job counts, pleasure lies all about after work. Why learn anything save pressing buttons, pulling switches, fitting nuts and bolts. . . . Life becomes one big pratfall, Montag; everything, bang, boff, and wow! (Bradbury, 1967, pp. 62–63)

Television's capacity to continuously amuse its audience produced an inherent conflict for many achievement-oriented Americans. Unlike many other pastimes, television did not come with a ready-made set of justifications. Leisure activities such as reading were considered admirable, sleep, restorative and exercise, invigorating, but what other value than the need to be entertained could possibly account for people's constant use of the medium?

While some would claim that television is "just another appliance—a toaster with pictures,"[1] others believe that the public's seemingly insatiable desire to be entertained has profoundly influenced people's enthusiasm and willingness to learn. Problems requiring complex thinking have been transformed to quick 30-minute solutions. The general push-button psychology has encouraged looking for the "easy way out." As a result, Neil Postman (1985) maintains that the television generation has produced a different type of adult—the "adult-

---

[1] Frequently attributed to Mark Fowler, Chair of the FCC.

child"—one who accepts as normal the childish need for immediate gratification, as well as the childish indifference to consequences.

The short-term gratifications theory argues that television has altered the very foundation of American values, those patterns traditionally committed to activity, sociability, and productive, goal-directed concerns. It is a thesis more suited to philosophers than social scientists. It suggests that television has fundamentally shifted basic societal values, from those which had previously been characterized by the willingness to defer gratification, to a new set of attitudes where the present is amplified all out of proportion. Once considered more congruous with lower class values and lower aspiration levels, (Schneider & Lysgaard, 1953), the desire for immediate gratification, as indicated by the minimal pursuit of education, is now seen as becoming the social norm (Geiger & Sokol, 1959; Postman, 1985).

In essence, these concerns are advancing two key issues. First, is the belief that the children of television will come to expect all of life to be entertaining; learning activities which require effort, time, and perseverance will be displaced in favor of the ready-made. Second, is the concern that this demand for entertainment will eventually lead children to be less enterprising and resourceful; creative problem-solving skills, through direct learning experiences, will simply never have the chance to develop.

These sweeping charges against television have not lent themselves to hypothesis testing. Perhaps more than any of the other theories, this one is characterized by the gap between pure speculation and scientific evidence. Why has this been the case? For one, the short-term gratifications theory lacks specification. Claims that the school children of today are different in their ability to tolerate frustration than the children of 35 years ago cannot be examined with great precision. Nor can the accusation that television is suppressing children's vocabulary, returning us to an oral culture and lower levels of thinking, and making us dependent on pictures (Postman, 1982) be adequately addressed. Second, even with greater specification, these concerns reflecting differences in learning styles and gratification patterns, require longitudinal studies. It is untenable, for example, to make dramatic statements of changes in children's attentional styles after they view only several episodes of *Sesame Street* in a laboratory experiment. Third, changes in children's interests, attitudes toward schooling, and learning expectations are so inextricably bound to other cultural changes that it is virtually impossible to isolate one particular variable from the others.

The villain-redeemer metaphor is particularly salient in the short-term gratifications theory. Unlike the villainous flickering screen, a cultural halo is thought to surround reading. Whether Shakespeare or Danielle Steele, print is regarded as the transmitter of higher levels of thinking, of culture and serious ideas. Thus, Postman argues that it is foolish to believe that the traditional goals of adulthood can be preserved because "television is not a book and can neither express the ideational content that is possible in typography nor further the attitudes and social organization associated with typography" (1985, p. 113).

Unfortunately, many of the charges against television are presented in such dichotomous terms. This chapter outlines each of the major arguments within the short-term gratifications theory, attempting to clarify and specify the means through which a relationship between television and changes in children's learning patterns is thought to occur. Throughout these discussions, it is clear that there are two prevailing ideologies operating here. One reflects a nostalgic wistfulness for the days before television. The other relates to a literacy bias—the assumption that thinking is primarily linguistic and that reading and writing is a precondition for all meaningful learning.

THE CRITICISMS EXAMINED

This section examines three aspects of the short-term gratifications theory. Unlike the other theories relating television viewing to literacy and schooling reviewed earlier, this theory tends to focus more exclusively on the *processes* of learning—enthusiasm, perseverance, concentration—rather than on cognitive outcomes. The concerns that follow are found most frequently in the literature.

Children Have Lost Their Zest for Learning

Central to this issue is the fear that television has created a generation of apathetic spectators, who lack initiative and the necessary energy to pursue intellectual ideas. Some critics assert that the entertaining features of television have led to intellectual passivity, by "feeding children information for which they might otherwise actively investigate" (Fader, 1983). Others suggest that viewing dulls the imagination or limits children's creativity as they engage in dramatic play (Cohen & Rudolph, 1977; Singer & Singer, 1983).

These concerns, raised initially when television was first introduced in communities, were reported to have no foundation in bench-mark studies by Himmelweit, Oppenheim, and Vince (1958), and Schramm, Lyle, and Parker (1961). They received new life, however, with the introduction of the innovative program, *Sesame Street* in 1969. Combining all the techniques that made commercial television successful, *Sesame Street* demonstrated that television could indeed provide an alternative learning environment for children. It was undeniably a turning point for children's television.

Sesame Street's triumph received mixed reviews from the educational community. While praised for its intentions, it posed a basic dilemma to teachers. Might not children get false impressions about learning? Would children confuse entertainment and education too much? Educational institutions paled in comparison to television. How could the typical teacher hope to compete with *Sesame Street's* flashy fast-paced techniques? Reports a third grade teacher, "I cannot change my body into different letters nor can I change color. But the lessons I consider exciting fall flat because I do not do these phenomenal things" (Cohen & Rudolph, 1977).

It was the unintended effects of *Sesame Street* that clearly concerned educators. Criticisms focused on two extremes of behavioral outcomes. Halpern (1975) found that the overstimulating pace of *Sesame Street* and other programs geared to preschoolers contributed to hyperactivity and frantic behavior. Others believed that the program unintentionally reinforced passivity by providing information that might otherwise be found in a book (Winn, 1977). In either case, *Sesame Street* was seen as seriously interfering with the development of reading (Cohen & Rudolph, 1977), and school-related behaviors (Trelease, 1982).

Testing these assertions, Tower, Singer, Singer, and Biggs (1979) examined the effects of two different styles of programming format on preschoolers' recall, concentration and imaginative play. Comparing the "fast-paced" *Sesame Street* and the "low-key" *Misterogers' Neighborhood*, with a control group who watched neutral films over a 10-day period, they found no group differences in the degree of imaginative play or concentration scores. Significant change scores in imaginative behavior for the less imaginative children, however, were reported in a second analysis, with results favoring *Misterogers'* over *Sesame Street*, leading the Singers to conclude that there were distinct advantages for the slower-paced program.

These findings, however, did not go unchallenged. Though widely quoted, this particular study had serious methodological difficulties. Lesser (1979) and Anderson and Collins (1988) suggesting a more cautious interpretation, noted that since all the low imaginative children in the Tower et al. study substantially increased their scores in concentration and imagination regardless of program type, and since scores from the *Misterogers'* group were lower to begin with, these differences might be accounted for simply by the phenomenon of regression toward the mean. In addition, other experimental research seemed to run counter to the Singers' claims (Anderson, Levin, & Lorch, 1977; Gadberry, 1980). For example, comparing the reactions of 72 preschoolers to rapidly paced and slowly paced segments of *Sesame Street*, Anderson, Levin, and Lorch (1977) found no differences between groups on impulsive behavior and persistence.

In contrast to these studies measuring the effects of *Sesame Street* on preschooler's play behavior, Salomon (1979) analyzed the factor of persistence in the elementary school setting. Comparing two groups of Israeli second graders, one of which watched eight days of *Sesame Street*, the other, adventure and nature films, he found major differences on a task of persistence. Children who viewed *Sesame Street* showed less perseverance for a "tedious" school-like task, than the comparison group.

One of the difficulties in interpreting these studies, as shown in Table 4.1, relates to the differences in the definition of terms and in measuring techniques. For example, can we assume that the factors of concentration, persistence, a lack of impulsivity in these studies all reflect the same construct? In addition, the specially designed measuring instruments in several studies, report no validity and reliability information. It is unclear whether these instruments do, indeed, tap the behaviors in question. Further, as Hornik (1981) accurately points out, this sort of experimental paradigm is not particularly helpful in investigating whether *Sesame Street* has seriously impaired the development of attention, concentration or persistence. Rather, the short-term gratifications theory suggests cumulative effects of television viewing over time.

Despite differences in findings and in several cases, questionable validity, these studies not only stimulated a good deal of controversy about the educational and emotional implications of *Sesame Street*, but about the larger issue of television's effect on school behaviors overall. Television programs were alternately described in the popular media as "relentless," "uncontrollable," and "highly distracting," fostering shortened attention spans and a low tolerance for learning. No longer were these assertions posed as "potential" effects; they were now assumed to be fact. An example, from an otherwise carefully researched article on the teacher crisis in *Time* magazine ("Help! Teachers can't teach!," 1980):

Table 4.1. Studies of Television's Effects on School Behaviors

Study	Relationship Analyzed	Dependent Measure	Instrument	Results
Anderson, Levin, & Lorch (1977)	Compared rapidly paced, slowly paced, or parents' reading	Perseverance Impulsivity	Puzzle Matching Familiar Figures Test	No differences
Tower, Singer, Singer, & Biggs (1979)	Compared *Mister Rogers'* and *Sesame St.*	Concentration	Observed extent to which a child remained with an activity, resisting distraction.	No difference in concentration for high imaginative children but low imaginative children scored higher on Mister Rogers'
Salomon (1979)	Compared SS with adventure and nature films.	Perseverance	Children crossed out a selected group of numbers from several pages of random digits.	Children who watched SS showed less perseverance.
Gadberry (1980)	6 weeks of restricting TV on IQ	Impulsivity	Matching Familiar Figures Test	Those who watched SS were less impulsive than others viewing commercial programs.
Zuckerman, Singer, & Singer (1980)	Correlated reading habits, TV, & school behaviors.	Enthusiasm Attentiveness	Teacher-rated 3-point scale	High enthusiasm was related to heavier viewing. Attentiveness and reading not related.
Singer, Singer & Rapaczynski (1984)	TV viewing and self-control	Restlessness	Waiting quietly Sitting still	Action programs were mildly related to restlessness.

A New York panel investigated declining test scores and found that homework assignments had been cut nearly in half during the years from 1968 to 1977. Why? Often simply because students refuse to do them. Blame for the shift in student attitude has been assigned to such things as Watergate, the Vietnam War, the Me culture. Also to television, which reduces attention spans.

Aside from anecdotal reports, the research evidence, supporting these claims, has been sparse. Two studies conducted at the Singers' television center at Yale University were among the few direct attempts to evaluate the association between heavy viewing and attentive behavior in school learning. Predicting that children who regularly watch such fast-paced programs as *Sesame Street*, cartoons, and action/detective programs might be unable to learn in the "calm, bland, environment of most public schools," they analyzed 232 third, fourth, and fifth graders reading habits, and as well as their attentiveness and enthusiasm for schooling.

Teachers evaluated students on a three-point behavioral scale. Enthusiasm, for example, ranged from "reads constantly and does extra projects of his/her own choosing in addition to the work assigned," to "has no desire to be in school or to participate in any learning activity whatsoever." The results of the study, however, ran counter to their expectations. Contrary to their hypothesis, those students reporting to be most enthusiastic in school, were the heaviest viewers; attentiveness and reading ability were not related to the amount of television spent viewing (Zuckerman, Singer, & Singer, 1980).

In a separate longitudinal analysis, Singer, Singer, and Rapaczynski (1984) measured the association between heavy television viewing and poor self-control for a group of 63 nine-year-olds. Children were observed for restlessness, measured by their ability to sit still "as if they were astronauts," and were also tested for their ability to wait quietly in an interview room. Using diary records of television viewing behavior, they reported that the viewing of action-adventure programs was mildly associated with restlessness in the waiting room and the ability to sit still. No correlations were reported for the total amount of television viewed and motor restlessness.

The Singers, however, provide us with no information on the validity or reliability of their measures. Interestingly, the two measures of restlessness correlated only $+.35$ with each other. It is also unclear whether these behaviors are related to school attentiveness or concentration. While they measured children's school adjustment, no data is provided on the relationship between these behaviors and viewing. Further, despite its intention, this research does not get at causation.

We are left, therefore, with little evidence to either support or reject claims of increasing restlessness due to television viewing.

In summary, despite claims that television causes "uncontrolled overactivity" (Halpern, 1975), "shortened attention spans" (Mankiewicz & Swerdlow, 1978), making it difficult for children to "apply themselves to tasks of any kind" (Cohen & Rudolph, 1977), none of these potential effects have ever been substantiated. There is no evidence at all that children have lost their zest for learning. Rather, perhaps as Himmelweit, Oppenheim, and Vince (1958) once suggested, these comments merely reflect a convenient way of expressing a basic prejudice against television.

Poor Kids Get Smarter; Rich Kids Get Dumber: The Mainstreaming Effect

Television represents the true "melting pot" of the American public, according to George Gerbner and his associates at the University of Pennsylvania's Annenberg School of Communication (Gerbner, Gross, Morgan, & Signorielli, 1980, 1982). The mix it creates, however, may have unexpected effects on children's educational aspirations and achievement. Contending that television makes "rich kids dumber," Gerbner reports (1985) that "TV represents a limitation for those who have had the advantages of our civilization" ("It's at home," 1985).

His thesis is based on the theory of mainstreaming. Born into the symbolic environment of television with its common images and messages, television is thought to cultivate changes in viewers' outlooks that transcend traditional barriers of literacy and mobility. Values held by heavy viewers, despite their differences in occupation or educational status, merge to form more homogeneous attitudes about society and life in general. Attitudes, therefore, over time tend to reflect how ideas are represented in the "television world." This process of convergence among heavy viewers is called "mainstreaming" on the premise that television's portrayal of life represents the mainstream of our culture.

Television's contribution to viewers' conceptions of social reality are particularly strong for those people who are least likely to be part of the mainstream of society—the high- and low-income groups. Through the synthetic world of television, their perceptions of the world regress toward the mean, blurring the traditional distinctions between social groups. Such a powerful influence, television viewing is thought to override or diminish the effects of other factors, including family environment and other personal characteristics that have traditionally differentiated these high and low groups.

Their research is based on two interrelated data sources: annual content analyses of prime-time and weekend television programming, and items from the National Opinion Research Center on the public's conceptions of social reality. The theory has gone through numerous refinements as it has been extended to areas dealing with sex roles (Signorielli, 1979), occupational conceptions (Gerbner, Gross, Morgan, & Signorielli, 1982), and educational achievements and aspirations (Morgan, 1980; Morgan & Gross, 1980).

The bulk of evidence on mainstreaming in the educational setting has been conducted by Morgan and Gross (1980) at Annenberg. As part of a cultural indicators study, Morgan and Gross reported the results of an investigation appearing to substantiate the theory of mainstreaming. Television viewing data, intelligence, and socioeconomic indicators were collected from a sample of 625 sixth through ninth graders. High IQ students who were heavy viewers tended mostly to get lower reading comprehension scores compared with high-IQ light viewers. At the other end of the spectrum, the opposite held true. There was a tendency, though slight, for the low-IQ heavy viewers to score higher than the low-IQ light viewers. Though the mean percentile scores between high and low IQ students remain far apart (a 38% differential), the tendency toward convergence is found to support mainstreaming.

Secondary analyses of other datasets led them to further evidence in favor of mainstreaming (see Table 4.2). For example, they found that the extent to which children devote attention to television was an interesting indicator of mainstreaming. Among light viewers, those who seem to attend most heavily to programs scored higher on achievement than those who watched while engaging in other pursuits. Heavy viewers who paid close attention to television, however, showed significant, negative relationships between the amount of viewing and achievement. "This not only shows sharp mainstreaming—it also suggests that the impact of television will be less among those who are not really paying that much attention to what's on" (Morgan, 1982).

Other indicators of mainstreaming, according to Gerbner and associates, are reflected in student's outside activities. The more studious, home-oriented students, who spend more time on homework, chores, religion, art, and music show stronger negative associations between television and achievement than their less intelligent counterparts (−.13, .02, respectively). Similarly, those students who have high educational aspirations get higher achievement scores, but they show stronger negative associations between amount of viewing and those scores (−.18, −.10). The authors conclude that in all cases, the results show mainstreaming—heavy viewers from high scoring groups con-

Table 4.2.   Summary of Gerbner et al.'s Findings on Mainstreaming

Dependent Measures	Results
Attention to television	High engagement with television yields stronger negative relationships between viewing and achievement. Low engagement show smaller associations.
Educational and occupational aspirations	Those with higher educational and occupational aspirations get higher achievement scores, but show stronger negative associations between the amount of viewing and scores.
Outside activities	More studious, home-oriented students show stronger negative associations between television and achievement.
Parent involvement	Students whose parents are less involved in their viewing show stronger negative associations than those who do.

Source: From Gerbner, Gross, Morgan, & Signorielli, 1984.

verge with their low-scoring counterparts. "These data suggest that the variations are not random, but part of a larger process. . . . The overall patterns show a systematic convergence of "otherwise" heterogeneous students. What it means is that television can override other powerful influences" (Morgan, 1982).

Others, however, would disagree. Far from being systematic, differences reported between heavy high achievers and heavy low achievers, seem to have little bearing on one another. For example, in Morgan's report on students' outside activities, differences in correlations are not far apart probably because all the relationships are very small. Out of 44 possible relationships, only 11 are significant; in fact, the largest correlation is only $-.16$. There is a marked absence of significant and meaningful relationships in each of their select findings. Even under Gerbner's criteria (i.e., size of an effect is less important than its consistency), these conclusions are suspect.

The logic of their argument is also difficult to follow. Presumably, according to their theory, lighter viewing students who attend more to their television viewing score higher on achievement, and heavier viewers score lower, demonstrates mainstreaming. But their tables do not indicate any partitioning of groups by social class or intelligence, a critical component of the mainstreaming theory. Without knowing what might "otherwise" be expected of high achieving groups, these data do not indicate any kind of convergence at all.

Finally, there is the issue of causality. Mainstreaming suggests that television "cultivates" changes in viewers' attitudes about society and life in general, indicating a causal relationship. Studies reporting these effects on educational achievement and aspirations, however, have been based only on correlations (Fetler, 1984; Morgan, 1980, 1982; Morgan & Gross, 1980). An examination of mainstreaming requires research designs that analyze causal relationships, measuring changes in viewers' conceptions over time.

Indeed, the statistical evidence and conceptual arguments for mainstreaming have been seriously challenged in several reanalyses by Hirsch (1980, 1981) and others (Hirsch & Carey, 1978; Hughes, 1980). Reanalyzing the NORC General Social Survey data and the content analyses that Gerbner et al. claim support the mainstreaming theory, Hirsch found a striking absence of significant or meaningful relationships between the two. While the theory proposes that (a) television presents a consistent set of images and messages, and (b) that these messages will be adopted by heavy viewers as their own attitudes and perceptions, there was no evidence to support these assertions. For example, Hirsch found that nonviewers tended to give "television answers" (according to their content analyses) more often than light viewers, while extreme viewers, watching more than eight hours daily, were less likely to adopt a television response than heavy viewers. In response to Gerbner et al.'s numerous refinements of the basic theory, Hirsch concludes:

1. The Annenberg group's formulation(s) is so inclusive that no matter what respondents answer on survey items, it can be argued to support one or another variant of the cultivation hypothesis. This treatment makes the assertion both irrefutable and untestable, almost by definition.
2. Our detailed reanalysis shows that notwithstanding their reformulated theory's growing ambiguity and lack of precision, the data analysis reported by the Annenberg team frequently overlooks standard statistical procedures. This makes it difficult for readers to infer which version(s) of their theory (if any) is supported empirically. (1981, p. 5)

These critiques call into question the Annenberg's basic approach as well as the theoretical underpinnings of mainstreaming. While intriguing, Gerbner et al.'s apocalyptic view of television's impact on society has clearly not been confirmed. Perhaps the claim that television democratizes education by "pulling the bottom up and the top down" is another example of the temptation to connect the assumed decline in school performance with the rise of television viewing.

The Sensory Orchestration of the Young Has Changed

Television's messages are expressed through oral language and visual images. Ideas are conveyed not through print, but pictures, speech, music and movement. Considering the significant number of hours spent viewing prior to schooling, some educators claim that television has profoundly influenced the nature of children's discourse and attitudes toward literacy (Fader, 1983). "The sensory orchestration of the young has changed, and the educational system must change to accommodate this mix" (H. Parker, 1974, p. 91).

Seeking the easy way out, children are thought to be reverting to more primitive modes of communications. Evidence for such reversion is cited in the increasing use of pictures instead of printed language in traffic signs, bulletins, and instructions (Carroll, 1974). Some critics even suggest that television might have a far more deleterious impact by altering the way the brain functions (Emery & Emery, 1976; Krugman, 1971). According to this view, television might enhance a stronger preference for visual representations (Zuckerman, Singer, & Singer, 1980). Others believe that television is returning us to an oral culture, and to lower levels of thinking (Postman, 1985). Lacking the sequential and linear demands of printed language, programs must rely on concrete actions, limiting imagination and abstract thought. Each of these views emphasizes television's fundamental role in altering perceptual development and learning in general (see Table 4.3).

Table 4.3.   Hypothesized Effects of Television on Children's Sensory Modalities

Hypothesis	Proposed By	Potential Result
Children will prefer pictures to words	Postman, 1979, 1982, 1985	Language and print will become less meaningful to the child.
Television viewing involves different brain functions	Emery & Emery, 1976 Krugman, 1971 Mander, 1978 Zuckerman, Singer, & Singer, 1980	Children will become less patient at making the effort to deal with reading materials.
Print develops cognitive abilities	Postman, 1979; Trelease, 1982 Winn, 1977	Television is an unsuitable medium for conveying ideas.

How has television influenced children's sense modalities? Postman (1982) argues that the most significant aspect of the medium's structure is that it expresses its content in visual images, not language. In contrast to the printed word, pictures are considered "cognitively regressive," calling upon people's emotions, not their sense of reasoning. "They ask us to feel, not to think" (p. 73). Even though language is certainly part of the code through which television communicates, it is the visual image that is thought to predominate.

Postman implicitly applies the principle of least effort (Samuels, 1970) to explain why these images interfere with learning. Given a complex stimuli (the auditory-visual symbol system of television), children tend to select that aspect of a total stimuli which more easily elicits the requisite information. Often providing redundant information to visual images, the language of television, is considered simply not to be necessary for children to intelligibly comprehend the medium.

Postman's analysis, however, ignores a large body of research on the comprehensibility of the medium. Particularly for young children, there is a strong linkage between looking and listening to television. Studies indicate that reducing the comprehensibility of auditory information has a distinct effect on reduced viewing, suggesting the importance of processing language while paying visual attention (Anderson, Lorch, Field, & Sanders, 1981). This pattern changes as children grow older and become more sophisticated language processors (Field & Anderson, 1985). Older children and adults are even more likely to monitor television by listening to programs rather than watching directly. This evidence strongly contradicts Postman's notion that television sensitizes children primarily to visual representations and less to language.

But his argument is resonant with a number of critics claiming television's nefarious effects on reading. Specifically, these critics rest their argument on the assumption that the two activities involve different brain functions (Krugman, 1971). Zuckerman, Singer, and Singer (1980), for example, assert that television viewing might bias the arousal of the right hemisphere of the brain. Since printed materials or complex verbal sequences seem to engage the left side of the brain, it is argued that when children enter their teens, they will "probably be less patient at making the effort required to process auditory verbal material, such as teacher's lectures, or to deal with reading materials." No evidence is provided by the Singers to substantiate these assertions.

Mander (1978) contends that television "dims the mind" by destroying the brain's capacity to integrate information. Citing a study by the

Emerys in Australia who acknowledge "with a certain degree of rage, that their findings are not based on great amounts of evidence," they conclude:

> The right half of the brain, which deals with more subjective cognitive processes—dream images, fantasy, intuition—continues to receive the television images. But because the bridge between the right and left brains has been effectively shattered, all cross-processing, the making conscious of the unconscious data and bringing it into usability, is eliminated. The information goes in, but it cannot be easily recalled or thought about. (p. 207)

Such claims that television has indelibly changed how children process information have not been subject to any serious methodological testing. Yet, surprisingly, the notion that television has disturbed the delicate balance in perceptual development has found a receptive audience among many educators who find viewing an anathema to reading. Some even claim that "rightbrainness" is a causal factor in reading disabilities (Carbo, 1983), though studies have failed to find any evidence to substantiate it (Torgesen, 1986). Despite the rather startling portrayals cited by Mander, the Emerys and others, none of the potential influences of television on brain activity has ever been established.

These charges against television, again, reflect a "literacy bias." In contrast to attitudes toward television, popular sentiment assumes that print is the medium of higher-level logical and abstract thinking. The very act of reading is thought to develop cognitive abilities as opposed to the immediate emotional gratifications sought through television (Trelease, 1982; Winn, 1977; Zuckerman, Singer, & Singer, 1980). Several fascinating ethnographic studies as well as historical accounts (Altick, 1957; Heath, 1983; Hoggart, 1957), however, find no such direct linkage. Analyzing the democratization of book reading in England, for example, Altick found that, to the dismay of the comfortable elite, the common people tended to gravitate toward lower-class fiction, without "any serious purpose in reading." Scribner and Cole's (1981) study of Vai literacy practices in Liberia also casts doubt on the belief that print, in and of itself, developed abstract thinking. Conducting a series of experiments that allowed them to control for the effects of schooling, they found clear-cut results indicating that literacy was not associated in any way with generalized competence in abstraction, verbal reasoning, or metalinguistic skills. Instead, the impact of literacy was restricted to the practices or functions it performed.

Literacy itself, therefore, does not directly contribute to the development of thinking skills. Used for mundane purposes, there is no reason to expect that reading will encourage intellectual growth anymore than watching a nonsensical movie or television show. The belief that "television is not a suitable medium for conveying ideas, because an idea is essentially language—words and sentences" ("TV's "diastrous" impact," 1981) is an example of this typical "literacy bias." Such views actually constrain the development of literacy by implying that thinking resides in a single technology.

Those who argue that television has irrevocably changed children's sensory orientation as well as their appreciation of the written word call for fundamental changes in curricula to "accommodate this new mix." Both Fader and Postman recommend more emphasis on spoken language in the schools and greater attention to the traditions and values of literacy to offset the volatility and novelty of television. Though their solutions are admirable enough, it is questionable whether they have correctly identified the true problem.

LEARNING AS A MULTIMODAL PROCESS

The short-term gratifications theory argues that television has fundamentally changed children's expectations toward learning, creating a generation of apathetic spectators who are unable to pursue long-term goals. These critics view television as a threat to the development of literacy, and to the perpetuation of literacy as the sole means of attaining knowledge. There is almost an exclusive emphasis in their thinking on reading and writing skills as a precursor to all meaningful learning.

But learning is a multimodal process, requiring a wide range of physical, perceptual, and cognitive skills. While the enormous value of literacy is undeniable, it is not without its limitations. Sometimes, visually presented images can instill competence in skills far better than verbal descriptions. Other times some type of motoric response is necessary. For example, it is virtually impossible to learn to drive or even fix a car just by reading a manual. Learning requires transformations of knowledge from many domains which are further translated into different types of experiences.

To not avail ourselves of other technologies for instructional purposes is dangerous and dysfunctional. Newer technologies do not in any way reduce the vital importance of competence in reading and writing. Rather, as the modes of communication expand, so, too, do our means of enhancing learning among all children increase as well. We now have the capacity to shape instruction to account for different characteristics of learners, different tasks and settings. It would represent a sad state of affairs to forego these options due to an anachronistic view of thinking and learning. A diverse culture demands diverse multimodal strategies to ensure that all children, regardless of their particular strengths and weaknesses, are given opportunities to learn.

5

The Interest Stimulation Theory

A child keeps in his mind a register of the actions and conversations of those who are about him; every scene he is engaged in is a book, from which he insensibly enriches his memory, treasuring up his store till time shall ripen his judgement, and turn it into a profit. (Rousseau, 1773)

Television's persuaders and entertainers opened up new gateways of learning for children. No longer were they confined to their immediate environment. With television, many of the conceptual and logical barriers to extending children's experiences posed by other media were virtually swept away. Its very accessibility meant that children were exposed to ideas, events, and places that were once reserved for adults alone.

The interest stimulation theory proposes that television can enhance learning by stimulating children's interests, and creating a hunger for further information. Once having viewed a program on a given topic, they will be more likely to display a greater interest in the classroom, or will read a book if they have seen the movie or the television show based on it. Implicit in the theory is that interests lead to action. In this respect, the benefits of television are potentially twofold: By stimulating new interests, young viewers will gain knowledge, and then will try to obtain even further knowledge on these same topics.

But exactly what kinds of interests are being sparked by television? While there was hope that children might be stimulated to learn about topics as unexpected as archaeology, there was a corresponding fear that they might be learning the wrong kind of things from television. The interest stimulation theory, therefore, has undergone a rather

107

complex history. Initial research focused on the interests and knowledge gained incidentally through television. Himmelweit, Oppenheim,
and Vince (1958), for example, analyzed the extent that television
stimulated children to take up new hobbies and interests. The 1970s
and early 1980s, however, saw an unprecedented effort to use television intentionally as a powerful motivating force to influence the
learning goals in the schools. Here, teachers were encouraged to directly intervene by linking children's interests in television and specific
areas of school curricula including social studies and language arts.

This chapter considers both incidental and intentional learning
from commercial television. It first examines television's role in stimulating children to seek information and new interests on their own. It
then analyzes the influence of parent and teacher mediation in constructing a learning environment for enhancing children's interests.
From this analysis, it becomes evident that greater collaborative efforts are required on the part of parents, teachers, librarians, and
publishers before the potentially stimulating capacities of television
are likely to be turned by children to their own intellectual advantage.

LEARNING FROM TELEVISION

Early investigations by Schramm et al. (1961), and by Himmelweit et
al. (1958) gave considerable attention to what children learned from
television. Indeed, it seemed hardly necessary to prove that learning
did occur. Anyone who had ever heard children recite commercials
verbatim, or recall stories and mannerisms of their favorite characters
was aware of it learning impact. Rather, their chief question focused
on whether the information gained through television significantly
contributed to children's general knowledge, interests, and school performance.

Their task was made more difficult by the nature of learning from
television. Children rarely go purposefully to the medium for useful
information. Most learning is absorbed incidentally as children spontaneously view for entertainment. Without any special effort at retention, attention may be divided among a host of other activities, some of
which may take precedence over viewing. What is learned, then, can
vary dramatically according to the circumstances seen as relevant to
young viewers.

It is difficult, therefore, to accurately gauge children's learning from
television. Even so, both Himmelweit and Schramm attempted to
measure gains from television using such indirect measures as vocabulary, visits to art galleries, and new hobbies. Both found that televi-

sion was "neither a distinct advantage nor a severe handicap" as far as children's performance in school was concerned. Neither did television markedly stimulate children's cultural, intellectual, or creative interests. Any interests aroused by television were fleeting, rarely leading to action.

More recent reports bear out these initial findings (Comstock, 1978; Liebert & Sprafkin, 1988; Salomon, 1983). The consensus of opinion is that incidental learning from ordinary entertainment viewing has only a minor impact on general knowledge and developing interests. Three reasons account for its small effects: first, Salomon argues that ordinary viewing does not call upon the requisite mental activities required for learning. Casual viewing, associated with "mindlessness" fails to activate cognitive processing. Only when individuals are encouraged to process for a given purpose can television significantly enhance learning. In Drew and Reeves' (1980) study of learning from news, for example, those children who understood that a particular news story was designed to give them new information were the same students that learned the most from it. Intentions help guide the processing of new information.

Second, most of television's entertaining programs are at a fairly low intellectual level. Programs might occasionally provide information but their impact is somewhat limited by the sheer redundancy of plots and characters with one another (Comstock, 1978). Such repetition might ensure that this limited range of information taught through television is thoroughly learned, but these lessons are probably grasped by a very young age.

Third, much of the incidental information conveyed in these programs is not retained for very long, particularly by children below the age of nine (Liebert & Sprafkin, 1988). Without opportunities to reinforce or practice what has been newly learned, a good deal of the new information is lost. Only those materials that appear to have some direct applicability to viewers are likely to be remembered and used.

There are, of course, a few outstanding examples where television has significantly increased knowledge and stimulated interest in a subject area. In a study reporting on the retrospective perceptions of *Roots*, over 37% of the sample cited increased knowledge and interest in issues of slavery (Fairchild, Stockard, & Bowman, 1986). But such cases are relatively rare. More often, incidental information is incorporated into already existing patterns of interests and ongoing activities.

Similarly, television has shown on occasion to be a powerful motivator of book reading. Following a special broadcast, book sales soar, though the data most often refer to the adult market (Hornik, 1981). But here too, these infrequent events can exaggerate television's customary role in stimulating reading interests. In the most recent Book Industry Study Group (1984) analysis of the juvenile market, only 4% of the children reported choosing a book on the basis of seeing or hearing about it through television. At best, what television seems to do is momentarily redirect existing reading choices. Neither the total amount nor the quality of children's reading has ever been affected by the interests whetted from television.

In sum, while entertaining programs may provide new information, their impact is limited due to the natural constraints of informal learning, and the characteristics of a medium viewed primarily as a vehicle of entertainment. Whatever interests are sparked by television, they seldom lead children to action. Some have argued that television's methods of presentation and choice of topics leave little opportunity for children to explore for more information (Himmelweit et al., 1958). But others suggest that it is probably due to children's perceived purposes for viewing, and the lack of guidance by adults who might otherwise spur these interests into creative activities (Schramm et al., 1961; Salomon, 1984). Without the capacity to provide feedback and reinforcement, television's role as a resource in learning new information and stimulating interests in a given topic is seen as rather minimal at best.

In light of these findings, rather than continue to focus on what television's content might bring to children, researchers turned to what seemed to be a more fruitful approach—an emphasis on the context of viewing, and how "significant others" might contribute to fostering children's knowledge and interests from television.

MEDIATED LEARNING FROM TELEVISION

When television first arrived, there was the fear that viewing would inhibit family conversations and personal interactions (Maccoby, 1954; McDonagh, 1950). Indeed, these fears appeared to be justified; 58% of the families in Maccoby's sample who had just acquired a set reported little or no talking while the television was on. Walters and Stone (1971), two decades later, reported roughly similar figures (52%), suggesting that the nature of family life in the presence of television seemed to be parallel rather than interactive.

But a recent body of studies, have challenged these findings (Alexander, Ryan, & Munoz, 1984; Bryce, 1987; Lemish & Rice, 1986; Messaris, 1983; Messaris & Kerr, 1983). These studies have focused on the many ways families process televised materials together, albeit in more subtle forms than found in previous surveys. Bryce, for example, found in the course of her three-month study that literally hundreds of question-and-answer sequences, expansions, and evaluations of television content among family members were made. These kinds of conversations, as reported in Table 5.1, were thought to have an enormous potential to mediate television-related learning.

Family conversations around the television set, often not intended to mediate television experiences, were reported to be both implicitly and explicitly educational. Some of the informational exchanges recorded in families from a study by Messaris (1983), for example, dealt with topic areas including history, geography, and natural sciences that are part of the standard curriculum in formal education. Other conversations extended beyond school content to skills and attitudes that may not be customary rewarded by standardized test scores. Thus, for example, when a young boy asks his father, "Was Eisenhower a good president?" he is establishing a link between his parent's knowledge, world views, and existing prejudices of his own. Messaris proposed that through these conversations, television might be providing

Table 5.1.   Types of Family Conversations in Television Contexts

Types of Family Conversations	Examples
Referrals Family members personalize TV content	6-year-old: "I'm going to marry Bill Cosby when I grow up"
Question and Answers Parent provides information at the request of the child	8-year-old: "Why do they cover their faces?" Parent: "Because they don't want anyone to know them."
Expansions Viewers supplement the television content	10-year-old: "See they used to be boyfriend and girlfriend but now they're not."
Evaluation Positive or negative comments about TV content.	10-year-old: "That's weird."
Participation Responds to TV content	TV commercial: "Have you driven a Ford—lately" Children sing along
Repetition Viewers mimic TV content	6-year-old pretends to walk like a monster

(Typology from Bryce 1983).

a context for learning that extends far beyond the formal educational process.

These studies are impressive because they suggest that the viewing context may have important implications for what children take away from the television set. But they also share two key problems. For one, none of these studies have detailed how often these conversations actually occur in the course of viewing. These types of verbalizations have been categorized but no frequencies have been tallied. Second, there is no evidence that these conversations really have had any modifying effects on learning or children's interest in a particular topic. The researchers might suspect that this is so, but the linkage between this research and learning has never been made.

Rather, these studies have relied on prior experimental research indicating that young children's learning can be significantly enhanced by intervention from adults (Corder-Bolz & O'Bryant, 1978; Corder-Bolz, 1980; Lull, 1980). This research paradigm emphasized explicit, formal learning rather than the implicit informal talk embedded in ongoing conversations in family settings. In a study by Corder-Bolz and O'Bryant, for example, preschool children viewed an episode of *Adam-12*, a police drama, in one of two conditions. In the intervention group, teachers made informational comments throughout the show, such as "another name for thieves and burglars is "robbers." In the nonintervention group, the teacher made statements designed for children to comply to instruction, such as "Let's all sit down and watch quietly." The results indicated that "intervention by a significant "other" could cause significant increases in the amount of information learned and the number of positive attitudes formed."

But can we compare such explicitly educational interactions in these experimental studies with the informal conversations reported from ethnographic studies? Are parents as distinctly mediational as the adults in Corder-Bolz's later work, saying such things to their children as "This mark is called an apostrophe," or "It is bad to fight. It is better to get help." Such laboratory-type studies can only describe the potential mediative power of parent or adult-child interactions. They cannot possibly describe how television is actually implemented in the daily lives of families.

With the dramatic increase in multiset households in the last 10 years, children are more likely today to watch alone, or along with their siblings than with adults. Entire families viewing together comprise only 36% of viewing time; mother-child viewing, only 6% of the time (Bower, 1985). Even in the most idealized circumstances, mediation of television is likely to be rather arbitrary, based on particular program preferences. In Field's (1988) study of 334 families of five-year-old children, for example, she found that parent coviewing was essentially a random event. Children were often left to their own devices when viewing as the parent engaged in other activities. Lemish and Rice (1986), in their observational study of mother-toddler interactions during *Sesame Street*, noted that parents rarely spent extended periods of time in the TV room, but rather interjected comments as they entered and exited frequently.

Family conversations might, on occasion, mediate children's comprehension of particular programs. But there is no solid evidence to suggest that these conversations affect the amount of information children take away from television. Since most of these studies have been designed to analyze the effects of coviewing on children's social behavior, no evidence exists on the influence of these conversations on enhancing children's interests in subject areas. Some researchers suspect, however, that the effects of most mediational references may be limited to facilitating only online comprehension and interpretation.

In this respect, while conversational exchanges might help children to master the television world, they are not sufficient to create a learning environment which inspires children to acquire more knowledge. Schramm and his colleagues (1961) argue that for television to be really effective in stimulating continuing intellectual or creative activity, it must be geared to an organization which is concerned with such activity. A place where children can freely ask questions, discuss ideas, or extend their understanding of issues by pursuing more information is necessary to systematize the learning from television. With these considerations in mind, it seemed only natural for the schools to be called on to take up the challenge.

LINKING TELEVISION AND LEARNING IN SCHOOLS

Commercial television's appearance in classrooms was motivated by two seemingly disparate forces. On the one hand, there was a great deal of concern regarding television's effects on children's social behavior (violent content, advertising, and social stereotyping). Since parental restrictions of television content were thought to be rather lax (Comstock, Chaffee, Katzman, McCombs, & Roberts, 1978), some educators believed that it was necessary for schools to take on the teaching of appropriate television viewing skills. Perceiving the "school as savior," critical viewing curricula were introduced in many classrooms with the intention that with good teaching strategies, television might become a positive force in society.

The second force, spearheaded by George Becker (1973) and Rosemary Lee Potter (1976), was the inclination to use the "television as motivator" in the schools. Here, the unsightly ills and abuses of commercial television were overlooked in favor of its possibilities in helping children learn specific subjects and develop their reading skills. Taking the perspective that commercial television is a sustained interest of most children, these educators encouraged others to use these interests to their advantage. Curricula linking television and school subjects were developed in the hope of capturing the attention of even the most reluctant learners.

Each approach attempted to change the nature of learning from commercial television. Far from being a by-product in children's search for diversion, expectations and learning intentions were now provided for entertaining programs. In constructing such goals, however, they not only changed the nature of learning from TV, but the functions of viewing. No small task, as educators soon discovered.

Schools as Savior

The notion that television had taken over children's lives, telling them what to eat, think, and value, spurred new efforts on the part of educators to influence what was learned from the medium. Recent publications seemed to indicate that children were being senselessly bombarded by television stimuli and that parents were either incapable or unwilling to control their viewing (Mankiewicz & Swerdlow, 1978; Winn, 1977). Without any sign of relief from either the FCC or community-minded broadcasters, the challenge to combat this apparent destructive influence was handed to the schools. The attitude that television education must begin in the classroom was typified by such comments as the following, reported in the *English Journal*:

> Helping society cope with television is one of the great challenges educators now face. Without education, the destructiveness of television will continue. With education, it may be possible for television to become an increasingly positive force in society. Perhaps someday, educators can point to a visually literate public as proof that teaching can make a difference. (English, 1981, p. 70)

Critical television viewing skills, as they came to be known, were conceived with two major goals in mind: One was to demystify television by exposing children to the technology of the medium. The other focused on visual literacy skills and the syntax and grammar of television. Like other media, television was thought to be a form of literacy that needed to be formally taught before it could be intelligibly understood. "After all, we would not give children books and expect them to read them without instruction; why then should we expect them to know how to watch television" (WNET/Thirteen, 1980, p. 8).

Four large-scale projects were funded by the Office of Education, covering all age levels from grade school to postsecondary education (Boston University, Far West Regional Labs, Southwest Regional Labs, WNET). ABC television, as well, sponsored a project for students in grades 3–5 (Zuckerman, Singer, & Singer, 1980). The national PTA, and a number of school districts and state boards of education (Indiana, Illinois) also became involved in developing critical viewing skills curricula (cf. J. Anderson, 1983, for a comprehensive review). While the individual curricula varied from project to project, their fundamental motivation was to teach children not to be easily persuaded, but to apply the rules of logic and critical thinking to their everyday television viewing. Table 5.2 describes the overall objectives of the critical viewing curricula.

Rather than rely on what may be learned incidentally from television, these projects encouraged children to form purposes for viewing. Watching to evaluate the plots of favorite stories, or to judge whether news stories were fact or opinion, or to critique the special effects of popular adventure shows, were now formalized as learning objectives taught in the school context. Further, many of the projects had follow-up activities to extend learning and interests beyond specific programs. In this respect, critical television viewing skills curricula proposed a radical shift from the traditional viewing of television. The casual, inattentive, pleasure-seeking young viewer was now actually supposed to take this light, entertaining medium seriously.

Unfortunately, these projects were on shaky ground when it came to evaluating their effectiveness. None of the four Office of Education

Table 5.2.   Critical Television Skill Curricula

1. How does television fit into your life?
2. What are the ingredients for a television story?
3. Who puts a television program together?
4. How do different types of television programs compare to each other?
5. How does television persuade us?
6. How do you analyze television news?
7. How does a television program get on the air?
8. What do you like about the television programs you watch?
9. How do you review a television program?
10. How can you become a more critical television viewer?

(Objectives from WNET, 1980.)

studies sponsored an evaluation component; consequently, no information was gathered on whether critical television viewing skills were learned or not. Two other projects, however, did conduct a limited evaluation. Dorr, Graves, and Phelps (1980) analyzed gains in kindergartners' knowledge about television and their reasoning skills after six critical viewing sessions. Differential effects were reported for facts about television, but not for skills that required reasoning. These results paralleled those of Singer, Zuckerman, and Singer (1980) in their ABC-sponsored study of third, fourth, and fifth graders. Students remembered the meaning of words such as "zoom," "sponsor," and "chromokey," but their critical skills while viewing remained essentially unchanged. Neither project, however, was able to measure whether changes in television knowledge affected children's behavior when viewing at home.

But an even more difficult issue emerged with the attempted implementation of critical television viewing skills curricula in the schools. Practical concerns like the availability of television sets, hookups, extension cords were always problematic. Scheduling became the greatest problem. Courses in critical television viewing skills had to either replace or become part of an existing course of study. WNET's (1980) project, for example, proposed that their curriculum could be used to teach standard language arts curricula, noting that "teachers will readily recognize most viewing skills and concepts are traditional reading/language arts skills." However the notion of equating the viewing of *Laverne and Shirley*, during class time with the reading of *The Wind in the Willows* could hardly be justified in most English curriculum programs.

Thus in their implementation phase, these critical television viewing skills programs tended to suffer a similar fate. School officials, principals, teachers, and parents had to seriously question their priorities. Was children's television viewing as important as the teaching of reading, social studies, and language arts? While some educators stood firm, believing that "without teaching, video idiocy will continue to grow like weeds" (English, 1981), others could neither justify the time nor the money to implement critical television viewing skills in the schools.

Curiously, the great impetus to protect children from television's excesses, as well as to enhance their selectivity and learning from the medium quickly faded after these projects were completed. Begun in 1980, most did not endure past 1983. Whether it was the failure to produce demonstrable changes in children's viewing habits or whether these curricula simply demanded too much from the schools can never be determined. In any case, it became clear that if the schools were to effect changes in what children learned from the medium, a new approach to linking television and teaching was sorely needed.

Television as Motivator

Attempts to curtail children's natural enjoyment of television had met with little success. Despite exhortations by educators and citizen's action groups deploring its excesses, television viewing continued to gobble up hours of leisure time. But not all educators saw this common source of data and language stimulation as a disadvantage. Unlike those seeking to protect children, these educators considered a very different strategy. Why not use children's interest and experience from television as a positive learning resource?

These educators recommended the use of commercial television as a motivating tool in reading and writing. No longer was television relegated to the role of frivolous entertainment. By "recycling the wasteland," television could now be integrated in everyday classroom experiences. "The time has come for teachers to stop criticizing TV and start using it effectively" (Rankin & Roberts, 1981).

Several approaches were undertaken. Publications by Becker (1973) and Potter (1976) encouraged teachers to use children's television experiences to build reading skills. For example, worksheets on dictionary skills or reference skills might use the TV guide as its resource rather than the typically colorless basal workbook pages. By doing so, reading might become more relevant by tying together functional uses of reading with children's interests and daily needs. Rankin and Roberts (1981), going one step further, even encouraged teachers to let students view daytime shows in their classroom and then use these programs to enhance comprehension skills.

Piloting a most innovative approach, Solomon and McAndrew created a "scripting" project for teachers in Philadelphia (Solomon, 1976). They taped popular television shows including *Gilligan's Island* and *I Love Lucy* and reconstructed scripts from the shows. Reluctant readers watched the program and read along with the script, while focusing on skills such as word analysis, creative expression, and comprehension. The technique was so successful that it was taken over by CBS, which through its affiliates, continues to offer students scripts of specially selected network programs.

Other organizations, as well, became involved in encouraging teachers to use television. "Prime Time School Television" and "Teachers Guides to Television" produced and distributed study materials on television specials and high-quality series programs. These guides included specific objectives for viewing (most often tied to language arts and social studies), questions to prompt discussion and comprehension of the themes of each broadcast, and suggestions for further reading, writing, and creative activities. Each attempted to take full advantage of the learning opportunities offered by children's interests in commercial television programs.

At the same time, new efforts were made to link children's television interests and book reading habits. A study by Feeley (1974) indicated that children's media preferences closely resembled their general interest patterns, suggesting an underlying pattern of taste that cut across both television and reading. Interests tended to cross media lines; students who enjoyed reading about sports also tended to view sports on television.

It made sense then to try and use television as a way to foster leisure reading. Several educators initiated programs using television to stimulate students to read. Hamilton (1976) conducted a survey analyzing the reading habits of 253 seventh graders. During a six-week period, participants were given the choice of reading or not reading books related to television (TV tie-ins). Students overwhelmingly preferred the television-related books, reading 7 tie-ins during the experiment compared to 3 customary titles. The tie-in approach was also used by ABC television in their project, "Watch the Program/Read the Book." Teachers were provided with background materials for "Afternoon and Weekend Specials," including biographies of authors, scenarios, and posters, all designed to encourage the reading of books in conjunction with programs.

There was great optimism about television's potential uses; commercial television was seen as an asset, offering teachers unparalleled opportunities to stimulate children's interests. "Television can be a strong ally to reading," reported a brochure published by the International Reading Association. Wary educators were encouraged not to condemn the medium but to capitalize on it. "Television will become a major teaching tool in the classroom and home by the year 2000" (Hardt, 1979).

But then the bubble burst. Interests in using television to motivate children gave way to more immediate and pressing problems in the schools. The National Assessment of Educational Progress (NAEP) revealed significant gaps in children's reading comprehension and skill development. Renewed calls for quality education, including the highly publicized Nation at Risk Report demanded more time-on-task for basic skills. Startling reports of a national decline in literacy brought concerns for "relevance" in schooling to an abrupt halt. Commercial television was, once again, relegated to the living room.

In retrospect, it is clear why commercial television's role in the classroom was short-lived. While providing occasions for stimulating information and enhancing children's interests, it remained a fragmentary approach at best for school learning. Teachers were required to be reactive, adjusting their curricular goals to meet the opportunities that television might provide. Rather than the motivational aide that was intended, it became a distraction, taking time away from the core curriculum.

Some educators and parents also had misgivings about commercial television's intrusion in the schools. After all, it seemed that children were already spending too much time watching television. Why use valuable school time on even more viewing, particularly with such banal fare as *Gilligan's Island* and *I Love Lucy*? And why encourage children to read TV tie-ins? In Hamilton's study, for example, children selected such books as *Cool Cos*, and *Mork and Mindy*, hardly classical literature. Rather, it seemed that the schools should attempt to raise children's expectations, and guide them toward higher quality reading.

There were, of course, a number of successful applications of commercial television in the schools. CBS's scripting program demonstrated some small gains on criterion measures of reading comprehension (Szabo & Lamiell-Landy, 1981). A case study reported by Cooper (1984) showed increased interest in reading a book following the viewing of a televised version. But, with these exceptions in mind, commercial television offered little to school programs. In the long run, the schools simply could not afford the time on such motivational activities without stronger evidence of learning improvement.

In sum, it was natural to assume that schools would be an ideal partner for enhancing children's learning and interests from the medium. But in many ways, they were ill-equipped for such a formidable task. Both the critical television viewing skill curricula as well as the motivational approach attempted to teach children strategies for processing and categorizing information from television which might lead to its more positive uses in the home. Such expectations, however, were far too ambitious; these approaches essentially tried to change the very nature of viewing as a leisure activity. In addition, there were some basic flaws in their argument. For example, both approaches hoped to improve the quality of television by creating more thoughtful viewers. Potter (1976, p. 113) argues that teachers should use even the worst commercial programs in schools "to help youngsters apply [their] thinking skills which will in turn help them to reject such poor programs." But there is no evidence to suggest that children have ever rejected a program on the basis of its lack of intellectual merit.

Despite their good intentions, these school curriculum programs did not appear to foster more learning from television. Objectifying viewing goals, creating educational experiences from popular television shows, criticizing television, all defied the basic functions for viewing. Television time is guarded preciously by most children as the very antithesis to schooling. They were not about to have it transformed into another classroom-like learning activity.

CONCOMITANT LEARNING

Parent and teacher mediational techniques proposed to broaden and activate children's interests from television through direct intervention. These strategies required that children be instructed either formally or informally by an adult, who proceeded to direct their attention to some aspect of learning. But children's natural viewing of television occurs in a much more spontaneous atmosphere. Their purposes for viewing are not consciously educational, no one typically directs their attention to explicitly instructional messages, and no specially designated learning goals are made.

Enhancing television's learning potential beyond mere incidental information requires a different strategy than learning in more formal settings. Modified from Borton's (1977) approach, one of the more promising techniques is called "concomitant learning." Concomitant learning consists of weaving educational messages in those times and programs that children do not perceive as being expressly educational. Concomitant learning is adaptive; it adjusts to the fact that something other than learning is the focal activity. "It is the art of teaching to divided attention" (Borton, p. 131).

Commercial television broadcasters have used concomitant learning strategies successfully on a number of occasions. ABC's spot announcements of *Schoolhouse Rock* were developed to teach basic computational and grammatical skills in one to two minute music and animated formats. Another format, first developed by CBS's *Fat Albert*, embodied prosocial messages in a cartoon story. In a test of its instructional effectiveness, 89% of a sample group remembered its messages (CBS, 1974).

More recently, the Center for the Book in the Library of Congress has initiated a number of concomitant learning projects linking television and reading. Developed in cooperation with ABC television, Cap'n O.G. Readmore, an animated cartoon cat who "knows a lot because he reads a lot," is featured in reading promotion spots aired during Saturday morning cartoons. Stars encourage viewers to "Read more about it" on selected CBS programs, by naming three or four relevant book titles available at their local libraries. New public service announcements on NBC have a "Books make a Difference" theme, describing the role of selected books in people's lives. Unlike educational programming, some of these shows are likely to attract at least 80 million people.

Another example containing elements of concomitant learning includes the highly successful "Project Literacy U.S." (PLUS) project, a collaboration between public broadcasting and ABC television. Designed to combat adult illiteracy, PLUS devised a media campaign strategy using spot announcements, documentary and entertainment programs. Perhaps most effective, thematic treatments of the trauma of illiteracy have been infused into entertainment formats. So successful in raising awareness and in motivating volunteer efforts, PLUS has been extended to serve school-aged youngsters as well.

All of these projects are examples of concomitant learning. They provide brief bits of instruction through a system designed and used primarily for entertainment. Integrated in regularly scheduled programs, they catch their audience in the midst of attending to something other than education. They are lengthy enough to allow learners to absorb the information, while at the same time, never distracting from the major purposes for viewing. Further, they do not require any adult intervention; instead, they use the medium to carry the instructional message.

These concomitant learning messages are far more than just a public relations ploy from the networks. With greater collaboration of resources, they can be used to enhance children's learning and interests from television in natural home-viewing conditions. But to do this more effectively, several essential coordinating efforts must be made:

Greater access to books related to television specials. Flashy displays in libraries and bookstores, promoting good reading on similar topics, can be used to attract and extend those interests generated from television. These need not be TV tie-ins which in many cases are mere derivatives of shows on television, but books which explore topical interests in greater depth. For example, following the viewing of *The Blue and the Gray*, book displays of nonfiction and fictional accounts of the Civil War might attract a good deal of attention.

Repetition of instructional messages. Attention to television is both divided and intermittent. Techniques using concomitant learning strategies, therefore, must adjust their instructional messages to "teach what can be taught when it can be taught" (Borton, p. 137). Since not much continuity is possible, it is particularly important that the subject matter be repeated, either in a number of different episodes, or often enough within a time period. Through such repetition, *Scholastic Rock's,* "Conjunction Junction," for example, became a mnemonic device for children studying grammar in the schools.

Greater linkages to other institutions. At best, concomitant learning merely introduces new ideas to children. The limitations of time hamper its capacity to delve deeply into any subject area. The usefulness of these instructional messages could be extended, however, by broadcasters providing telephone numbers of local agencies to contact, as well as additional backup reading materials for those who are interested in obtaining more information. Such interagency cooperation clearly supported the powerful impact of the PLUS project, where over 100 organizations joined forces with the networks on the adult literacy initiative.

Better coordination of instructional messages. Concomitant instructional messages are able to cover only a small body of information at one particular time. Their effectiveness as a learning strategy, however, could be enhanced through accretion, slowly over time. For example, messages could all be tied to a particular theme or subject matter, teaching small bits of information at a time. Or ongoing messages could be connected to an umbrella campaign, such as "The Year of the Young Reader," supporting other existing projects to encourage more leisure reading. Such concerted efforts could use television's motivational capabilities to concentrate on a few top educational priorities.

Concomitant learning may turn out to be one of the more promising approaches to stimulating children's interests in topics from television. Well suited to their typical viewing patterns, its educational messages are subordinated to the entertainment context. No limitations are placed on children's freedom to wander in and out of the television room, and no specially designated learning requirements are made. In this respect, it is intended only as a voluntary learning opportunity which children may make use of or not. Along a spectrum of incidental and intentional learning, concomitant learning as a mediational technique may represent an important move toward middle ground.

SUMMARY

The interest stimulation theory proposes that television can enhance learning by stimulating children's interests, and augmenting their knowledge related to school subjects. In the course of viewing for entertainment, the theory argues that interests will be sparked which will lead children to seek new information through reading or other activities. However, only occasionally has television actually reached its potential. Most of what is learned incidentally from television has little effect on school learning. Interests aroused from television tend to be fleeting, rarely leading to any action.

Considering the sheer number of hours spent watching television, how might the medium be used to better enhance learning? The answer from educators was to create intentional learning goals which might serve to define (and sometimes constrain), what children should learn from television. But television entered and exited the classroom fairly rapidly. Even the most liberal educators had difficulty buying the notion of "viewing as a language art."

Important lessons have been learned from these efforts. Foremost is that any attempts to change what children acquire from television should take heed of typical home viewing conditions. Children were not going purposefully to the medium to seek information when television first arrived, and they are not now. Rather, a different strategy must be used to enhance learning and arouse children's interests from television. Concomitant learning holds promise as one approach for using the medium to enhance children's interests.

6

Is Television as Bad as It Seems?

And when she was good, she was very, very good, but when she was bad, she was horrid. (Mother Goose)

Television usurps so much of our children's time. Surely it must influence their reading growth and developing reading interests. Its lack of intellectual substance, its rapid pacing, its cluttered mixture of visual movement and sound—television's role in the precipitous decline in achievement scores and school standards seems so plausible, so blatant. How could it be that for all these theoretical discussions, there is no relation between television, literacy, and schooling outcomes?

Broadly defined, two schools of thought have emerged in answer to this question. One claims that there simply are no effects. While viewing may have some relation to achievement, its impact, according to some authorities, may be just too minor to be worthy of consideration (Cook, Curtin, Ettema, Miller, & Van Camp, 1986). The second view argues that the strength of the effects may be masked due to flaws in research designs (Hornik, 1981). Weak or unreliable measures of viewing behavior, lack of statistical controls, nonrepresentitative samples may have all led to ambiguous results and limited progress in the field.

These next two chapters argue that neither school of thought adequately explains the nature of the relationship between television, reading and school achievement. Viewing, alone, cannot be considered a "cause" with resultant effects on individual achievement. Just what is learned from any one source (media or otherwise) is tempered by innumerable other educational and potentially educational experiences in children's lives. Rather, television has become so much a part of the fabric of everyday family life in the United States that it is

125

impossible to examine its effects as an isolated phenomenon. As such an integral family member, television is embedded in children's literacy activities, in their play, and in their conceptions of stories, suggesting a relationship that is far more complex than has previously been assumed.

To make this argument, a new series of studies conducted by the author are reported in the next two chapters, measuring television's influence on reading achievement, school-related behaviors, and leisure activities. Specifically, these studies will address the following questions:

- Does television affect children's reading achievement?
- Is television displacing outside independent reading?
- How does television relate to children's other leisure activities?

In carrying out this inquiry, both quantitative and qualitative methodological strategies are used to examine television's effects on such direct product measures as achievement, as well as those processes and conditions which might indirectly affect children's developing literacy skills and interests. This chapter gives a brief overview of the study designs, then proceeds to report findings pertaining to each of the questions above. In the next chapter, the processes of how children use television and reading activities in the home environment are explored through an ethnography of three families. Here, a new theoretical framework is proposed—one that argues that for moderate viewers, a potential synergy exists between children's media activities and their growing literacy development.

AN OVERVIEW OF THE STUDY DESIGNS

The data reported in this chapter come from a series of studies conducted from 1986–1989 on television and reading. This section briefly describes each study and the methods used to reveal learning outcomes.

Study 1: The Displacement Effect: Assessing the relation between television and reading performance (1988).

Using data from eight statewide reading assessments (California, Connecticut, Illinois, Maine, Michigan, Pennsylvania, Rhode Island, and Texas) and the 1984 National Assessment of Educational Progress (NAEP) Reading Test, the study analyzes the relation between self-reported television exposure and measures of scholastic achievement and out-of-school activities. With a sample size of over two million children in elementary, intermediate and secondary grade levels, broad trends are identified, along with the magnitude and direction of the relationship between television and reading to characteristics such as grade level and socioeconomic status.

A secondary analysis of the 1984 NAEP, in particular, provides profiles of children's leisure activities including voluntary reading habits and their relation to television viewing for three subgroups in the sample. Representing students at all levels of schooling, these cross-sectional data describe patterns of media preferences as they change over time.

Study 2: Television, leisure reading and the home environment (1986)

The relationship of the home learning environment and children's television and leisure reading preferences are explored for 122 fifth graders. Using a home environmental questionnaire designed to measure seven process characteristics typical of parent–child interaction, five aspects of children's voluntary reading habits and television viewing patterns are measured from weekly diaries and parental reports.

Study 3: The relationship between television viewing and the quality of children's leisure reading choices (1982, 1988).

The quality or maturity level of leisure reading choices are analyzed for students identified from an initial survey as representing either the upper or lower quartiles in terms of their leisure reading behavior (as measured by the number of books read during the month) as well as their television viewing habits (as measured by the average number of hours watched per week). Using a modification of the Gray and Rogers "Maturity in Reading Scale," children's leisure reading choices, over a period of four weeks, are coded on three qualitative dimensions and related to the amount of television viewed they watch weekly.

Study 4: Medium effects on children's story comprehension (1988).

The impact of different media presentations is investigated with 44 third graders' story comprehension. The study analyzes whether a treatment using a televised version of a story as well as an illustrated storybook, might influence the way in which a story is remembered and understood. Children's story retellings are analyzed for five aspects of story structure, as well as measures of expressive language and cued recall.

Study 5: Television and reading in the lives of young children (1989)

Three families participated in a year-long study of children's television and reading behavior. Using participant observational techniques, this study examines how seven children, ranging in ages from 2½ to 10 years old, use television and reading in their everyday interactions, and in their play, and how these processes may relate to their emerging literacy development.

Table 6.1 gives an overview of the characteristics of each study. These studies provide the bases for addressing the major questions of television's impact on literacy and school achievement.

DOES TELEVISION AFFECT READING ACHIEVEMENT?

Implied in the question of whether television affects reading achievement is the issue of causality. Does television cause poor reading, or does it stimulate reading? Neither statement, of course, can be made

Table 6.1. Characteristics of Study Designs

Study	Research Question	N
Study 1 A research synthesis	Displacement effects of television and reading	2 million children 9, 13, 17
Study 2 Television, reading and the home environment	Relation between home learning environments and children's uses of television and reading	122 fifth graders
Study 3 A qualitative analysis	Relation between television viewing and the quality of children's leisure reading	200 4, 5, 6 graders
Study 4 Medium effects on children's comprehension of stories	Effects of television and reading on children's understanding of stories	44 3rd graders
Study 5 An ethnographic study	Analysis of children's uses of television and reading in the home environment	3 families with 7 children, ranging in ages from 2½ to 10.

from current research designs. Unfortunately, the opportunity for such broad-scale natural experiments (like those of Schramm and Himmelweit and colleagues) no longer exists in cultures where television has become ubiquitous.

But a synthesis of statewide reading assessments representing such a sizable population from all geographical areas of the United States can at least determine the magnitude of the relation between television viewing and reading achievement for children at different age levels. Each of the eight states in their reading assessments in Study 1 measured a broad array of reading skills (field-tested for validity and reliability), along with questions of television viewing time. In this respect, such a synthesis has some important advantages over the small-scale studies conducted with different age groups, using very diverse methodological strategies (as reported in Chapter 2) and, therefore, may be particularly useful in identifying important developmental trends in children's academic and leisure behaviors over the course of their school years.

Television and Reading Achievement

Before examining the question of whether television influences reading achievement, it is critical to differentiate between those students who view an average amount of television and those who watch exces-

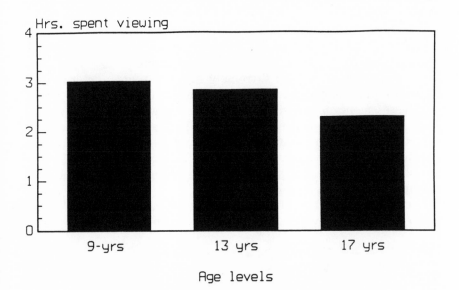

Figure 6.1. Average Hours of Daily TV Viewing

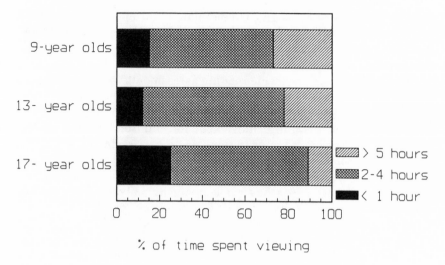

% of time spent viewing

Figure 6.2.   Percent of Leisure Time Spent Viewing

sively. For example, Figure 6.1 describes typical viewing behavior for elementary, intermediate, and high school level students from these assessments. These data indicate that, on the average, students are watching approximately three hours of television daily at the elementary level.[1] Viewing then declines just slightly over the next several years, until the high school level where viewing typically is at its lowest amount.

These averages, however, obscure the range of viewing behavior. As noted in Figure 6.2, some children in each age group rarely view, while others appear to do little else with their free time.

These differences become extremely important when determining the issue of television's impact on achievement. Reading proficiency in these assessments is measured largely in terms of three key skills: vocabulary, comprehension, and study skills (see Table 6.2). Broadly defined, the vocabulary items measure word meaning, the comprehension questions tap students' understanding of main ideas and their applications, and the study skill items assess the ability to find and interpret information from other sources.

To examine the extent of the relationship between television viewing to reading achievement for students at three age levels, mean

---

[1] These figures are slightly less than those of the commercial rating services indicating 24 hours weekly (Nielsen, 1987). As mentioned in Chapter 2, it is known that rating service estimates are heavily biased by the use of announced "sweeps"—measurement periods occurring four times a year.

Table 6.2.   Reading Skills Measured in Statewide Assessments

Skill	Sample Item
Vocabulary	
Word meaning	The bread is still *fresh* and warm.
Word in context	
Antonyms	The opposite of *fresh* is
Synonyms	
	a. white
	b. stale
	c. sliced
	d. new
Comprehension	
Main topic	The story says that John
Reading for details	a. plays tennis
Predicting outcomes	b. enjoys hiking
Critical reading	c. likes to paint
	d. write stories
	From this story, we know that John probably:
	a. has few friends
	b. is shy and quiet
	c. is good at sports
	d. watches a lot of television
Study skills	
Dictionary	Using this dictionary, how many meanings does *bulletin*
Graphs	*have:*
References	a. 1
Table of contents	b. 2
Index	c. 3
	d. 5

standard scores were plotted by state and grade level for each of the reading subskills. Using least-squares procedures, the curves that follow describe the relation between television viewing time and vocabulary (Figure 6.3a), comprehension (6.3b), and study skills (6.3c). In all three figures, the vertical axis indicates the standardized reading score, represented in tenths of a percentile to better illustrate the shape of the curve. The horizontal axis indicates the number of hours children spend viewing on a daily basis. The data points represent the skill scores for each of the three grade levels from each state.

These curves show strong evidence of a curvilinear relation between the amount of viewing and reading skills. Looking at the patterns of relationships across all three skills, it becomes obvious why any discussion of the television-reading relation depends so strongly on whether children's television viewing habits are defined as either "moderate" or "excessive."

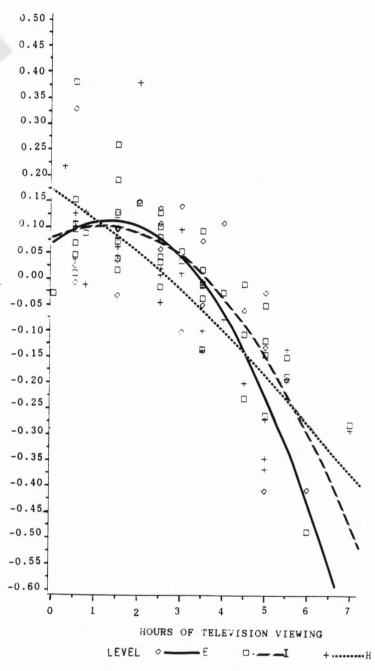

Figure 6.3a.

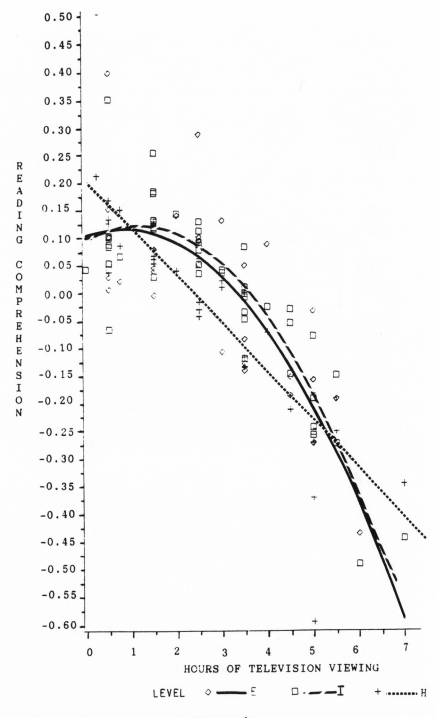

Figure 6.3b.

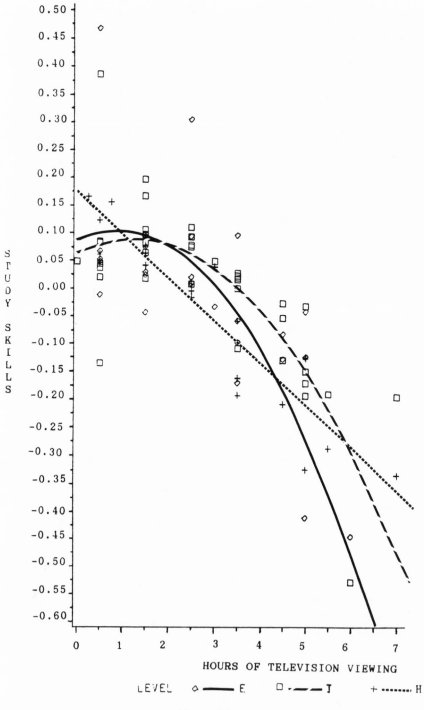

Figure 6.3c.

For example, up to approximately 25 hours per week of viewing at the elementary and intermediate levels appears to be associated with higher levels of reading. Differences between the high and low means for scores between 0–4 hours of viewing on the three skills are modest, indicating that the average amount of television typically viewed by these students neither helps nor hinders their reading achievement. But beyond this amount, extreme cases demonstrate extreme differences. Those who watch more than four hours of television per day have significantly lower achievement scores.

Scores at the high school level reveal a somewhat different pattern; here, students viewing little or no television scored initially higher on each reading skill than those at the elementary and intermediate levels. Differences in scores between light and heavy viewers are also larger for high school students, where the magnitude of the effect is about .4 of a standard deviation. Most likely this relationship reflects changes in viewing patterns. As indicated in Figure 6.2, more students at the high school level are viewing television for less than one hour, and fewer students are viewing for more than four hours. Again, those who view beyond the average amount of television consistently show poorer reading proficiency than others.

The power of this analysis is the high degree of convergence across various assessment instruments measuring a broad array of reading abilities. These results indicate a modest increase in children's scores, at the elementary and intermediate levels, for those watching a moderate amount of television per day. Beyond this amount, however, achievement steadily diminishes with increased viewing. Five or more hours of television viewing per day invariably relates to lower reading scores for all grade levels. Further, this pattern does not substantially change across different socioeconomic status groups, for either gender or in different regions of the country.

Clearly these data suggest that for a small minority of students, very heavy television viewing is associated with low achievement scores. But what are the underlying causal mechanisms? Is it something in the act of watching television which influences reading? Or is it possible that beyond 25 hours a week, time conflicts begin to interfere significantly with homework or other more intellectually stimulating activities that are indirectly tied to achievement? Would children spend more time on outside academic activities, if not for viewing?

Television and Homework

It is doubtful that television is seriously inhibiting the amount of time spent on homework activities. One of the more discouraging findings from the National Assessment of Educational Progress (NAEP) in Study 1 is the lack of homework generally assigned to students. These findings essentially confirm the results from other studies (Walberg & Shanahan, 1983; National Commission on Excellence in Education, 1983), reporting that homework assignments receive little attention from teachers and their students. Whether teachers are skeptical about giving homework because they fear students will not complete it (perhaps choosing to watch TV instead), as argued by Roberts and Rockman (1986), or whether the demands for correcting so much paperwork make it untenable, is not known. In any case, the distributions from the NAEP analysis in Figure 6.4, describing the time spent the previous day on homework activities, indicate that students spend little of their discretionary time outside of school on academic study.

Approximately one third of the 9-year-old students in the NAEP analysis, report receiving no homework assignments. Of those that do, over 40% spend less than one hour completing assignments. This time allotment at the fourth-grade level is certainly not unusual. But what is unexpected are the strikingly low figures on the amount of time spent on homework at the upper grade levels. More than one-third of the students at age 17 report not being given or not doing homework the previous night. Only slightly over one quarter of the 13- and 17-year old students spend between one and two hours per night on assignments. Most students at the high school level report studying less than an hour per night. These figures suggest that outside academic activities represent a relatively small portion of the older students' leisure time.

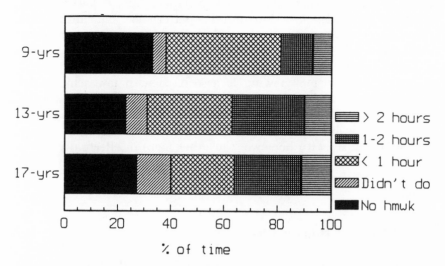

Figure 6.4. Hours Spent Daily on Homework

There are some educators who suggest that it might be television viewing that significantly interferes with homework. However, this appears unlikely. Relationships between television viewing and homework are negative, but quite small at the upper two grade levels (intermediate, $-.08$; high school, $-.10$), Rather, Patton, Stinard, and Routh (1983) argue that the television viewing–homework relationship is more complicated than those who might argue simply for television's interference. Their study indicates that a surprisingly high percentage of students tend to do certain homework tasks in conjunction with television; in some cases, students report that television is actually "helpful" in facilitating homework completion. Students seem to adjust their study environment according to the demands of the homework task.

It would be wrong to assume that television viewing merely replaces the time students would normally spend on homework. Instead, there may be far more complex issues at work. Walberg (1984a, 1984b), for example, argues that homework completion tends to be connected to a separate nexus of factors, among the most important, teacher monitoring practices. His studies indicate that when teachers grade students' nightly assignments, more homework is completed and more learning is accomplished.

These findings suggest that the relationship between excessive television viewing and low reading scores is still in need of explanation. One hypothesis is that these consistent patterns might reflect differences in the personalities and home-related factors of average versus heavy viewers. It is easy to imagine that children who view television to the exclusion of other free time activities may have fewer demands made upon them or may have fewer available options outside of school that those who view less. Might the linkage, then, between poor achievement and children's viewing be tied to certain characteristics in their home environment?

Television, Reading, and the Home Environment

Television and reading behaviors are, indeed, embedded in a complex set of family influences. The home environment study of 122 families of fifth-grade students (Study 2) focused on process characteristics demonstrated in previous research (cf. Bloom, 1981) to be most significant in defining a home learning environment: parental expectations, guidance, the degree of independence and responsibility given to the child, encouragement, and organization of time and space for learning in the home. These dynamic characteristics, unlike the more static variables of occupation or economic level, concentrate on the kinds of parent–child interactive patterns seen in the home.

Of these families in the initial study, two distinct groups were selected to provide an in-depth profile of the nature of parent-child interaction and media practices: (a) Children who were heavy television viewers and light readers, and (b) Children who were light television viewers and heavy readers. Parents and children from each of these groups were individually interviewed, using closed and open-ended questions. Figures 6.5–6.12 describe these findings.

Overall, this study indicates that children's media preferences tend to follow the examples set by their parents. Those who came from reading households, read more; others from homes where television predominated, spent more time viewing (see Figures 6.5a and 6.5b). However, these patterns appeared to be based not only on children's observation of parent behavior alone. Rather, it seemed to reflect the priorities set by these families. In other words, parents who themselves enjoyed reading were often familiar with popular children's books, could discuss them, and recommend specific book titles to their children. One parent, for example, suggested that her child read *Black Beauty*, remembering how meaningful the book had been in her own childhood. In contrast, in homes where television was watched a great deal, the interviews revealed that parents often encouraged children to view along with them.

Interestingly, both groups of parents said they attempted to monitor television program content and restrict viewing time; however, these rules seemed ineffective in limiting the time heavy viewers actually spent on the activity (Figure 6.6). Perhaps as a result of their inability to restrict viewing, these parents approved of fewer programs than others, referring to typical program fare, as "garbage" or "junk." De-

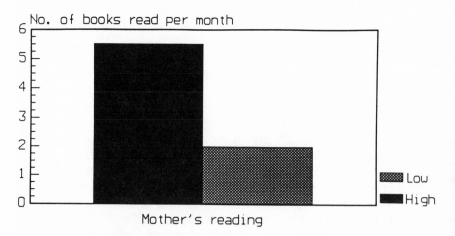

Figure 6.5a. If Child's Book Reading Was:

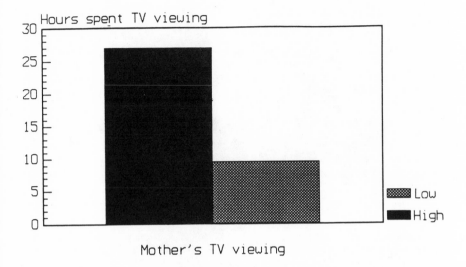

Figure 6.5b.   If Child's TV Viewing Was:

spite their uneasiness and intention to guide their children's viewing, these families reported that most of their television viewing remained virtually unsupervised.

These different media patterns were linked to differences in parents' attitudes toward learning. For example, parents of those who were heavy readers often involved their children in family outings, as well

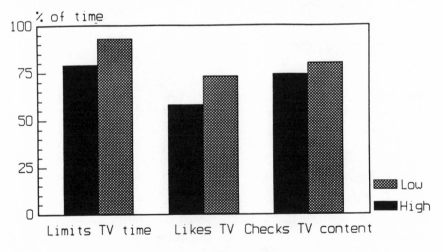

Figure 6.6   If Child's Viewing Was:

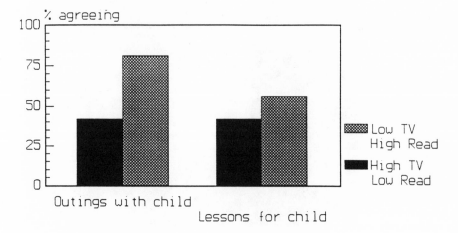

Parents assessment of the importance
of child's outside leisure activities

Figure 6.7. If Child's Media Behavior Was:

as organized activities and lessons, seeing themselves as responsible for developing their children's interests and believing that educational and recreational activities are an important part of their family life (see Figure 6.7). In one case, a mother who enjoyed writing as a hobby encouraged her child to become involved in editing activities during her leisure time. In contrast, those families who viewed more heavily, seemed to involve their children less in outside activities, generally

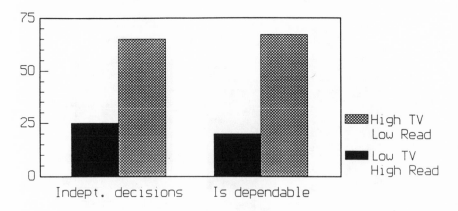

Parents' attitudes toward child's
independence and responsibility

Figure 6.8. If a Child's Media Behavior Was:

considering themselves to have limited influence and power over their children's future.

Children who spend more time reading were often given greater independence and responsibility than others (see Figure 6.8). Parents not only encouraged their children to explore the world around them, but make fewer restrictions on them to do so. Children were allowed to earn their own money, go to the movies alone with their friends, and develop new acquaintances. In the heavy television group, parents seemed to discourage these opportunities, expressing concern about the safety of their children and their neighborhoods.

Parental priorities were clearly evident in the kinds of stimulating activities available in the home. Parents of children who were heavy readers established a fixed routine early on of reading to their children when they were young (see Figure 6.9). Naptime and bedtime stories were said to begin as early as six months of age. In the other group, these reading habits were regarded more flexibly; parents read with less frequency at times when the child was free from other activities. These priorities continue to be reflected in the patterns set by these families. For example, parents of heavy readers reported subscribing to at least one children's magazine such as *National Geographic World* or *Ranger Rick* and spent a good deal of dinner time conversation sharing their reading and school activities with other members of the family. In contrast, television often dominated the family meals in the light reading group.

Expectation factors seem to vary according to media orientation. Parents of those children who read more expressed greater expecta-

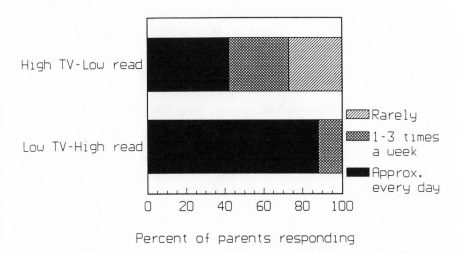

Figure 6.9.   Time Spent Reading with Child When He/She Was Young

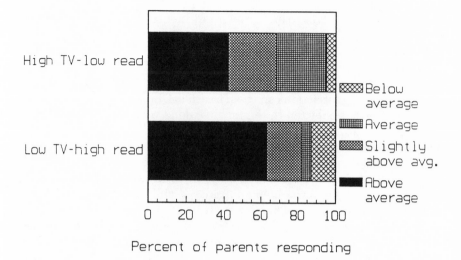

Figure 6.10.   Expectations for Child's Performance in School

tions of their child's future performance in school than others (Figure 6.10). These expectations, however, did not translate into fixed goals. Statements such as "Whatever my son wants to do will be fine" or "I'd like my daughter to decide whether she wants to go to college—that will be her decision," indicated that these parents were rather relaxed and confident of their child's future. However, the parents who described their child's school performance as only average or below, tended to be more concerned about their future goals—"He could go to Harvard if he'd only apply himself." In addition, a number of parents were less concerned about specific career aspirations than about monetary considerations—"I don't care what he does as long as he makes money."

Parental guidance, quite minimal for both groups, tended to be related to children's progress in school (Figure 6.11). Those children who did well at school, often received little help; their parents tended to be rather relaxed about setting time guidelines for homework, confident that the child would take care of it on his/her own. Those who had difficulty structuring their homework time often needed help from members of their family. But the amount of parent guidance was often confounded by a number of factors: Work schedules at times inhibited the time available to help children with school work, and a number of parents could not do the homework due to the difficulty of the assignment (math, in particular).

Parents of children who read more were likely to consider their child's involvement in recreational or academic activities to be more

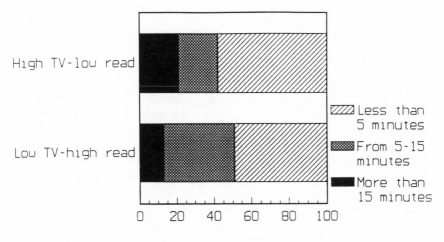

Figure 6.11.   Parental Guidance with Schoolwork Each Night

important than household responsibilities. However, most children, regardless of media preferences, were required to do very few chores (Figure 6.12).

Together, these process measures and parent-child interactions suggest some very real disparities in the home learning environments of families with different media orientations. These differential patterns indicate that, in contrast to technological determinist beliefs, television, like other media, tends to be integrated into common family

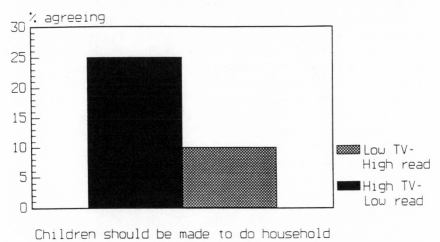

Figure 6.12.   Expectations for Child's Participation in Household Chores

patterns and values. Among these values are the expectations that parents place on their children's learning, literacy and future achievements.

Previous studies have analyzed the powerful influence of the home environment on either children's literacy or their television viewing (Chaffee, McLeod, & Atkin, 1971; Morrow, 1983; Whitehead, Capey, Maddren, & Wellings, 1977). But this research suggests that there are indeed, important linkages between both television and reading activities and these home environmental process characteristics. By describing these patterns, this line of inquiry begins to solve the seemingly inexplicable relationship between excessive viewing and poor achievement. They indicate that average versus heavy viewing habits cannot be explained simply in terms of differences in children's intelligence, or in parents' socioeconomic status. Or, for that matter, that children choose television strictly because other alternatives are not available. Rather, they suggest that television and reading behaviors are closely embedded in the way parents interact on a daily basis with their child. These family processes have an enormous capacity to influence children's overall attitudes toward achievement, literacy and schooling in general.

There will be some researchers who claim to see a clear-cut causal relationship between viewing and achievement, that is, excessive viewing "causes" a lack of interest in literacy. It is a dramatic claim, but a misleading one. Family values, patterns of interactions, and habitual behaviors form a coherent whole. No single experience, heavy viewing or, for that matter, excessive playing of sports or listening to music, could represent such a singular, "causal" factor.

Returning to the basic question that framed this inquiry: Does television viewing affect reading achievement? Not meaningfully. The synthesis of data measuring over two million children's reading achievement in vocabulary, comprehension, and study skills indicates that the overall effects are small. A recent study measuring television using detailed diaries of children's viewing patterns and outside leisure activities for periods ranging from 8 to 26 weeks reported similar findings (Anderson, Wilson, & Fielding, 1988). It is the family environment in which television is a part of that has the power to influence the child's use of the medium.

DOES TELEVISION TAKE TIME AWAY
FROM LEISURE READING?

If not for all that television viewing, according to Marie Winn, "children would calmly spend more time looking for something good at the library" (1977, p. 58). It is a compelling indictment of television for many educators and parents. This relationship is said to occur not only on the basis of the amount of time available, but on television's functional similarity with book reading. Given limited time, children will be more likely to sacrifice other media activities that appear to satisfy the same needs as television, but do so less effectively.

In Chapter 2, it was argued that children were not spending much time reading before television was introduced, and they are not reading very much now. A number of critics contend, however, that time alone may not be the appropriate measure of interest. Indeed, there may be more subtle indicators of deterioration in the way children read today than in the pretelevision era. Notable declines in children's reading of fantasy have been reported, according to Winn and her colleagues (Larrick, 1975, Trelease, 1982). In addition, they say that the quality of children's leisure reading choices since television's introduction has seriously diminished.

In this section, children's self-reported leisure reading behaviors from the 1984 NAEP will be reported, along with their relation to television viewing time and reading achievement. In addition, a qualitative analysis of a month's reporting of leisure reading (Study 3) will be explored to answer the charges that television has significantly affected children's reading choices, making our children, according to some critics, into a nation of "nonbook" readers.

Time Spent Leisure Reading

Trends in children's leisure reading from the NAEP analysis, reported in Figure 6.13, tend to agree with other smaller-scale studies on the amount of time spent reading outside of school (Greaney, 1980; Whitehead et al., 1977). Two different questions were asked in the analysis: one, which measures time spent with print of any kind (including magazines, newspapers, letters), and the other, which focuses more exclusively on book reading. In both cases, the trends are similar. Nine-year-old students read the most; almost half of these students spend at least some time reading every day. This age level is typically regarded as the height of the "reading craze," a time when children have learned to become independent readers and enjoy exercising their increasingly developed skills. But following this period, interest in leisure reading declines. Changes in book reading habits are particularly dramatic; less than one quarter of the 17-year-olds report spending some free time with book reading.

Leisure reading does not appear to play a large role in children's lives. For comparison purposes, the frequency of book reading habits are analyzed in Figure 6.14, along with children's other favorite activities. One of the striking findings is the differences at all levels in

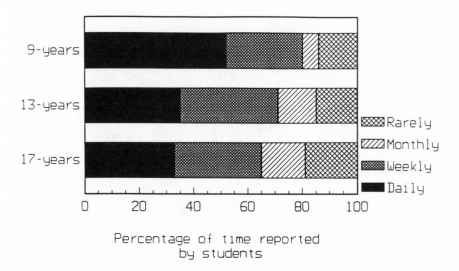

Percentage of time reported
by students

Figure 6.13.   Frequency of Time Spent Leisure Reading (as reported on NAEP-84)

children's preference of television over reading during their free time. Indeed, any free time activity fares better than reading for the 13- and 17-year-olds.

But why is this the case? Are children sacrificing reading for viewing? Apparently not. Actual relationships between out- of-school leisure reading and television viewing time are extremely small at all

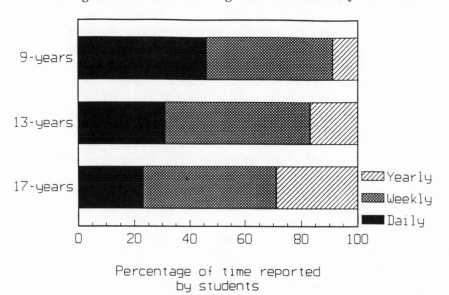

Percentage of time reported
by students

Figure 6.13.   How Often Do You Read a Book?

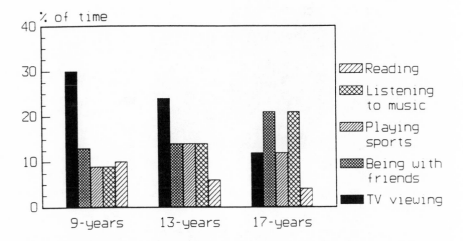

Figure 6.14. Frequency of Time Spent on Leisure Activities (as reported on NAEP-84)

three levels (−.01, −.03, and −.05, for the 9-, 13-, and 17-year-olds respectively).

Even more telling, however, are the reported relationships of reading achievement scores, hours of daily viewing, and the frequency of leisure reading in Figure 6.15a–i. Once again, there is continuing evidence at the elementary and intermediate levels that watching some television is better than none. Highest scores for children at these ages are recorded for those watching 2–4 hours per day and reading on a daily basis; children who rarely read or watch television, score lowest in reading achievement.

There are at least two possible reasons for these relationships. One is the tendency during these years for brighter children to do more of everything—television viewing, reading, playing and so on, than the less able students who show little initiative in any activity. The second relates to an intriguing hypothesis, backed recently by some evidence, that new vocabulary is actually "picked up" while viewing (Rice & Woodsmall, 1988), much as it is during leisure reading (Nagy, Anderson, & Herman, 1987). However, unlike books, the narrow range of spoken vocabulary found in most television programs limits its influence over time, as indicated by the leveling of scores at the high school level.

As expected, different patterns are found for the 17-year-old students. These interactions are complex, making it difficult to draw clear-cut conclusions. One possible reason for this lack of conclusiveness is that so few students at this age level are reading during leisure time. Even those who reportedly do read daily, however, perform lower

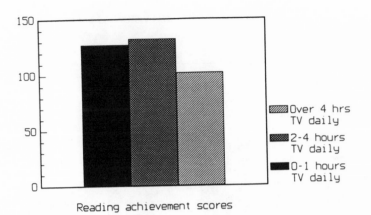

Reading achievement scores

Figure 6.15a. Reading Achievement Scores for 9-Year-Olds Reading Daily (as reported in NAEP-84)

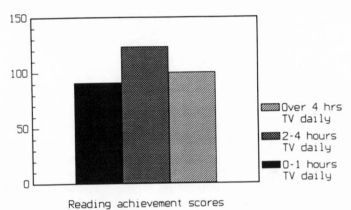

Reading achievement scores

Figure 6.15b. Reading Achievement Scores for 9-Year-Olds Reading Weekly (as reported in NAEP-84)

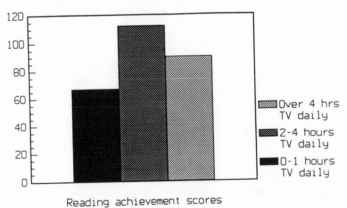

Reading achievement scores

Figure 6.15c. Reading Achievement Scores for 9-Year-Olds Reading Rarely (as reported in NAEP-84)

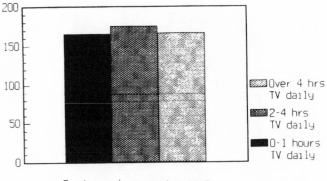

Reading achievement scores

Figure 6.15d. **Reading Achievement Scores for 13-Year-Olds Reading Daily (as reported in NAEP-84)**

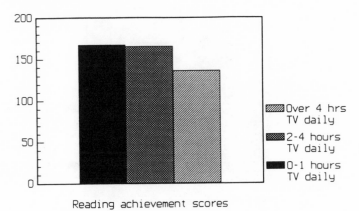

Reading achievement scores

Figure 6.15e. **Reading Achievement Scores for 13-Year-Olds Reading Weekly (as reported in NAEP-84)**

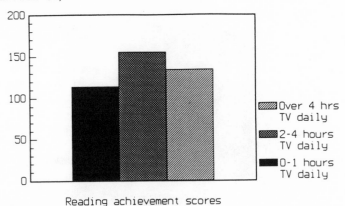

Reading achievement scores

Figure 6.15f. **Reading Achievement Scores for 13-Year-Olds Reading Rarely (as reported in NAEP-84)**

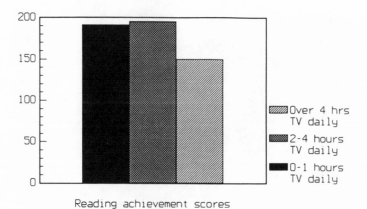

Figure 6.15g. Reading Achievement Scores for 17-Year-Olds Reading Daily (as reported in NAEP-84)

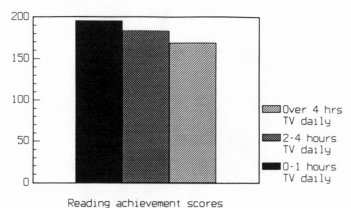

Figure 6.15h. Reading Achievement Scores for 17-Year-Olds Reading Weekly (as reported in NAEP-84)

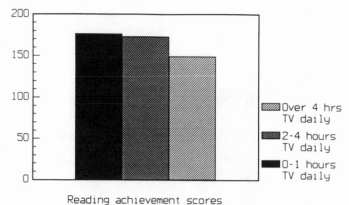

Figure 6.15i. Reading Achievement Scores for 17-Year-Olds Reading Rarely (as reported in NAEP-84)

Table 6.3.   Correlations of Leisure Reading Variables with
Frequency of Leisure Reading as Reported on NAEP

Variable	Frequency of Reading
Reading importance	.02
Perception of Reading Level	.10*
Purpose of Reading	
Read to do certain activities	.006
Read to play games	.02
Read for enjoyment	.34**

*p < .01
**p < .0001

on achievement than do all others if they watch six or more hours of television per day.

These patterns of relationships indicate that television viewing is not displacing leisure reading. Children are not choosing to sacrifice their reading time for an activity they regard as similar, but serving their functional needs better. For example, even though viewing declines for the 17-year-olds, time spent reading books and newspapers during free time still does not increase. Therefore, targeting television as the source of children's lack of interest in leisure reading is simply too easy an answer to a much more complex issue.

Why does reading occupy such a minor role in their leisure time? The reasons probably lay elsewhere. Turning the question around, several attitudinal reading variables were examined along with their relation to the time spent leisure reading. Two significant associations were found: time spent leisure reading is positively related to children's perceptions of their reading ability, and their reading enjoyment. Children who believe they are good readers, and enjoy reading, spend more time on the activity (see Table 6.3).

These relationships, of course, seems obvious. These findings, however, may strike at the critical issue in determining how children select one leisure activity over another. Free time may not be the determining factor. Rather, the primary consideration in selecting one media activity over another may be perceived satisfaction. So strongly associated with school achievement, "leisure" reading may not be regarded as "leisure" at all by children who are searching for an effortless, relaxing activity.

The Quality of Leisure Reading

Children's leisure reading habits may be changing from pretelevision behavioral norms, though perhaps more subtly than measures of time alone can adequately analyze. After all, leisure reading tends to be rather episodic in nature, varying from week to week, depending on such factors as availability of materials, and time of year. It could be that changes have occurred not so much in the time devoted to the activity, but in the quality of children's reading preferences. In fact, an early study by Parker (1963) studying the effects of television on library circulation, indicated a net reduction of more than one book per person, with fiction being affected more than nonfiction. He related these results to Schramm, Lyle, and Parker's hypothesis that television satisfied fantasy needs, and thus served to displace fiction, while reading related to people's reality needs.

Of course, these findings represented only an initial exploration of television's impact when first introduced in a community. They may not be terribly informative for understanding how television has affected children's reading preferences today. This research, however, raised important questions regarding the nature and quality of what children read outside the school setting. Have children's interests in fantasy been displaced by the fantasy content on television? Has television cheapened or debased the quality of leisure reading?

These questions were examined by asking 122 parents and children in the 4–6 grades to keep a television viewing and reading log including the number of books, newspapers, magazines and comic books read, for one month. On the average, children reported reading few books; girls read about three books, while boys, less than two for the month. Magazines and comic books were rarely read; newspapers sections (following along rather sexist lines, with the boys reading about sports, and girls reading the living section) were glanced at several times during a month.

But the interest of the research was less on the number of books read than on the quality of the children's leisure reading choices. Specifically, the study was designed to measure whether the amount of television viewed related to the quality of leisure reading—the tendency to choose "serious materials which promote a growing understanding of one's self, and problems of a social, moral, and ethnic nature" (Gray & Rogers, 1954). In order to examine the quality of leisure reading, a modification of the Gray and Rogers, *Maturity in Reading Scale* was used. This scale, measuring fiction and nonfiction materials, identifies three key factors in the quality of books read: intellectual challenge, complexity of the treatment of ideas, situations, or characters, and the richness of ideas, insights, and understandings presented (see Table 6.4).

Over the four week period, 340 book titles were recorded by students: 79% of these books were fiction, 21% nonfiction. These figures correspond to those from the Book Industry Study Group analysis (1984), indicating children's preference for fiction over nonfiction

Table 6.4. Indicators of Maturity in Fiction

Fiction Books

I. Plot
Level 5—Plot is used to illustrate universal problems and truth.
Level 4—Plot, and points it illustrates, are above average but lack universality.
Level 3—Plot is used to illustrate some point beyond mere story for story's sake.
Level 2—Plot still primary; ideas, probability, consistency are sacrificed to plotting.
Level 1—Plot is important for its own sake. Hackneyed standard plot formula. *Deus ex machina* solution and devices.

II. Characters
Level 5—Characters stand up both as individual characters in the book and as symbols of broader implications.
Level 4—Characters individualized, with some psychological insight.
Level 3—Characters may be used to illustrate a particular characteristic or point of view.
Level 2—Characters are stock characters.
Level 1—Characters are introduced merely to act as vehicles for the action.

III. Richness of Ideas
Level 5—Contributes to the development of a scale of values and/or a philosophy of life.
Level 4—Ideas (of some originality) with implications of wider importance than immediate situation but readily grasped without too much intellectual effort.
Level 3—Some original twists on familiar ideas—or a fairly new idea of limited scope.
Level 2—Introduces some new ideas, but treated in a pedestrian way.
Level 1—Plot is end-all and be-all; story for story's sake; commonplace and hackneyed ideas and plotting.

Nonfiction Books

I. Subject Matter
Level 5—Subject matter involves issues of a social, cultural, historical or political nature; several frames of reference for viewing subject are presented.
Level 4—Subject matter involves specific incidents, biographical portraits, or descriptions usually limited to one frame of reference.
Level 3—Subject matter involves avocational interests and hobbies.
Level 2—Subject matter deals with specific methods, processes, problems, and techniques related to the practical demands of daily living.
Level 1—Subject matter is superficial; material designed for purposes strictly of amusement or shock value.

II. Intellectual Challenge
Level 5—Presentation is as stimulating as the materials presented; thorough research coupled with logical implications.
Level 4—Accurate presentation of factual material with additional interpretive data but failure to extend to fullest implications.
Level 3—Accurate presentation of factual material; some biases or limitations may appear in the presentation.
Level 2—Reporting may be accurate but is oversimplified and pedestrian.
Level 1—Unsuccessful attempt to make report adequate.

III. Richness of Ideas
Level 5—Represents an original contribution to the world's thought.
Level 4—Important problem dealt with in a competent and/or stimulating way.
Level 3—Good coverage of purely factual material.
Level 2—Ideas introduced but not original; attempts to stimulate thought based on sensational or sentimental appeals.
Level 1—No ideas; mere reportage of unimportant or trivial matters.

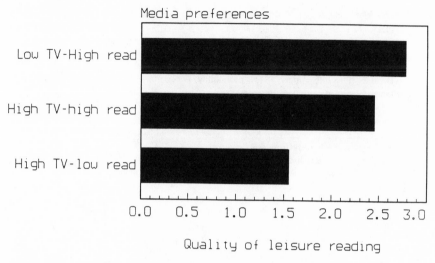

Figure 6.16.   Quality of Leisure Reading Choices for Fourth, Fifth, and Sixth Graders

books. From these data, it is apparent that despite those who claim otherwise, television's fantasy content has clearly not displaced children's interests in reading fiction.

Most children at these ages do not select particularly high quality books. Average fourth through sixth grade readers generally preferred rather simplistic plot structures, stock characters, involved in immediate situations and pedestrian themes. As expected, the more sophisticated readers are girls, who were bright and proficient in reading. These students, representing only 7% of the sample, not only read more books per month (over 7), but books of higher quality than others. The average quality rating for the most avid readers was 2.8, indicating a moderate level of maturity in their leisure reading choices. In comparison to most of the other students, these avid readers were far more likely to spend their free time on reading than television, reporting only seven hours a week of viewing.

Two other groups of media preferences were isolated from the larger sample to measure the relation between viewing and the quality of leisure reading choices. Figure 6.16 describes the scores of those who were the heaviest television viewers in the sample, along with their leisure reading habits. This analysis indicates that the students who were both heavy readers and viewers received quality scores that were basically undifferentiable from those of the most avid readers, while students who were heavy TV viewers and light readers chose books of a significantly lower quality than the others in the sample ($p < .05$).

These data suggest that television viewing, alone, does not relate to the quality of children's leisure reading choices. The profiles of media preferences argue against such an naive explanation. Rather, it appears that children's selection of sophisticated reading materials may be tied to a different, but recurring pattern of choices. In this analysis, as before, intelligence and reading proficiency were strongly related to quality scores, indicating that the less proficient readers favored poorer quality reading materials. This association is probably related to two factors: readability level, and the time devoted to leisure reading as a free-time activity. Sophisticated reading materials usually include more difficult vocabulary, and require more reading time— factors which might prove too overwhelming to the struggling reader.

In this respect, a vicious cycle seems to occur: Those students who would be most likely to benefit from outside reading, do less reading. When they do read, they tend to limit their exposure to poorer quality materials, which have fewer ideas, and provide less stimulation than materials at higher levels. In addition, unlike quality reading selections, these materials serve only a very narrow set of functions. The effects of reading lower quality books over time could mean that, in contrast to the "rich get richer" or cumulative advantage phenomena, such poor reading habits may inhibit further growth in reading ability. This has led some researchers (Stanovich, 1986; Walberg & Tsai, 1983) to speculate that subsequent achievement is based on the "Matthew Effect," after the Gospel according to Matthew: "For unto everyone that hath shall be given, and he shall have abundance: but from him that hath not shall be taken away even that which he hath" (XXV:29).

These findings are particularly important in light of recent research suggesting that the patterns established at young ages tend to be highly predictive of later achievement and interests in media preferences. Children who display interests in higher quality materials are likely to gravitate to similar content in adult life. Taste for strong stimulation (violence and adventure), as well, seems to show similar continuity over time.

In sum, leisure reading is not an activity that is established by simply turning off the television set, or by setting aside a time when reading is required. Instead, the nurturance of leisure reading occurs over time, as teachers and parents make children aware of its pleasures and its functions. Bettleheim and Zelan (1981) suggest the importance of these first instructive lessons in reading:

> We teach children to read in the hope that what they read will have meaning for them. But a skill that was not intrinsically meaningful when we first learned it is much less likely to become deeply meaningful later on. (p. 42)

These first lessons must include the joys, skills, and uses of reading as an activity. Reading aloud to children, incorporating timely materials from newspapers and magazines to everyday events, encouraging discussions of reading, providing access to high quality materials, all make reading a more effective, purposeful activity to children who are becoming increasingly interested in the world around them.

DOES TELEVISION TAKE AWAY FROM OTHER LEISURE PURSUITS?

Children only have so much leisure time. Considering the inordinate number of hours they seem to spend viewing, some activities must suffer, or be severely reduced. If not homework time, or leisure reading, might it be the more casual, unstructured activities, such as playing with friends, sports, and "free time" that are being sacrificed in favor of viewing?

Himmelweit and her colleagues found that in the first phase of television's introduction, children seemed to make room for viewing at the expense of "marginal or fringe" activities. These were the pastimes for which children placed little value, or which were of an unspecific, indefinite character, rather than the more organized or clearly purposive ones. Spending time on solitary activities, taking walks, doing nothing at all, these were the times that were reduced as children's lives became inevitably more crowded.

In this section, some of these unstructured activities from the NAEP study are examined, along with children's television viewing time. Unlike other research on children's uses of leisure, this analysis has the advantage of looking at children's free time activities at three different age levels, thus providing important information on how leisure time priorities might change over time.

Time Spent on Unstructured Activities

Over 12 different leisure activities were assessed in the NAEP analysis. In a series of questions, children were asked to rate the activities they engage in most during their free time. Reported in Figure 6.17 these trends indicate rather striking changes in leisure as children get older. Television is clearly the favorite activity of the 9-year-olds. Time is also spent, though to a lesser extent, on playing sports and being with friends. The majority of free time, however, is devoted to the more solitary activities, including TV viewing, video games, and reading.

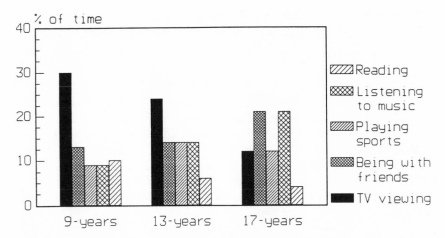

Figure 6.17. Frequency of Time Spent on Leisure Activities (as reported on NAEP-84)

This pattern, however, begins to change at the intermediate level. Here, children are still watching a good deal of television, but they are beginning to move their activities in a more social direction. Book reading goes down, along with video game playing, as spending time with friends, and playing in sports goes up. By the high school level, television is no longer the favorite leisure activity. At this age, listening to music takes over as the most popular medium, and friendships and social activities become a higher priority.

To measure the potential relationship between these marginal fringe activities and television viewing, three of the more popular unstructured activities were correlated with viewing time: spending time with friends, sports activities and listening to music. In all cases, viewing time was not related, either to friendships (.00, −.02, −.02, for each age level), or sporting events (.01, .00, −.02), or music (.00, −.01, −.01). These results provide fairly strong evidence that television is not affecting unstructured leisure activities considered to be important to children.

These data, of course, cannot measure whether children would place greater value on such activities as doing extra homework or writing a letter, if not for viewing. But it is doubtful that given all the available leisure options today, television's absence would encourage children to become involved in these types of unstructured activities obviously held in such low esteem. The unwritten assumption that children would be engaged in more worthwhile pursuits if the television set could only be ousted from the home is an illusion. Royko (1982) probably describes children's behavior more accurately:

The fact is, given a choice between doing something constructive (like homework) and something useless, 98% of all children will do something useless. If you make it impossible for him to do one useless thing, he will find something other useless thing to do.

It can be assumed, therefore, that television does not take up children's time from other more constructive activities. Rather, time spent watching is a measure of how much time children perceive to have free from other activities.

The patterns of leisure activities for children 9, 13, and 17 show strong evidence of change over time. Television viewing time, once the primary activity, diminishes as students grow older and as new demands are placed on their time. But the changes in television viewing are probably not only related to availability of time. The independent and solitary activities of television viewing and reading make way for the more social activities that become dominant in students' lives. Activities that give children access to and control over their environment become increasingly important as they grow older. In this respect, the individual selects media based on its functions.

Thus, rather than asking what activities are being sacrificed in favor of viewing, the question becomes how is television being used to satisfy needs. For the majority of students, the hours spent watching television as the primary leisure activity are tempered by the increasing demands of schooling and by the onset of activities associated with teenagers' more active lives. Only for a small minority of students are these options perceived as not being available. It is then that television most likely fills that gap.

SUMMARY

Television is a wonderful nemesis for those inclined to fret over the education of the young. It has been accused of robbing youngsters of childhood, reducing attention spans, and impairing children's ability to think clearly. Critics blame television for the decline in basic traditional academic skills and for problems ranging from dropping S.A.T. scores to illiteracy. Young viewers are presented as bleary-eyed addicts, incapable of the mental effort needed to sharply focus on ideas in a sustained manner.

This chapter has found no evidence to support these claims. While television is clearly not an educational panacea, the charges against the medium have been unwarranted. Television viewing has replaced neither book reading nor homework, and has not lessened the desire for achievement. Rather, the medium is used selectively by children to serve their functional needs. And what they and their families chose to do with television is closely interwoven with expectations for future achievement and overall educational goals.

Children's literacy patterns, as well, are based on their perceptions of functionality. Reading and writing activities, closely tied to overall performance in schooling, are perceived as serving a different set of needs and gratifications from home television viewing. These differences in the uses of each medium account for the consistently small relationships found between viewing and achievement.

Conceivably, recreational reading activities outside of school should serve similar functions as television viewing, and thus vie for children's available time and attention. Yet, there is no contest. In this analysis, as well as other surveys (Greaney, 1980; Whitehead, Capey, Maddren, & Wellings, 1977), little time is spent leisure reading, representing at most 8% of children's free time. Their apathy should not be taken, however, as evidence for displacement or competition between media, but rather a reflection of their attitudes toward reading. This analysis indicates that for many children, leisure reading is not seen as an enjoyable activity. Changing these existing attitudes, then, is critical in attempting to encourage leisure reading as a free-time activity. Unless regarded by children as a pleasurable activity, one serving their multiple needs, reading will always be cast in the shadow of other pursuits.

That television has not seriously constrained children's intellectual achievement and interests in reading should not be interpreted as unqualified support for the medium. Television, can indeed, be overused. A small, but significant proportion of school-aged children do report to be watching over six hours of television per night. These figures, however, tell us more about the characteristics of home environments that are far more deleterious to learning than about television viewing itself.

The chorus of frantic voices warning that children are helpless victims of the television set have unfortunately concentrated on this subset of children. One can understand their concern. But it is misleading to generalize from the small numbers of children who overuse the medium to the bulk of average viewers. Most children, watching between 2–3 hours daily, are successfully achieving and are developing higher-level literacy skills than previous generations. In homes where literacy is prized, television becomes another resource to enhance children's knowledge and critical thinking. The key, then, lies in the quality of the family learning environment, and not in the medium of communication.

7

Television and Reading in the Lives of Young Children

> In grasping the character of a society, as in judging the character of an individual, no documents, statistics, "objective" measurements can ever compete with the single intuitive glance. (Auden, 1962)

Television viewing and leisure reading activities are embedded in family life. These activities are established and valued through a loosely woven web of influences from the child's home environment. In this respect, children's ways of approaching media are inextricably linked to the complexity of these family processes. Research that bears on the particular processes of how television and reading activities are used, therefore, must be examined within the situated contexts in which they naturally occur.

Consequently, there are tradeoffs in employing quantitative and qualitative methodological strategies. Quantitative research studies are highly valuable in determining the relationship between television viewing and a number of important aspects of the reading process. These studies can provide important indications of which factors may, indeed, be causally linked to reading and school achievement. But this research paradigm cannot adequately describe the processes of influence and or clarify the proximal chain of cause and effect. Such clarification requires qualitative or naturalistic procedures to directly observe the behavioral and cognitive aspects of television and reading in the lives of young children.

To examine these processes, this chapter reports on a year-long ethnographic study, analyzing television and reading in the lives of three families. Ethnographic procedures were used in order to explore the ways in which families interacted with these activities in their everyday life. After identifying some of the assumptions reflecting on the time children spend on these activities, this chapter describes how television and reading were used in the lives of three families. Then, it focuses on the implications for further theory development and for practical applications in the home.

COMMON ASSUMPTIONS

Central to the charges against television is its extraordinary hold on children's time and attention. Many theories, as shown in previous chapters, have proposed different causal mechanisms to account for the potentially deleterious effects on children's developing literacy. Nevertheless, the element common to most of this research has been their reliance on the factor of time. In practice, it may be argued that most of the weight of interpretation for television's effects has rested on some variation of the displacement theory.

As we have seen, however, no direct evidence indicates that the amount of time spent reading has essentially changed since the introduction of television. Still, a great number of critics support the view that television may be indirectly related to reading. Some authorities consider that viewing may harm the acquisition of reading skills by displacing activities thought to be associated with children's emergent reading and writing (Elkind, 1981; Singer & Singer, 1983). Such negative displacement is believed to occur when viewing substitutes for an activity that provides opportunities for skill practice, active participation, and exploration (Gadberry, 1980; Gaddy, 1986). For example, it has been suggested that problem-solving skills may develop more slowly if viewing replaces an ability-enhancing activity such as imaginative play (Singer & Singer, 1983).

Judging from the research (Gadberry, 1980; Roberts, Bachen, Hornby, & Hernandez-Ramos, 1984; Singer & Singer, 1980) as well as theoretical accounts (Beentjes & Van der Voort, 1988; Greenfield, 1984; Hornik, 1981; National Institute of Mental Health, 1982), three common assumptions, reflecting the processes of spending time with television and children's learning to read, are thought to underlie these views:

1. Television stifles children's imagination and creativity: By presenting concrete visual images and fast-paced entertainment, television substitutes for self-generated imaginative activity. This assumption suggests that television is essentially a reactive, passive

activity, which may later transfer to a lack of mental effort or incentive in learning how to read.

2. Television takes time away from more worthwhile pursuits: Time given to television displaces out-of-school activities that might otherwise facilitate the development of reading skills. This assumption implies that television may reduce cognitive growth as it displaces more beneficial home-based activities such as drawing, or time spent reading.

3. Television is functionally equivalent to alternative leisure activities: Television displaces activities serving children's needs for novelty, social reinforcement, and information. This assumption suggests that children might favor spending time with the vicarious learning experiences of television rather than become involved in an activity more directly.

Following a description of the participant families, each of these assumptions are addressed in this chapter. In analyzing these issues, however, one should recognize that the goal of this naturalistic inquiry is in the discovery of the meanings of family actions and events, and not at a generalizable explanation of the patterns of all families.

THE PARTICIPANT FAMILIES

Since young children tend to be heaviest consumers of television (National Institute of Mental Health, 1982), the focus of the research was on families with children in the primary grades. A number of studies have suggested that television's effects might be particularly strong at the critical juncture of school entry where children are beginning formal reading instruction (Gadberry, 1974, 1980; Zuckerman, Singer, & Singer, 1980). To examine this potential association, then, families were selected in which one of the children was just about to enter the first grade in the following September. Three families were chosen in an effort to look at the potential differences in family experiences as well as the commonalities among these parents and children.

The Clarkes, living in a well-to-do suburban neighborhood, were the first family selected for the study. At the time, Claire was a full-time homemaker, and Rob, a management consultant. Three of their five children were currently living at home: Harry, Eddie, and Stephanie, ages 6, 8, and 10, respectively.

Also agreeing to participate in the study, Mary Alice Conley, a single parent, lived in what she described as a "Betty Crocker" district in a local suburban area—a mostly white, lower-middle-class rental neighborhood. Mary Alice was chiefly responsible for the two children, Stacey, age 6, and Alex, 2½, even though the father frequently called and spent occasional weekends with the children. As the president of a fledgling public relations company, Mary Alice was often busy at meetings and called on her friends to help in taking care of the children. When I first started observing, Robbie, an old acquaintance, was living in the house, because he was "down on his luck." During the year, there were a succession of young women from France who became "au pairs," helping with housework and the children in return for free rent.

In contrast to the Conley family, the Diamonds lived in an older, transitional neighborhood, where large homes were being renovated by young middle-class families. The Diamonds were selected to explore displacement in a home where the children had greater free time available during the day. Having taking a sabbatical year from preschool teaching, Caroline wanted Jennifer, age 5, and Leah, age 2½, to have some time off from day care, and her husband, Peter, a computer salesperson, strongly agreed with the decision. Few extra activities were scheduled for the children; Leah was picked up daily from the preschool at 12:00 and Jennifer usually arrived home by 3:00.

My role in the family was that of a participant observer. As noted by Leichter and her colleagues (Leichter et al., 1985; Taylor, 1983), establishing oneself in a home environment is difficult, involving a process of negotiating how to be perceived by the members of the family. In order to become familiar with each family's natural patterns of interactions, therefore, it seemed most appropriate to become a participating member of the household, helping with chores and the children, babysitting at times, eating meals, and spending time informally chatting with various family members.

Since television viewing time is likely to vary from week to week due to perceptions of available time (Bower, 1985), it was also necessary to make observations over a sufficient time span and over a variety of time periods to obtain a picture of seasonal, weekly and daily cycles of the family's life. Scheduled visits occurred at different time periods on all days of the week except Sunday over a 12-month period. Approximately 314 hours of observation, in all, were conducted.

During these visits, I carried a small notebook which allowed me to note important points, situations, and comments in shorthand form, often using a catch-phrase to get the gist of the account. After each observation, these notes were more fully transcribed, detailing the behaviors and contexts observed, the hours and family members present, the seasonal variations, as well as any personal and theoretical notations.

On occasion, family storybook readings and conversations around the television set were audiotaped. These recordings allowed me to capture the intimacy of the parent–child interactions during storybook reading when observations were intrusive; it also permitted me to examine the typical "family talk" that occurred when the families spent time watching television together.

These ethnographic procedures provided an opportunity to observe young children's television viewing and reading activities within the context of their other daily patterns. In this respect, it was a useful strategy for analyzing the ways in which television is mediated by the family environment and how displacement is thought to occur. But this approach also has its limitations. One, of course, is the number of families. While the types of families selected enable contrasts and comparisons, this discussion rests on young children who may be considered to be broadly within the middle class. In addition, these particular parents, demonstrating considerable skepticism about television, all controlled children's viewing time and to some degree, the type of content to be watched. None of these children would be regarded as excessive viewers. Consequently, the patterns described here reflect moderate viewers and average readers. The basic characteristics of these families are shown in Table 7.1.

AN ETHNOGRAPHIC LOOK
AT TELEVISION AND READING

This section describes how television and reading were used in these three families, in light of the common assumptions of displacement. Following this analysis, the next section will look at the implications of these observations on further theory development.

Displacement of Cognitive and Imaginative Activities

It is frequently claimed by some critics that television viewing weakens children's active thought processes, decreasing their imaginativeness and ability to be creative (Singer & Singer, 1980; Winn, 1977). These arguments are largely based on the issue of cognitive overload (Mander, 1978; Singer, 1980; Trelease, 1982). Television's pacing, its constant sensory bombardment is thought to maximize an involuntary form of attention, preventing children from strategically processing or generating hypotheses from televised content. Without the time necessary to assimilate incoming information, it is argued, that children become transfixed by the medium (Singer & Singer, 1983).

Table 7.1.   Summary of Characteristics of Participant Families.

Characteristics	Families		
	Claire & Rob Clarke	Caroline & Peter Diamond	Mary Alice Conley
Children in study	Stephanie, 10 Eddie, 8 Harry, 6	Jennifer, 5 Leah, 2½	Stacey, 6 Alex, 2½
Parent's profession			
Mother	Homemaker	Homemaker (on sabbatical) from school	President, public relations
Father	Management Consultant	Computer Salesperson	Salesperson
Housing	Owned home	Owned home but rented out second floor	Rented two family home
Non-Kin Household Members	None	None	1 (4 different people in year)
Number of TV sets	2	1	2
Videotape owned	yes	yes	yes
Approximate amount of weekly TV viewed by children (varying by season)	21 hours	14 hours	18 hours
Attend public library	Weekly	Weekly	Rarely
Involvement in community activities	Sports Church-related Lessons	None	Sports

Such inactivity is though to impede the development of reading ability on two grounds: (a) The cognitive passivity of television viewing may be internalized, and later generalized to more demanding processing tasks like reading (Salomon, 1984), and (b) television's concrete visual images may obviate the need for children to spontaneously produce their own mental images (Tower, Singer, Singer, & Biggs, 1979). This may exert a destructive influence on children's imaginative play, considered to be associated with emergent narrative competence (Pellegrini, 1985).

To examine these assertions, observations were analyzed first to examine how children watched television. It seemed fair to assume that if children spent a large proportion of their time passively incorporating television content, with little evidence of cognitive activity, then they might be less prepared to engage in higher level processing tasks, like reading.

The television viewing context. Children did not appear to be cognitively passive at all while watching television. In contrast to the conception of the child just sitting and staring blankly at the television, observations indicated that there were wide variations in the way the children responded to television. Sometimes, these response patterns gave clear indications that children were actively engaged in processing the televised content. For example, Harry tended to be highly participatory, as he responded to television with both physical and verbal activity:

> We are watching *The Cosby Show*. The story is about Bill Cosby who is trying to fix the plumbing in the bathroom.
>
> *Harry:* "Maybe he might need the plumber (starts imitating what a plumber might do).
>
> (Some minutes later) Probably that's not real glue, probably they use plastic or something.
>
> (A couple of minutes later)
> Most plumbers don't do that—they don't take down a wall.
>
> (later) I know where the sledge hammer is—(that Cosby was using to break down a wall)—its under the tub."

Other times, however, children made few overt responses while viewing. In the past, this lack of motor involvement has been taken as evidence that little processing occurs (Mates, 1980). Such an interpretation, unfortunately, has not allowed for the alternative explanation that children may be actively processing the content, albeit covertly (see Table 7.2).

Table 7.2.   Different Ways of Watching Television

Viewing Styles	Examples
The participatory viewer	Harry is watching a commercial on television and starts singing, "Have you driven a Ford, lately."
The reflective viewer	Stephanie is watching a fight from the movie *Rocky* on TV. "They're not really hitting each other. See they're using water to make it look like sweat, and red stuff to make it look like blood, and false teeth to make it look like their faces are bulging.
The strategic viewer	Stacey watches TV while playing with her new stamp album. She only occasionally looks up at the TV set, as she tells her mother all about her new book.
The zombie viewer	Jennifer is watching a tape of *Charlotte's Web*. As she turns it on, her mother asks her a question. "Shhh, it's now beginning, and never says another word until the end of the show.

Evidence for children's covert involvement was observed through their questions and comments during breaks from their viewing. For example, often annoyed by her brother's running commentaries, Stephanie's viewing style tended to be reflective, as she watched a program intensely without saying a word. Her comments during the commercials or following the show, seemed to belie the conventional view of passivity, as she revealed her attention to even the smallest story details, as well as her inferencing from story content:

Stephanie has just finished watching *A Different World*.

Stephanie: Where is Princeton?

Mother: New Jersey.

Stephanie: Is it warm in New Jersey in February?

Mother: No, but why did you think so?

Stephanie: Because everyone on the show is wearing short sleeves and so I thought it must be warm out.

Similarly, in the Conley home, there were no outward signs to suggest that Stacey comprehended and interpreted story sequences on television. Displaying a very different style from Harry or Stephanie, Stacey, was a strategic viewer, using the music and sounds to key into significant story events. Staring only occasionally at the set, she simultaneously engaged in a host of other activities, as in this example:

Stacey is sitting on the bed, talking to her Dad on the phone, and then her step-sister Heather. She is discussing her upcoming birthday plans. At the same time, Isabel, the current 'au pair' is yelling at Alex, "it's time to go to bed." She chases him around the room, and he bites her. Stacey continues to talk, occasionally saying in her grown-up voice to Alex, "it's time to go to bed." These events are simultaneously occurring as she watches *Who's the Boss*, and *Growing Pains*. When the programs are over, I ask:

SBN: Those programs were pretty sophisticated—I mean what do you think?

Stacey: They both teach you things.

SBN: Oh, like what?

Stacey: Oh, I don't want to tell you. OK. The first, *Who's the Boss* teaches you not to tell a lie because remember how she got caught, and the second, *Growing Pains* that you shouldn't marry too young.

Though monitoring several other events, Stacey was obviously able to comprehend the essence of the plots from each of the television narratives.

In contrast, Jennifer's viewing style often resembled the popular characterization of the "zombie" viewer. She tended to watch as if she were in a stupor, neither responding to comments or questions from any one in the room. But even this trance-like behavior, suggesting extreme passivity, was somewhat deceptive. For example:

Jennifer is watching *The Cat in the Hat* on television.

Mother: What's he doing?

No answer.

Mother: What's happening?

No answer.

Mother: What's that?

No answer.

After the show is over,

Jennifer: Now I want to read the book. (She runs upstairs to get *The Cat in the Hat*).

While it was impossible to gauge how much Jennifer was actually absorbing from the program, the outward appearance of passivity may, in this case, have reflected her intense concentration. "Zombie viewing" in Jennifer's situation interacted with program content; during unfamiliar shows, she seemed transfixed, while she was clearly more participatory when watching reruns or tapes.

Jennifer's mother puts on the Winnie-the-Pooh tape that they own.

Jennifer: You've got to watch my favorite part. See—
(Tigger is buried under a big snow drift)

Jennifer: It's old long ears. (She laughs)
I wish I were Roo.
(Someone falls)

Jennifer: That's so funny.

Leah: That's so funny.

Jennifer: I wish I were Roo.

Variations in viewing styles, therefore, suggested that there was no one typical "active" processing style. Children, who were active, were not always physically or verbally participating in the televised action; instead, many times, they were absorbed or gave intense concentration to the television screen. These variations in viewing, however, did not seem closely tied to the children's abilities to predict and interpret television content. Thus, those who have argued that television is a passive cognitive activity may be confounding viewing style with the processing of televised content. In contrast to the assumption that children are held captive by the set, the pacing of information, nor the multiple stimuli from television did not appear to hinder their ability to generate ideas, nor to prevent different strategies for viewing. In fact, television viewing may have given children opportunities to practice these processing skills.

Outside the television-viewing context. It may be the case, however, that television's impact on children's active thinking processes and imaginative activities takes place on a more long-term basis. Thus, its influence may be only evidenced in a different context apart from the actual viewing of television. Since children's imaginative play activities have been strongly associated with their developing sense of narrative (Heath, 1983; Pellegrini, 1985), observations were examined to analyze the potential linkages between television and children's free play activities at home.

Observations indicated that, rather than inhibit play, television content was often used as a point of departure for children's imaginative play activities. Generally, this occurred over two stages. At the first stage, the children seemed almost to duplicate the televised story in their pretend play. Caroline, for example, found Jennifer actually acting out a favorite *Rainbow Brite* story, assigning specific character roles to her friends, and using the dialogue directly from the show. Once familiar with the characters and themes, the children at the second stage, invented whole new adventures of their own, while at the same time, conforming to the underlying story structure.

Not all of children's viewing, however, was a resource for pretend play. Rather, the selection of television content reflected children's already existing play themes. For example, Jennifer incorporated the character of Heidi in a familiar play theme of family after watching only a few minutes of a Disney cartoon; programs including *Sesame Street* and *Misterogers' Neighborhood*, for which she devoted many hours, never related to any of her play scenarios. In this respect, television was not just uniformly incorporated in their play; instead, children used its content selectively to satisfy their needs.

Three factors were associated with the television content selected for pretend play: (a) The characters had clearly identifiable behaviors, (b) uncomplicated plot structures, and (c) general familiarity among many children.

Television characters used in pretend play reflected distinguishable character traits, such as "Big Bird" who according to Alex was "always afraid" or "Carebears" who had "magic in their stomachs" and engaged in highly predictable behaviors, such as "Snuffelupiguss" who "always gets into trouble," and "My Little Pony" who had "so much smooze and so much witches and so much monsters." These characters were used in such common play themes as good versus evil, marriage and family, and fear of monsters.

Children selected television content with highly formulaic plot structures for their pretend play. After viewing the program *The Carebears* on television, for example, it became a frequent variation in Jennifer's good versus evil play theme. The plot of the televised version followed a simple formula involving the magical Carebears, living in the land of "Care-a-lot," who fight against the evil spirits that would remove all caring from the world. Retaining the basic theme from the story, Jennifer and her friends created a new story of their own making:

Jennifer: (swinging on a hammock) That cloud—it's a care-a-lot cloud.

SBN: What's that?

Jennifer: The carebears live there. The carebears shaped me. I just jumped from the cloud. I helped take care of the teensie-weensies and kept them away from Dark Heart, who has red eyes and he can turn into anything he wants. He trapped the grown-ups and I have the key. Me and Lara, she had the other key and I had the key to the babies and Lara to the adults. Star and Heart were the helpers. And more and more children came, and the adults were away, and we saved the care-a-lots and flew home.

The basic plot structures from *Rainbow Brite, My Little Pony, Brady Bunch*, and *Family Ties* were among the many television-related pretend play activities observed during the year.

In order to sustain play, it was necessary to be familiar with the televised "script." It was not uncommon for the children to invite particular friends over to play a mutually-shared favorite of *Family Ties* or *Carebears*. On some occasions, the older children invited their younger brother or sister to join in, but only if they were able to follow the story structure. When they did not, play was interrupted, as in the case when Jennifer yelled to her sister "C'mon Leah, remember in Rainbow land you have to have a problem." Such awareness of the implicit rules of a television story argues against the conception that, for Jennifer, viewing was merely reactive.

These observations, both in the television viewing context and in children's pretend play activities, suggest that, rather than stifle their imaginative capacities, television may embellish children's play by offering new variations of content on well-established play themes. In this respect, television as a common cultural experience may serve the important social function of helping children to initiate and interact with others (Anderson & Collins, 1988). James and McCain (1982), in their observational study in preschools, found that when play involved television-related content, more children actually joined in. Thus, in contrast to preventing symbolic play, a moderate amount of viewing age-appropriate content may involve children in the production and comprehension of decontextualized language associated with literate behavior.

Displacement of Worthwhile Pursuits

A central concern of displacement is that the time spent watching television diverts children away from more worthwhile activities (Hornik, 1981). This assumption implies that children's emerging literacy skills may be inhibited by displacing activities, both directly and indirectly, which are thought to facilitate general cognitive development (Gaddy, 1986). Among the activities that are considered to be most likely, and directly, affected is leisure reading. Presumably, if television is taking time away from leisure reading, then the development of reading skills and fluency might suffer. Activities that are thought to indirectly impair children's reading skills might include such ability-enhancing pursuits as drawing, homework, or even resting (Gadberry, 1980; Maccoby, 1954; Schramm et al., 1961).

For television to be displacing more worthwhile activities, it is logical to assume that children must be viewing during the times when they would otherwise be engaged in these valuable activities. To examine this assumption, observations were analyzed focusing on when television viewing and reading occurred most often and for what general purposes they were used by these families.

When television viewing occurs. Observations indicated that, in contrast to displacing organized activities, children's patterns of viewing tended to reflect the times perceived to be free from these other pursuits. Established family routines, indicating parent's educational and social priorities, served as an important mediational influence in structuring children's time. Such routines included formal lessons, as in the case of the Clarke children who were scheduled for a particular activity every afternoon. Or they might simply include care-taking responsibilities, such as the evening bath, or the bedtime reading routine. In either case, however, these routines, consciously or unconsciously, controlled when children were able to view television and what purposes it served for these families.

For the Clarke children, for example, television was turned on immediately after they entered their house around 5:00, following their heavily scheduled day. Soon interrupted by dinner at 5:30, then homework and other responsibilities, viewing was only allowed to be resumed after (or if) other activities of greater priority were completed:

> Rob is giving instructions to the babysitter before he goes out.
>
> *R:* Stephanie must first go up and do her homework and have it checked. (to Stephanie) Good piano lesson today, sport. Remember you have to practice piano before TV. Otherwise, no Cos. (to babysitter) Then if she has finished she's allowed to to watch *Cosby* and *A Different World*.

Television viewing in this family was often used as a reward system, serving to encourage and reward the children for fulfilling their responsibilities.

For the Diamond's children, television viewing occurred during the latter part of each afternoon from 4-6 p.m, when the children were either tired or getting fussy after playing with friends. Caroline prepared dinner while the children viewed either a video tape or educational programs, like *Reading Rainbow* or *Sesame Street*:

> I usually have the children watch *Sesame Street* in the afternoon to calm them down when they get a little wild. Or when Jennifer is in a bad mood, when nothing Leah can do is right. Jennifer's a bit too old for it, really. But it puts her out. She doesn't think about it. Television just makes her rest.
>
> My father gave us a videotape with many of the family occasions together. The tape is filled with family and relatives, and with long segments of Christmas and playing in the backyard of our house. Leah watches "her video" every day, generally falling asleep for a nap on the couch after 15 minutes.

In addition to these functions, television served as a time clock in the Conley family. Children watched *Sesame Street* while dressing every morning for school, came downstairs for breakfast and *Misterogers'*, then viewed "whatever was on" following dinner and their evening bath from 8:00–8:30 each night before going to bed. Living in a busy neighborhood, the children either played outside or in the house with friends in the latter afternoon; nighttime television was reserved for relaxation and escape:

Mary Alice: After dinner, it's quiet time. No friends over. The children
can play with their coloring books, and watch a bit of TV.
Sometimes Alex listens to a music tape before he goes to
bed, but no more playing.

Afternoon television was discouraged in all three families for reasons that "the children could be doing something better with their
time, like playing." Generally these parental restrictions were followed, as noted by Harry in his school diary:

The thing I like best about my mother is when she doesn't let us watch
TV. It makes me feel happy, because in Spring, I can always go outside to
play.

By establishing priorities and routines, parents exercised their influencing potential in helping children structure their time. In doing
so, they confined children's choices in selecting television content, and,
to a great extent, controlled the time available to watch television. In
these homes, television did not replace active involvement in alternative activities; instead, television was used primarily as an activity to
mark the end of a busy day. Even with these limitations on time,
however, children were able to free approximately 14–21 hours per
week for watching television.

When storybook reading time occurs. Associated chiefly as a
night time activity, storybook reading typically vied for children's
attention at the same time as television viewing, and thus had the
greatest potential of all free time activities to be displaced. Observations indicated varying degrees of displacement; to the degree that
storybook reading was incorporated as a structured family activity, it
was not displaced by television. However, when book reading was
regarded by children an optional activity, it was not only often displaced by viewing, but by other activities as well.

As expected, television viewing, occurring only in the late afternoon, did not compete with the nightly storybook reading in the Diamond home. Here, the nighttime story was a highly ritualized event,
beginning right after dinner:

About 6:00-6:30, the children begin to go upstairs. They put on their PJ's,
brush their teeth, and then they both go to Jennifer's room, unless Peter
is home and he takes one of them, and I take the other. Then Jennifer
either reads to Leah in front of me, or I read about 5 or 6 stories to them.
Then I sing a song like "Twinkle twinkle" and Leah goes to bed. After
that, I read to Jennifer alone out of a chapter book, and then I sing her a
night time song.

Night time, however, was more complicated in the Clarke family. Parent meetings, and varying reading interests among the children, sometimes interfered with the regularly scheduled storybook hour:

> We read almost every single night. But it's getting kind of split up now. I read to Eddie and Harry together, and Stephanie separately, cause she's into different stuff. Then the children are allowed to stay up ½ hour past the time they are put into bed to read. Stephanie and Eddie listen to a tape and read along with it—Harry just listens to a tape.

Book reading time, however, was indeed a candidate for displacement when the structured story hour did not take place or when the children had the option to choose between other activities:

> A babysitter is taking care of the children. Checking on the children for bedtime, she sees that Stephanie is watching *The Breakfast Club* on television.
>
> *Babysitter:* Stephanie, it's 8:30. You said you were supposed to read. When are you going to do that?
>
> *Stephanie:* I'll go to bed at 8:45, and then I'll read until 9:00. I've got to have lights out at 9:00.
>
> The babysitter leaves and comes back at 8:45.
>
> *Babysitter:* You need to go to bed.
>
> *Stephanie:* Please please, just let me watch one little bit more.
>
> *Babysitter:* You promised to read.
>
> *Stephanie:* Please, please.
>
> *Babysitter:* Why don't you get in your pajamas, brush your teeth, and you can watch 10 more minutes.
>
> *Stephanie:* OK, only ten more minutes.

Even when television viewing was not possible, during the half hour designated as individual reading time before bedtime, reading was easily replaced by other activities. At night, I often found Eddie playing with his cars in bed, Stephanie sewing a hook rug in her room, and Harry only occasionally listening to a music or *Curious George* audio tape. Yet at the same time, Eddie complained, "I never have any time to read. During the day, I'm too busy, and then at night, I'm too tired."

Unlike the other two families, there was no bedtime story in the Conley home. Having many late business meetings, Mary Alice left the night time routine to the "au pair," who knew little English, and would send the children off to bed following the nightly prime time television program. Even when Mary Alice was home, however, other commitments took precedence before book reading; instead, television was used by her as a substitute for the night time story, as described in the following examples:

> Alex brings a book into his mother's room and asks her to read him a story. Mary Alice ignores this, and puts on a *Bill Cosby* videotape.

> Mary Alice puts Alex to bed by kissing him and talking to him. She tells Stacey that its time to go to bed, but Stacey brings in a story about *Madeline* to read. Mary Alice starts making a phone call.

> *SBN:* Do you read a story before bed?

> *Stacey:* No—we watch TV. Mom never reads to us because she's too busy. Only when we have babysitters do we read books.

Observations of these episodes suggested that Stacey and Alex did not actively choose to substitute television viewing for book reading. Rather, television was selected in the absence of any book reading opportunities. Given television's accessibility to the very young child, viewing, in this respect, may be conceptualized as a "default option" for those who have a limited set of alternatives during the evening hours.

These observations argue for a more complicated pattern of displacement than has been described in previous research. Unlike television viewing, storybook reading for young children is a dependent activity, one that is facilitated by an adult's encouragement and supervision. Without parental support, it may be that television is watched because it happens to be there when other, even possibly more attractive activities, are not. Thus, in the case of young children, the displacement theory might provide a more accurate description of a parent's behavior rather than his/her child's.

Television viewing, however, did replace book reading on occasion for the older children, who were capable of reading on their own. But, again, these patterns are complicated, revealing a fundamental paradox about book reading. Even when viewing was not possible, other activities such as playing, or music, often displaced reading, suggesting that the very flexibility of the book reading activity, may, at the same time, allow it to be more easily displaced than some other activities. Further, as a relatively effortful activity, books may not be considered "leisure" for young children who are tired at the end of a day.

Concurrent activities. One of the problems in interpreting the displacement of worthwhile pursuits, however, is that some activities are not mutually exclusive with television viewing. Studies involving extensive videotaping of viewing behavior, for example, have indicated a variety of other activities are likely to be time-shared with television (Anderson, Field, Collins, Lorch, & Nathan, 1985; Bechtel, Achelpohl, & Akers, 1972). Beentjes and Van der Voort (1988) have argued that some of these activities may be qualitatively displaced because of the distraction provided by the TV.

Over half of the children's viewing time in this study involved both viewing and other activities, including playing, eating, reading and homework. Observations suggested that, in contrast to qualitative displacement, the children seemed to strategically allocate their attention to television according to the demands of the time-shared activity.

For example, though not allowed to do so, sometimes Stephanie combined viewing and homework activities:

The Clarkes have given instructions to the babysitter that Stephanie is to complete her homework before watching TV. After her parents leave, however, I find her upstairs watching *Wheel of Fortune* while doing her homework. She is trying to guess at the missing letters.

SBN: Stephanie, I don't think you are allowed to watch and do your homework.

Stephanie: Oh, I only put this on as background. I find something that doesn't bother me when I do it.

For Stephanie, this homework assignment, which was completed by the end of the program, presented little challenge, allowing her to expend more effort on watching the television show.

Contrary to the opinion that these time-shared activities suffer when combined with television, observations indicated that it was often the television that was neglected.

It is 7:30 on Thursday at the Clarke home, and the children are getting ready for *The Bill Cosby Show*, a family event. Claire makes popcorn and the boys decide to build a fort, with gym mats and large tubes in the TV room. They turn the TV on, watch for a moment, and then continue to play in the fort. Claire turns the TV off, but no one seems to notice, as they are now playing hide and go seek in their fort.

Particularly for the younger children, who were rarely in control of the program selected, these other activities at times drew them away from the TV set when the program was of little interest or comprehensibility:

Alex and Stacey are watching *Growing Pains* while coloring in their new coloring books. Alex, looking up at the TV only occasionally, takes a magic marker, and begins to tell a story about the pictures in the book,

"That's my old buddy Burt. Burt is going to catch a ball, and there's me and Stacey. Stacey is hugging me." As he turns each page, he tells a new story about his old buddy, Burt. After about six times, Stacey, who is trying to watch the program, suggests that I read the coloring book to him. Alex comes over to me and continues to tell his stories, ignoring the TV show altogether.

These observations suggest that young children adjust their attention to television and other activities on the basis of their interest and the amount of mental effort required for each activity. Children's differential attention seems to involve a strategy of attending more closely to the activity that demands the higher level of concentration, while investing less effort in the other. This interactive pattern contrasts sharply with the view that the quality of time-shared activities is invariably displaced while viewing. Conceivably, it is possible that in some cases, the viewing environment may even support children's engagement in these other activities.

The enhancement of worthwhile activities. Generally, the displacement theory assumes a negative relationship between viewing and other pursuits; that is, television is thought to take away from these other, more valuable cognitive activities. Only rarely has television been thought to facilitate children's involvement in reading-related activities. Of those few scholars that have supported this view, television's role has alternately been cast as an information-providing experience (Dorr, 1986), a boost to the reading of specific books (Hamilton, 1976), or a strategy for reluctant readers (Potter, 1976).

In these family contexts, however, I observed not a one-way, but a reciprocal, ongoing relationship between viewing and print. Children's interests often crossed media lines as they looked for opportunities to spend time with their favorite characters and stories. For example, Caroline describing Jennifer's current interest:

> Jennifer's just in love with *Charlotte's Web* right now. She tries to read a chapter when she wakes up in the morning. We got the video and I thought, "Oh dear"—here she was reading the book. But the video helped her get back into the book again, which surprised me. It brought her back to the book.

> She just loves Templeton. The video makes it so funny. And she laughs about that. And then when she gets in the book, she laughs because she knows what's going to happen. Whereas, I could never get into Templeton—he was the terrible one. So I think the video has given her a new angle on Templeton.

In this case, Jennifer's interest in *Charlotte's Web* first began with her teacher reading the book at school. But at other times, Jennifer became interested in reading as a result of watching television. For example, having seen *Rainbow Brite* on television, she bought a little golden book that she learned to read independently. Later, with her mother's help, she used these resources to write and illustrate her own book. Such similar cross media patterns occurred with *Winnie-the-Pooh*, *The Cat and the Hat* as well as *The Carebears*, which Jennifer described in a message to her mother: "Carebear my fafrit movie the carebear storybook."

For the Clarkes, television was occasionally used to directly encourage reading. Scanning the Disney Channel guide each week, Claire videotaped a number of classics, including *The Lion, the Witch and the Wardrobe*, and *The Lord of the Rings* that she wanted the children to eventually read. The videos were used as a way of "getting into" the story, which she later read during their evening storyhour.

Cross-media connections were also evident in the Conley's home, where television often substituted for the children's storybook hour. Alex's and Stacey's interest in *The Velveteen Rabbit*, first introduced by their respective teachers, was transferred to the home via a videotape, bought through the school book club. With no one to read the story to him, Alex repeatedly watched the video with intense interest, waiting for his favorite scene, "when all the toys get fired."

In this home, television was often used explicitly by Mary Alice as a catalyst for the children's literacy interactions. Linkages between Alex's interests in *Sesame Street* and print, for example, were seen in a calendar in his room, a primary vocabulary (and picture) learning game, an alphabet videotape, a Big Bird jigsaw puzzle, a subscription to the *Sesame Street* magazine and a Big Bird Cookbook. Similarly, Mary Alice joined the *Fraggles* Book Club for Stacey, who was just beginning to read on her own.

The sheer variety of connections between television and print suggested that children's interests tended not to remain medium-specific. Seeking time beyond the immediate television or reading experience, children pursued their favorite stories and characters through multiple exposures with different media. In fact, the distinctions between media became increasingly blurred, as the children moved freely back and forth from visually oriented media (i.e., television, videotapes, movies) to print-oriented media (books, toy books, advertising circulars). Thus, contrary to displacing worthwhile activities, these observations indicated that television often served as a resource for children's emerging interests. Rather than conflict, there was a complementarity between children's media activities; interests in one medium often sparked similar interests in the other.

In sum, these observations argue that the consequences of television viewing are more complex than are indicated in the hypothesis for displacement. There was no consistent or strong evidence that television viewing displaced valuable cognitive activities. Rather, children often viewed in the absence of stimulating activities. For example, there were indications that children replaced reading with viewing when there was a lack of parental guidance, or when the option for being read to was unavailable.

However, there were also instances when viewing was concurrent with, or facilitated children's involvement with print activities, either directly by encouraging them to read TV-related books or indirectly, by generating or sustaining interests in activities associated with reading. Thus, it was the children who were active agents in their choices of leisure activities: their uses of the media were guided by their interests and their practical assessment of attractive alternatives.

Displacement of Functionally Equivalent Needs

A related assumption of displacement is that television is functionally equivalent to alternative leisure time activities. Here, it is argued that television displaces activities serving children's similar needs, but requiring more effort than viewing. Because it is continuously available and instantly gratifying, television is thought to subsume children's needs for excitement, information and social reinforcement (Gadberry, 1980; Gaddy, 1986). Thus, from this perspective, television may induce children to become mentally and physically lazy, preferring vicarious learning experiences rather than those requiring active exploration. Such an assumption implies that children would be less interested in learning to read and less prepared to invest the mental effort required by reading.

Children's viewing and reading behavior, however, have been shown to be influenced by the models set by their parents (Bryce, 1980; Neuman, 1986b). Such influence may be exercised by parent's attitudes toward each medium or by personal example. Presumably, if parents use television to the exclusion of reading or other activities, it might reasonable to assume that their children would be likely to follow their model. To examine this assumption, therefore, observations were analyzed for examples of how parents may guide, implicitly or explicitly, their children in the uses of television and reading and how these lessons seem to be internalized by their children.

Lessons about television. Observations indicated that parent's beliefs about television exerted a strong influence in their children's perceptions about the medium. These influences, however, did not tend to be manifested in the amount of time children actually spent on viewing; in all cases, the children's viewing time far exceeded the models set by their parents. Rather, these informal lessons appeared to play a significant role in the way children watched television and in their definition of its uses to serve their needs. In this respect, parent influences served as an important constraining factor in television's capacity to displace other potentially, similar activities.

The strong educational orientation in the Clarke and Diamond homes, for example, exerted its influence on their children's attitudes and uses of the medium. In both families, time was regarded as too precious to waste on noneducational activities; television, though sometimes informative and enjoyable, should be used only sparingly to the degree that it is not substituting for more active, worthwhile pursuits.

Different mediational styles, however, were evident in the way these families elected to exercise their influence. For example, with older children, the Clarkes monitored the frequency of their children's viewing, but with the exception of violent programming, not its content:

> I want the children to learn to self-regulate. I rather have them come to see these things in the home rather than somewhere else. When they watch, I answer all their questions even if its a little embarrassing. I like them to analyze what they see and hear on television. Occasionally, though, if I'm in there reading and Stephanie is watching something like she was last night, I'll say this is trash, this is really stupid, you must have something better to do with your mind!

The children were well-aware of their parent's orientation toward television. In his school diary, Harry drew a picture of a television as an example of an activity he did that grown-ups hated. Similarly, when a teacher-strike disrupted school and Stephanie got caught by her mother watching *The Price is Right* in the afternoon, she quickly turned it off, then rationalized, "I was just learning how to estimate."

In contrast, viewing in the Diamond home was monitored for both its frequency and content. Here, television was limited primarily to educational fare:

> Time is so valuable. I'd rather the children play or something. But if they're really exhausted they can watch one of the educational programs like *Square 1* or *Reading Rainbow*, something really useful.

Monitoring, however, became more difficult when cable television, along with a remote control panel, was installed in the home. Spot checking, Caroline noticed that Jennifer was changing channels to noneducational daytime television. Arguing that television was "getting out of control," new restrictions were instituted:

> The children can chose anything they want, like *Square 1* or *3-2-1 Contact*, but they can only have it on for one hour. I think they're having more fun doing things as a result of less television.
>
> *SBN:*   Jennifer, what do you think you're doing more of?
>
> No answer.
>
> *Caroline:*   Oh, I think the kids are just playing more, playing with their dolls, doing more drawing. Hasn't it been fun Jennifer?

Jennifer (playing with her doll):   Yeh.

Television viewing for the Diamond's children, therefore, was carefully controlled by their parents: the medium was to be used as an enhancement for learning, or it was not to be used at all. Even with educational fare, however, the Diamond's clearly communicated the message that active involvement in playing or other activities was always preferable to viewing.

Unlike the other two families, there was a strong social orientation in the Conley's home. Being a single parent, Mary Alice encouraged her friends, relatives, and business associates to stop by or telephone each night. Television often served as a backdrop during these informal social occasions; TV jokes were remembered and repeated to her children and her friends around the kitchen table. Similarly, Stacey used television for social purposes, memorizing jokes from her favorite shows and sharing them with her friends:

> *Stacey:*   I've be telling everybody at school these riddles from the *Bill Cosby Show*. Here's one. A boy went into the hospital and the doctor said that it was impossible to operate because the child was family. The doctor was not the father—who was it?
>
> *Boy next door:*   I don't know
>
> *Stacey:*   It was the mother, get it?

In this family, television did not substitute for social interaction; rather, its content was used as part of their social exchanges with friends. In fact, these jokes were so successful that Stacey later borrowed a *Bill Cosby Joke Book* from the library and started memorizing jokes from *Discovery* magazine. Thus, in contrast to displacement, television content served to enhance this family's social involvement with friends.

Bryce, (1980) in an ethnographic analysis of families and television, argued that the uses of the medium are inextricably related to the values and patterns by which family groups organize their lives together. "Television is a new dimension in an old system" (p. 359). In homes, where education and active exploration are valued, television does not replace such ability-enhancing activities; similarly, where social activities are important, television content may be used to provide more opportunities to practice these skills.

Lessons about reading. Parents beliefs about reading, were similarly transmitted to their children by their attitudes and actions. Though different in their goals, reading held an exalted status in all three families. Children received a very clear and distinct message from their parents that their success in reading was symbolic of their success overall.

While there were books, newspapers, and magazines in all the nooks and crannies of each house, there were variations in the models set by the parents and the functional uses of reading in two of the three families. In the Clarke and Diamond homes, for example, one of the parents in each family was a heavy reader; Claire Clarke read books from 10–12:00 each night, and Peter Diamond was a voracious reader of business-related and more classical fiction.

In these families, reading served an important communication function, as a way for the parents and children to spend time together. On family trips, for example, Caroline and the children made language experience books to remember their favorite vacation activities, then she bound these books for the children's library. Similarly, Rob, who had many late meetings, would use the opportunity of the night-time story to catch up on the children's daily events.

Reading also served as an important source of information; the library was used as a frequent resource when planning gardens, house renovations, and organizing family vacations. By their actions, parents were emphasizing the way they believed their children should be exposed to reading. For example, Caroline, frustrated with Jennifer's reading program at school, remarked:

> The teacher doesn't seem to link ideas together. You see, in our house, if the children see something, like a raccoon, we'll go and open up a book and find out more about raccoons. In this class, Jennifer said they worked on raccoons, but in truth, they only heard a story about raccoons.

The uses of reading for purposes of escape or coping with difficult times was also communicated to the children. Claire sometimes used reading as anesthesia, "I read one murder mystery after another when I'm hurt or angry." Similarly, when Stephanie was going through a difficult period socially in school, Claire bought her "Sweet Valley Twins" books, which addressed and attempted to resolve young children's problems of jealousy, friendships, and sibling rivalry.

The models established by these parents emphasized the multifunctional nature of reading. Books were not confined to school-related activities; rather, by their examples and their own behavior, parents demonstrated the importance and usefulness of reading in their daily activities at home. In this respect, parents used their influencing potential to introduce children to a variety of reading experiences and circumstances for which gratifications from reading might be derived.

In contrast, there was a greater emphasis on "product" in the Conley family. Like the other two families, Mary Alice was keenly aware that reading was central to her children's later success. Just three years old, Alex was formally tested by the school on his prereading skills because she was worried that he was "a little bit behind." Similarly, Mary Alice proudly reported after a conference that Stacey was "at the top of her class, in the top reading group." But not being much of a reader herself, Mary Alice was less interested in the reading process than in Stacey's progress in school, as noted in this example:

> Stacey shows her mother a picture with a language experience story from school.
>
> MA: That's great Stacey, look your teacher says 'lovely'—Stacey you're doing so well in school.
>
> Stacey: Let me tell you how I did it. This poem was written on the board. See, I read it over and over again, and I think about it in my mind. Then I make the pictures that come to my mind.
>
> MA: (as she's cleaning Stacey's lunchbox) Oh, that's great Stacey, that's really nice.

Here, the functions of reading seemed more narrowly defined than in the other two families. There were virtually no observances of Mary Alice's direct guidance or involvement in reading at home with her children. Rather, reading appeared to be regarded as a skill learned in school, one that must be acquired in order to perform well in later life.

Though differing widely in the scope of functions these parental models represented, children in each family received strong messages that reading was important. Accomplishments in reading were highly praised, rewarded, put prominently on display on refrigerator doors, and walls, framed for others to see. In this respect, reading was held separate from all other subjects and leisure activities that children engaged in during their busy day. Thus, in contrast to the assumption of functional equivalence, parents helped to distinguish the importance of various activities and set priorities for their children. Reading, as a result, appeared to be tied to a very different set of needs and gratifications for parents and their children from alternative leisure options, including television viewing.

In sum, according to the displacement of functionally equivalent needs, it has been assumed that given a choice, children may prefer the vicarious experiences of television in favor of alternative activities, requiring greater physical or mental effort. Salomon (1984), in his conceptualization of the amount of mental effort (AIME), for example, argued that the relative ease of watching television may produce a general tendency not to expend much effort in other domains as well.

There was no evidence, however, to suggest that children transferred their notions of the perceived ease of television viewing to other situational demands. Rather, each family through their own values and examples, guided their children in the uses of each medium. Parents made categorical distinctions between these media; above all, reading was equated with successful achievement, while television, with novelty and entertainment. Even at such an early age, there were indications that children internalized these values, if not directly the behaviors associated with them. Maccoby (1954) hypothesized that these internalized models, though failing to be overtly displayed at a young age, may be manifested in later in adulthood. As evidence of this argument, Himmelweit and Swift (1976), in a 20-year follow-up of their benchmark television study, found that parent's orientation toward the media appeared to be exhibited in their child's subsequent media behavior in early adulthood.

In contrast to the view that children may substitute television for other activities, observations indicated that in instances where there was a choice between an active, socially- related activity, or the more sedentary activity of viewing television, children invariably selected the more active experience. These findings substantiate Schramm, Lyle, and Parker's (1961) classic study indicating that the vicarious pleasures children attain through viewing tend to be hierarchically less satisfying than the ones derived from direct experiences, providing, of course, that these experiences are available. Consequently, it seems fair to assume that the satisfactions children gained from television did not displace their ongoing interests for intellectually stimulating and socially reinforcing activities.

IMPLICATIONS:
A THEORY OF SYNERGY

Common assertions about television have centered on its potentially deleterious influences on children's developing cognitive abilities and emergent reading skills and interests. Specifically, it has been argued that television's rapid sensory bombardment encourages intellectual passivity, stifling children's imaginative capacities and ability to infer and reflect (Singer & Singer, 1983). Other charges argue that television may impair the growth of reading skills by displacing activities useful for general cognitive development or for enhancing reading practice and skills (Corteen & Williams, 1986; Gadberry, 1980; Hornik, 1978). Further, some critics consider that children may replace the more effortful activities such as reading in their lives for the relatively undemanding pastime of television viewing (Salomon, 1984).

Observations of the children's activities from these three homes casts a great deal of doubt on these common assertions. In these families, children exhibited a number of viewing styles, engaged in many imaginative activities related to television content, and appeared to generate inferences during and after their viewing. There was no evidence, at least at these ages, to suggest that children's imaginative or inferential abilities were adversely affected by television. Further, rather than displace valuable cognitive activities or reading, television and reading preferences often converged as children pursued their interests in multiple media presentations. More often than not, viewing was regarded as "the last resort" in the absence of other stimulating alternatives. Finally, the gratifications derived from television did not seem to substitute for the children's interests in learning to read, social interactions, or involvement in other ability-enhancing activities. Reading and television activities appeared to serve functionally different needs for even the very young child.

These sets of observations argue against the acceptance of a deterministic model of displacement as a mechanism for explaining television's influence on reading development. Rather, it maintains that television's use is conditioned by environmental circumstances. For example, it is possible that television may indeed replace leisure reading sometimes when children are given an option between the two activities. But it is also true that, at other times, the more attractive alternatives of being read to or of spending time with friends may replace children's involvement in television viewing. Television's influence cannot be measured simply for unidirectional effects.

A conditional model may better account for the synergy of children's media experiences found on many occasions in the three family contexts. Rather than displace one activity for another, the children often engaged in what appeared to be a spirited interplay between the media. As interests were established, children alternated between video-based and print-related experiences on the basis of its accessibility, and their capacity to make optimal uses of the particular medium. These activities seemed to be guided by children's rather consistent patterns of interest, instead of the specific medium presentation.

In homes with established educational priorities, moderate viewing habits, and multiple leisure alternatives, the concept of synergy describes the relation between children's viewing and emergent reading more accurately than does displacement. The notion of synergy is based on two propositions: (a) that there are qualitative differences in the content of each medium's messages, and (b) that the skills acquired from media act conjointly in helping children construct meaning and generate inferences in new contexts. Each of these propositions is briefly described.

The first is based on the premise that media convey information in distinctive forms. McLuhan (1964), for example, theorized that these qualitative differences emerge on the basis of the different symbolic systems employed by each, and the manner in which these codes are used to represent content. A printed story requires children to treat language as text; television demands both the integration of sound and visual images through movement.

But the distinctiveness of media derives from other critical aspects as well. Among these differences are the particular rules and conventions various media use in its treatment of material, the kinds of content it makes available, its historical legacy, as well the particular critical mass audience required by the economics of the industry to stay viable in the marketplace. All of these factors suggest that while, different media may seemingly convey similar material, each will do so in a qualitatively different form.

Initial studies at Project Zero, as noted in Chapter 3, and subsequent research (Meringoff et al., 1983) suggests that children use these distinctive features of each medium in interpreting stories from each medium. For example, children's retelling of a televised version of a story relied more on character actions—a storybook version on their expressive vocabulary.

Researchers following this tradition have suggested that the repeated exposure to a particular medium may accumulate experiences with some types of information more than others, resulting in the cultivation of cognitive skills preferable to that medium. Thus, it has been argued that television's capacity to enhance children's visual literacy might lead to the detriment of their language or vocabulary skills. These conjectures, however, have been based on experimental studies analyzing single observations of cross-media effects on comprehension.

In contrast, this ethnographic analysis suggests a second premise, namely that the skills and information children acquire from their innumerable experiences with media may act together in building children's background knowledge so critical for constructing meaning.

As children engage in each activity, they are acquiring domain-specific and strategic knowledge that may be used in making sense of subsequent events and actions. Thus, the inferences children may make when viewing television cannot be attributed solely to their experiences with television, but to many events (media-related and others) that help shape these expectations. Prior work on media differences have relied on a deficit model; here, it is argued that, with moderate viewing, the relationship is synergistic.

With their distinctive characteristics, each medium's physical features, its structure, its method of handling material, adds a new dimension to children's knowledge and the means they employ to attain new knowledge. Thus, rather than detract from literacy, some moderate amounts of television may expose children to an additional set of processing tools, which in combination with others, contributes to their ability to interpret events. Since children apparently engage in inferencing strategies while viewing, it is possible that these cognitive abilities are refined through practice and enhanced through their application in another medium. For example, in examining third graders' recall and inferential abilities, I found that the students who were given multimedia exposures of a similar story recalled more story structural elements than those students receiving repeated exposures through one medium alone (Study 4).

Consequently, there may be a spiraling effect. A greater facility to process information may enhance children's capability to acquire new information. Such an analysis might account for the replicated finding that a modest amount of viewing appears to be positively related to young children's reading scores (Neuman, 1988; Williams, Haertel, Haertel, & Walberg, 1982).

While the concept of synergy surely requires further hypothesis testing, this area of research suggests several important implications here for practice in the home. First, whether or not, or to whatever extent television may be "the vast wasteland" (Minow, quoted in Barnouw, 1977), it is clear that children's interactions with television are not immune to influence from their environment. What they take away from the medium, how they use it, and how literate they become as viewers is shaped, to a large extent, by the way television is mediated by the family. For example, though differing in pattern, each of the families in this study exercised controls over the amount and type of their children's viewing. Television did not consume an inordinate amount of time in any of these family's daily lives, but rather was balanced with other interests and activities.

Second, on many occasions, parents influenced the educative potential of television by linking these interests directly with literacy-related materials. Cross-media connections were made intentionally to spark reading interests. In this respect, children interests were taken seriously by their parents, were shaped and transformed to reflect the educational priorities established by their families. Consequently, in contexts where the mediational influences reinforced literacy practices, children's experiences with visual media served to support and enhance their emerging conceptions of print.

Finally, there are skills involved in viewing television. Cues provided by the medium itself which direct and guide viewers in their watching can be informally taught through conversations by parents and children around the television set. For example, in several cases in this study children were made aware of some of the diverse technical elements of television, were encouraged to ask questions and critically evaluate the explicit and implicit values in content. Acquiring this set of skills is an important process in orienting children to the language and grammar of television, and this process enables children to come to understand and anticipate story events.

While the virtue of books is widely accepted, television's assets have been only rarely acknowledged. However, it should not be ruled out that television can serve a modicum of intellectual stimulation to the young child. What this means is that, while its limitations must be acknowledged, the medium's attributes should be appreciated and used constructively for learning. Just as children are exposed to a diverse diet of genres and levels of reality and fantasy in reading, so too, should they be exposed to stories in a variety of media presentations. Such experiences may enrich children's understanding of stories and events, thus extending their engagement in literacy practices.

8

The Complementarity of Media

In this question of television and the book, we have here a melodramatic example of the displacive fallacy, the fallacy that an invention is a conqueror and makes the predecessor surrender. This is not so. (Boorstin, 1978)

When watching the shimmering images from the electronic box for the first time in 1937, E.B. White predicted television's potential power as being either "an unbearable disturbance" or "a soaring radiance in the sky." In fact, the television medium has fulfilled both predictions. It has shown us on many occasions its enormous capacity to inform, and at others time has displayed its penchant to cater to the very lowest levels of popular taste.

In its short lifetime, the bulk of public discourse on television's effects has been extraordinarily negative. Television has been accused of damaging children's ability to think clearly, of reducing their imagination and creativity, of seriously influencing their educational aspirations by destroying independent thinking and the pursuit of scholarly activities (National Institute of Mental Heath, 1982). None of these charges, unfortunately, have been pursued in the past on any consistent basis through research or further inquiry.

This book has focused on a specific subset of these charges: Television's effects on children's literacy and school achievement. It has attempted to look beyond such rhetorical accounts claiming that "TV alters brain waves," or "encourages deceptive thinking" to take a fresh look at the scientific evidence for the television-print relationship. To do so, the book has examined four basic themes that thread throughout these discussions: theories relating to time and energy displacement, changes in children's abilities to effectively process information, differences in gratification patterns and attitudes toward schooling, and the learning of instrumental information through television.

In the following section, the main conclusions for each of these issues are briefly restated, followed by practical suggestions for parents and teachers.

Displacement

It has been argued that since television consumes approximately 20 hours a week for the average child, it must displace "something." And indeed, it does. Television has substantially replaced a number of functionally equivalent entertainment media, including cinema, radio (for certain age groups), and has virtually destroyed the comic book industry. In spite of some claims to the contrary, however, none of these media activities have ever been shown to be more intellectually valuable for school success than the act of television viewing itself.

While most anecdotal reports "agree" on the decline in literacy skills and practice due to the time spent on viewing, there is no evidence to suggest that any major changes have actually occurred in the time children devote to leisure reading at home. In fact, the amount of leisure reading has remained amazingly stable over time: In 1945, children were reading about 15 minutes a day, and today, they are still reading approximately the same amount of time.

As to the hypothesized effects of television on homework activities, again, there is no consistent finding arguing against viewing. Since many students are not assigned homework regularly in the first place, it is difficult to evaluate whether a linkage actually exists or not between homework time and viewing. While some teachers have claimed that there is a causal relationship, arguing that they refrain from assigning homework because of the competition with television, there is no evidence to buttress this claim. It is true, however, that a great deal of homework is done concurrently while viewing, with no apparent adverse effects on quality. Children seem to choose a study environment according to the demands of the homework assignment.

Little evidence, therefore, hinges on the assumption that leisure reading or homework have been substantially influenced by television viewing. Without a reasonable causal mechanism to explain how the time spent viewing might affect school-related activities, the case for the effects of displacement on children's literacy skills or school achievement is weak.

Information Processing Theory

It has been claimed that television's symbol system—its characteristic mode of conveying information—influences children's information processing activities. Undoubtedly, certain media attributes, such as the ability to "zoom" into details or "animated modeling," have been shown to activate certain mental activities, like cue attending and the ability to produce visual images. The key controversy, however, has lied not in whether these symbol systems can be shaped in such a manner for learning to occur, but whether it is the symbol system, itself, that enhances these cognitive skills.

Recent evidence argues against the unique contribution of symbol systems on learning. Rather, this evidence suggests that learning is most likely to occur when a particular symbol system is manipulated to represent the critical features of a cognitive task. In this respect, it is the modeling of these attributes into a form that is understandable for the learner, and not the attributes themselves, that is most important.

In contrast to those who claim processing differences, here it has been argued that the actually cognitive skills used to comprehend information share a remarkable similarity across medium. Comprehension in both media require children to activate schema-driven processes of attending, predicting, interpreting, and applying their prior knowledge. Thus, it is hypothesized that while symbol systems may be influential during the initial stages of decoding information, they may not affect higher levels of reasoning and inference generation. From this perspective, viewing and reading activities may be engaging children in experiences that require similar processing tools.

The Short-Term Gratifications Theory

Some scholars maintain that television has fundamentally changed children's expectations toward learning, creating a generation of spectators who rely more on vicarious experiences than on active involvement in learning. This attitude is thought to affect school learning in two ways. First, exposure to the effortless activity of viewing television may lead children to believe that all activities require such effortlessness, and two, that the rapid pacing of television may induce shortened attention spans and cause hyperactive behavior. It is even suggested that the continual exposure of television may bias the arousal of the right hemisphere of the brain, permanently affecting children's ability to process print.

There is no evidence at all to substantiate these claims. To an unfortunate extent, these critics perpetuate a "literacy bias," the notion that thinking resides in a single technology. There is the belief on their part that television will reduce the vital importance of reading and writing.

In contrast to this view, it is argued that learning is not acquired through a single medium, but an integration of knowledge from many domains of experiences. To not avail ourselves of other technologies as a means to foster literacy and learning on the basis of such an ideological issue, therefore, is dysfunctional to both parents, teachers, and learners.

The Interest Stimulation Theory

There have been a few sanguine voices for television's impact on literacy and learning. Here it has been argued that, under some conditions, television can enhance children's motivation to learn by stimulating their interests and encouraging them to read materials after viewing them on television. Even in the course of viewing for entertainment, it has been thought that children may incidently learn important instrumental information which may then be applied to school learning.

Contrary to this view, there are no data indicating that the immediate interests generated from television lead children to seek new information through reading and other activities. Rather, these interests appear to be rather fleeting and rarely lead to action. Efforts to enhance what can be learned from television, through intentional teaching strategies, have also failed to show increases beyond temporary readjustments of interests, in reading and school achievement.

Concomitant strategies, consisting of weaving educational messages in entertainment fare, are one of the more successful approaches that have been used to enhance learning from television. With better coordination, and greater linkages to institutional learning, concomitant strategies may hold promise for using the medium to stimulate children's interests as they watch for entertainment.

A DIFFERENT UNDERSTANDING
OF THE RELATION BETWEEN MEDIA

From this research evidence, it is obvious that television as a medium is neither "intrinsically" good nor bad. In contrast to popular conceptions, it is a resource which like any others, may be used or abused. Unfortunately those who have condemned the television set as a "mechanical rival," prescribing to do away with it altogether, have failed to weigh its strengths and weaknesses. In doing so, they have ignored the possibilities of television as a means of extending children's interests and knowledge. These critics have also created an unnecessarily adversarial distinction between what has traditionally been defined as "entertainment" and what is classified as "education"—a relationship which, in fact, may be more complementary than conflicting.

It is true that by design, television is not an instrument of teaching. Yet the medium may have much to offer in educational value. For example, television is a remarkable disseminator of information. It has undoubtedly contributed to the public's knowledge and understanding of current social and political events (Comstock, 1978). Similarly, television is a primary medium in which many children today are introduced to a wide variety of stories and genres. These opportunities could be used more fruitfully to help children see the important connections between their traditional school subjects and the different facets of our culture.

Too often many adults, particularly those in the educational community, have chosen to ignore television or even worse, have virulently attacked all uses of the medium. Articulating this perception in a public address, Jankowski reported (1986):

> It is a source of constant amazement to me that the television set, an inert, immobile appliance that does not eat, drink or smoke, buy or sell anything, can't vote, doesn't have a job, can't think, can't turn itself on or off, and is used only at our option, can be seen as the cause of so much of society's ills by so many people in education.

Unfortunately, the assumption that media draw children's attention away from learning has fostered a rather narrowly defined view of how literacy develops and how learning is thought to occur. Reading graded materials, such as basal readers, has been viewed as the sin qua non in schools, sometimes at the cost of equally important hands-on experiences or activities involving other forms of symbolic representation. However, if children's ability to acquire literacy is said to be based on their prior knowledge, their conceptual understanding of language, and their uses of a variety of strategies, then there might be many paths to that goal, some of which may actually lie outside the printed page. For example, background knowledge derived from television, radio, and other sources surely contributes to an individual's understanding and critical thinking when reading about similar events in newspapers and texts. In this respect, rather than compete, media may serve complementary functions.

Indeed, children's interests in stories are often enhanced by their presentation in more than one medium. Cooper (1984), for example, found that after watching a televised version of a popular children's story, even the youngest children wanted to discuss its meaning, to explore the fiction further, to mull it over, and to go back to the book. We need to appreciate the special qualities inherent in each medium, to expose children to multiple genres and media presentations, and to build important connections between them.

It is a fact that many children today are watching a great deal of televised fare that is inappropriate for their age and sophistication level. This concern raises two possible courses of action. If we take the position of technology determinist Neil Postman that "it is pointless to spend time or energy deploring television or even making proposals to improve it," then the only response is to lock the television set up, or do whatever is necessary to keep it away from the innocent eyes of children. But if we believe that television can offer the potential to complement and enliven children's literacy experiences, it is imperative that greater efforts be made both to improve the quality of programming, and children's viewing habits. These efforts need to involve not just parents, but all those concerned with children in our society. As Schramm, Lyle, and Parker found (1961):

> We have a resource in children and a resource in television. We are concerned that television should strengthen, not debilitate, the human resource. This end can be accomplished most easily not by unilateral activity on the part of the TV industry, or by parents or schools, but rather by mobilizing all the chief forces in society which bear on the television-child relationship. It must be a shared effort to meet a shared responsibility. (p. 188)

Television has the potential to extend learning and literacy well beyond the classroom walls. Whether it actually realizes its potential depends on the cooperative efforts and sense of public responsibility of broadcasters, the guidance and supervision of parents, and the skills and vision of educators building linkages between home and school learning.

IMPLICATIONS AND SUGGESTIONS

Many of the suggestions that follow regarding the appropriate uses of media are not new; indeed, there has been a great number of thoughtful articles on how children and parents may develop better television viewing habits. Several of these ideas are restated, however, because they are central to using television as a complementary resource in children's literacy development. In other words, these suggestions are derived closely from the actual data reviewed and thus attempt to focus more specifically on the television-reading relationship.

Greater Attention to Television Content

One general conclusion from this research is that the focus of public concern on television's effects on reading has been misplaced. There has been a great deal of public anxiety about the effects of the long hours of viewing on children's developing reading proficiency and school learning. The bulk of studies, as noted in Chapter 2, focuses on this question of how time spent viewing relates to school achievement. Findings from Chapter 6 suggests that, with the exception of those watching an excessive amount of television, the relationship between television time and reading behavior is really quite negligible. Of much less concern, however, has been on the effect of what children are viewing—the actual nature of the programs they see. Yet if television is to work in children's interests, there needs to be a great more attention paid to the type of programs they are allowed to view. This is not to suggest that viewing be restricted only to instructional programming, for a good deal of knowledge can be acquired from entertaining shows. Instead, the more important issue is whether any of the programs children are viewing contribute to their growing understanding of people and situations outside their immediate environment. Children's interests can be broadened by what they see; in a similar vein, they can be restricted by a steady diet of stereotypic or violent-oriented programming.

It is critical for parents and teachers to be aware of what children are watching on television. Clearly this is important not only to prevent them from seeing what is harmful, but even more important, to encourage them to view programs in their general interest. Up until now, the bulk of public attention on television has been on the destructive and negative; far less time has been spent on lending support to the worthwhile.

In truth, it is difficult to adequately supervise children's viewing. Even though highly desireable, parents often have responsibilities that require their attention far more immediately than watching television along with their child. But even a limited attempt to reinforce quality viewing content is preferable to no attempt at all. Several strategies might be helpful:

1. Parents can more easily influence the content of what children watch when the television set is placed in a public area in the

house. Though not ideal, even casual monitoring of content will provide parents with important information on children's viewing interests, and at the same time, provide a modicum of supervision of program choices.

2. Indiscriminate viewing often occurs when children have no particular program to watch. Parents can encourage more selective viewing by offering several options, or by circling programs in a television guide that might be of interest to them. Good quality entertainment shows also have merit for children. Key questions that might determine whether such a program is suitable for children include:

(a) Is the program developmentally appropriate in terms of children's social, emotional and intellectual needs?

(b) Does the program handle content in a creative, imaginative manner?

(c) Does the program spark their interests and curiosity beyond their immediate environment?

3. Children should be encouraged to watch a diversity of program genres. Just like books, there is a wide variety of fare on television that may never be tapped by children without direct encouragement. If we consider television's storytelling and informational functions seriously, then it is important to expose children to high quality animated programs, situation comedies, superhero adventures, documentaries and animal series, and others, all of which may inspire them to picture the world in new ways.

4. Whenever possible, discussions of favorite programs provide a rich opportunity for exploring children's views about various topics. Though viewing similar programs, differences in prior knowledge between parents and children often lead them to reach dissimilar conclusions in stories. It is these differences in understanding that enable family members to benefit from discussions with one and another. Such discussions need not be formalized; in fact, casual conversations are often far more informative. By sharing their viewpoints with others, children are revealing the scope and the limitations of their individual perceptions. It also allows parents and teachers to correct faulty assumptions, to help children identify alternative solutions to problems, and to reinforce valuable experiences they see on television.

Setting Limits

While children's content choices should be of primary concern, still some limits need to be set on the amount of time spent viewing. Excessive viewing of generally over three hours per day is clearly related to lower proficiency scores in reading as shown in the analysis of over two million children in Chapter 6. Left to their own devices, some children clearly take advantage and misuse television, watching merely to fill a vacuum of free time.

How much television should children view? It is impossible to fix on a set number of hours that are appropriate; too much depends on children's age level, the number of resources available in their immediate environment, and the family's attitudes and patterns of viewing. Given television's easy accessibility, very young children often watch a good deal of television, and gain quite a bit of information and vocabulary from quality programming. But as they grow older, so do their options for alternative activities and information gathering. Typical television fare, at this point, tends not to offer much in the way of novelty and learning. Viewing diminishes sharply as most adolescents chose to spend their time on more social activities and increasingly demanding school work. The assessment of how much television is appropriate to view, therefore, must really reflect on the nature of what children are getting from the medium, and what other options are likely to be available during their free time.

Interestingly, even though parents tend to express a good deal of concern about television, Comstock et al. (1978) report they do little in the way of controlling their children's viewing directly—particularly the amount of it. The limited restrictions that are reinforced tend to focus merely on setting the bedtime hour. Even more perplexing is that in the cases where parents do report having more restrictive rules, apparently their children are often not even very aware of their existence. Thus, rather than relying strictly on parental rules, we need to consider alternative strategies in attempting to limit children's viewing time.

Perhaps the most useful approach to controlling television's use is through providing attractive alternative activities to viewing. Much of children's viewing time is relatively casual as they plop down on the couch and flip the dial looking for the "least objectionable program." Children, however, have a deeply ingrained need for activity and sociability; the more active or social an alternative experience, the more likely it is to compete for children's time and attention with television. Activities that include spending time with friends, supervised sports, lessons, and youth group events are generally far more compelling to children than the sedentary activity of viewing. Involvement in such a diversity of leisure activities is also linked positively to children's interest and the time they spend on leisure reading.

In addition, established family routines discourage indiscriminate viewing, and at the same time, prevent parents from having to constantly supervise the time spent with television. As described with the

Diamond family in Chapter 7, such routines may include the nightly bedtime story, the hour (s) when homework is to be completed and reviewed, and a list of family responsibilities and chores that must be completed before viewing. It is also useful for children to select certain favorite programs to watch regularly, lending an air of anticipation to their viewing. Choosing a weekly program to watch as a family event is another way to reinforce selective viewing and discourage the unquestioning use of television.

Linking Viewing with Other Activities

Television often stimulates children's interests, but as summarized in Chapter 5, only briefly. Generally these interests rarely lead to action because of the lack of accessibility to further activities or materials. Parents can help maintain these interests by linking television directly with other print-related activities. For example, there are many cross-media connections between children's favorite television characters, books, and films. A great number of popular books are selected and written for screen adaptation; similarly, books based on television-related characters and events, known as TV tie-ins, tend to flood the juvenile marketplace. Available through supermarkets, bookstores, and book clubs in schools, these materials add a dimension to children's viewing experiences, not only by directly linking them to print, but by allowing them to experience their favorite characters and events in a different contextual setting.

In addition, many libraries today offer a wide variety of videotaped renditions of popular books, including such favorites as *The Velveteen Rabbit*, *Charlotte's Web*, and *Curious George* adventures. Encouraging children to borrow these tapes is useful on a number of accounts: (a) it generates interest in visiting the library, (b) it allows parents to more carefully control the content of what children are viewing on television, and (c) it gives children the opportunity to view the content repeatedly until they have mastered the story. Just like rereadings of favorite storybooks, children's comprehension of a televised story is enhanced by repeated presentations. Further, they often enjoy returning to the book after watching filmed versions of their favorite stories.

Teachers, as well, might use a wider variety of media materials in the classroom to enhance children's interests in stories. By showing similar stories across different media, children may become aware of the unique characteristics of each medium, as well as how the subtle distinctions within each contributes to differing adaptations and, occasionally, interpretations of characters and events in their favorite stories.

Finally, magazines tend to be an underutilized resource in linking children's interests in television and print. Magazines offer a diversity of content at children's reading levels in a brief, yet highly interesting format. Many of their favorite television characters, jokes from popular shows, and themes are featured in articles from such popular magazines as *Dynamite, Penny Power, 3-2-1 Contact,* and *National Geographic World.* These magazines are also an excellent resource for inclusion in classroom libraries, particularly for those students who are reluctant to read book-length materials.

Parent Models

Parents' own television behaviors critically influence their children's viewing habits. Simply stated, parents who view excessively can expect to have children who do likewise. In our reading clinic, for example, we found that one of our children was being kept up every night until 2:00–3:00 in the morning to watch television with his mother. The young boy arrived in school generally around 1:00 in the afternoon and very often fell asleep shortly after. We found that it was impossible to influence his habits of viewing until we attempted to modify his mother's. Unfortunately, using television to compensate for family interaction and companionship sometimes occurs on too frequent a basis.

The influence of parental models on children's viewing behaviors, however, is said to decline as children mature (Dorr, 1986). Since adolescence is characterized by turning away from parental influences, it is certainly not atypical for teens to react independently rather than emulate any adult model. These findings, however, have lead some critics to suggest that parent modeling may have only a small effect on the nature of children's viewing (see Comstock et al., 1978, for review).

But what these research studies have not adequately measured is the long-term effects of parent models. Some researchers suspect that while children and young teens may fail at the time to internalize their parents behaviors, these models are likely to be manifested later in adulthood. Himmelweit and Swift's (1976) 20-year follow-up study, for example, suggests that there was a remarkable similarity between the pattern of media preferences and behaviors that occurred among parents and their children as older adults.

Thus, if the television set is on continuously, and parents themselves watch indiscriminately, discouraging children from asking questions because they might interrupt the program or challenging its content, then it is most likely that their children will view equally unselectively and unthoughtfully. Likewise, if parents selectively watch programs from a range of news-related and entertainment fare, discuss and encourage their children to explore new ideas without fear of reprisal, then their children are far more likely to view more of this type of content and use it more wisely as well.

Similarly, parents who themselves spend time reading, who read to their children and provide them with a wide variety of print-related materials are sending a powerful message about the functions and pleasures of reading. Like television viewing, these models might not immediately influence the time and effort children devote to reading in their free time. Rather, these parental examples tend to be internalized by children and serve an inestimable role in laying the foundation for later successful reading. When parents take a special interest in children's literature, share their own favorite childhood stories with their youngsters, help them to relate their reading of newspapers, magazines and books to everyday events—all of these activities develop and nurture reading as an integral part in children's lives.

PROMISING DIRECTIONS

Television is a unique mass medium, capable of transferring information and experiences, widely, quickly, vividly with a realism and immediacy hardly matched by other mass media. We have not adequately explored its potential uses. In contrast, our focus to date has been on "saving" children through either harnessing, eliminating, and discouraging television use. In only a few unique instances, have we actually tapped the power of the medium to serve educational purposes. Surely our conceptions of its capacity to enhance children's learning and literacy have reflected our narrowness of thinking rather than our vision.

Young children today enjoy a far more sophisticated knowledge of political and social events, are likely to possess richer vocabularies and a greater familiarity of story genres, all of which have been influenced by the vast array of informational resources available to them. These sources of information need not be in competition with one another. Instead, they must be brought together in order to provide greater opportunities for learning and knowledge acquisition for an increasingly pluralistic society. Indeed, rather than banish new technologies, we must rejoice in the marvel of expanding knowledge bases, and explore ways of using this larger network of information to enrich children's lives and further their understanding of what it means to be truly literate.

References

Adams, A.H., & Harrison, C.B. (1975). Using television to teach specific reading skills. *The Reading Teacher, 29,* 45–51.

Alexander, A., Ryan, M.S., & Munoz, P. (1984). Creating a learning context: Investigations on the interaction of siblings during television viewing. *Critical Studies in Mass Communication, 1,* 345–364.

Altick, R. (1957). *The English common reader.* Chicago, IL: University of Chicago Press.

Ames, L. (1979, March 6). TV helps out. *New Haven Register.*

Anderson, D.R., & Collins, P. (1988). *The impact on children's education: Television's influence on cognitive development.* Washington, DC: U.S. Department of Education, Office of Educational Research and Improvement, Contract No. 400-86-0055.

Anderson, D.R., Field, D.E., Collins, P.A., Lorch, E.P., & Nathan, J. (1985). Estimates of young children's time with television: A methodological comparison of parent reports with time-lapse video home observation. *Child Development, 56,* 1345–1357.

Anderson, D.R., Levin, S., & Lorch, E. (1977). The effects of TV program pacing on the behavior of preschool children. *AV Communication Review, 25,* 159–166.

Anderson, D.R., & Lorch, E.P. (1983). Looking at television: Action or reaction? In J. Bryant & D.R. Anderson (Eds.), *Children's understanding of television: Research on attention and comprehension* (pp. 1–33). New York: Academic Press.

Anderson, D.R., Lorch, E., Field, D., & Sanders, J. (1981). The effects of TV program comprehensibility on preschool children's visual attention to television. *Child Development, 52,* 151–157.

Anderson, J.A. (1981). Research on children and television: A critique. *Journal of Broadcasting, 25,* 395–400.

Anderson, J.A. (1983). Television literacy and the critical viewer. In J. Bryant & D.R. Anderson (Eds.), *Children's understanding of television: Research on attention and comprehension* (pp. 297–330). New York: Academic Press.

Anderson, R.C. (1984). Role of the reader's schema in comprehension, learning and memory. In R.C. Anderson, J. Osborn, & R. Tierney (Eds.), *Learning to read in American schools: Basal readers and content texts* (pp. 243–257). Hillsdale, NJ: Lawrence Erlbaum Associates.

Anderson, R.C., Hiebert, E.H., Scott, J.A., & Wilkinson, I.A.G. (1985). *Becoming a nation of readers.* Washington, DC:U.S. Department of Education.

Anderson, R.C., & Pearson, P.D. (1984). A schema-theoretic view of basic processes in reading comprehension. In P.D. Pearson (Ed.), *Handbook of reading research* (pp. 255–291). New York: Longman.

Anderson, R.C., Reynolds, R.E., Schallert, D.L., & Goetz, E.T. (1977). Frameworks for comprehending discourse. *American Educational Research Journal, 14,* 367–382.

Anderson, R.C., Wilson, P.T., & Fielding, L.G. (1988). Growth in reading and how children spend their time outside of school. *Reading Research Quarterly, 23,* 285–303.

Angle, B.D. (1981). *The relationship between children's televiewing and the variables of reading attitude, reading achievement, book reading, and IQ in a sample of fifth grade children.* Doctoral dissertation, The University of Akron. (*Dissertation Abstracts International, 41,* 3501A.)

Auden, W.H. (1962). *The Dyer's hand and other essays.* New York: Random House.

Baggett, P. (1979). Structurally equivalent stories in movie and text and the effect of the medium on recall. *Journal of Verbal Learning and Verbal Behavior, 18,* 333–356.

Ball, S., & Bogatz, G. (1970). *The first year of Sesame Street: An evaluation.* Princeton, NJ: Educational Testing Service.

Ball, S., & Bogatz, G. (1972). *Reading with television: An evaluation of "The Electric Company."* Princeton, NJ: Educational Testing Service.

Banker, G.S., & Meringoff, L.K. (1982). *Without words: The meaning children derive from a non-verbal film story* (Tech. Rep., Harvard Project Zero). Cambridge, MA: Harvard University.

Barnouw, E. (1977). *Tube of plenty.* London: Oxford University Press.

Beagles-Roos, J., & Gat, I. (1983). Specific impact of radio and television on children's story comprehension. *Journal of Educational Psychology, 75* (1), 128–137.

Bechtel, R.B., Achelpohl, C., & Akers, R. (1972). Correlates between observed behavior and questionnaire responses on television viewing. In E.A. Rubinstein, G.A. Comstock, & J.P. Murray (Eds.), *Television and social behavior: Vol. 4. Television in day-to-day life: Patterns of use* (pp. 274–344). Washington, DC: Government Printing Office.

Becker, G. (1973). *The positive uses of television.* Newark, DE: International Reading Association.

Beentjes, J. (1989). Learning from television and books: A Dutch replication study based on Salomon's model. *Educational Communication and Technology Journal, 37,* 47–58.

Beentjes, J.W.J., & Van der Voort, T.H.A. (1988). Television's impact on children's reading skills: A review of research. *Reading Research Quarterly, 23,* 389–413.

Bettleheim, B., & Zelan, K. (1981). *On learning to read.* New York: Alfred Knopf.

Bloom, B. (1981). *All our children learning.* New York: McGraw-Hill.

Bobrow, D.G., & Norman, D.A. (1975). Some principles of memory schemata. In D.G. Bobrow & A. Collins (Eds.), *Representation and understanding: Studies in cognitive science* (pp. 131–149). New York: Academic Press.

Bogatz, G., & Ball, S. (1971). *The second year of Sesame Street: A continuing evaluation.* Princeton, NJ: Educational Testing Service.

Book Industry Study Group. (1984). *Reading and book purchasing: Focus on juveniles.* New York: Author.

Boorstin, D.J. (1978). Opening remarks. In J.V. Cole (Ed.), *Television, the book, and the classroom* (pp. 7–8). Washington, DC: Library of Congress.

Borton, T. (1977). Reaching them where they are. *Curriculum Inquiry, 7,* 131–143.

Bower, R. (1985). *The changing television audience in America.* New York: Columbia University Press.

Bradbury, R. (1967). *Fahrenheit 451.* New York: Simon & Schuster.

Bransford, J., & McCarrell, N. (1974). A sketch of a cognitive approach to comprehension. In W.B. Weimer & D.S. Palermo (Eds.), *Cognition and the symbolic processes.* Hillsdale, NJ: Lawrence Erlbaum Associates.

Brown, J., Cramond, J., & Wilde, R. (1974). Displacement effects of television and the child's functional orientation to media. In J.G. Blumler & E. Katz (Eds.), *The uses of mass communications* (pp. 93–112). Beverly Hills: Sage Publications.

Bryce, J. (1980). *Families and television: An ethnographic approach.* Ann Arbor, MI: University Microfilms International.

Bryce, J. (1983, April). *Family talk in television contexts: The case for "significant interaction."* Paper presented at the American Educational Research Association Conference, Montreal, Canada.

Bryce, J. (1987). Family time and television use. In T. Linklof (Ed.), *Natural audiences* (pp. 121–139). Norwood, NJ: Ablex.

Busch, J.S. (1978). Television's effects on reading: A case study. *Kappan, 59,* 668–671.

Calvert, S., Huston, A., Watkins, B., & Wright, J. (1982). The effects of selective attention to television forms on children's comprehension of content. *Child Development, 53,* 601–610.

Carbo, M. (1983). Research in reading and learning style: Implications for exceptional children. *Exceptional Children, 49,* 486–494.

Carroll, J.B. (1974). The potentials and limitations of print as a medium of instruction. In D. Olson (Ed.), *Media and symbols: The forms of expression, communication, and education* (pp. 151–180). Chicago, IL: National Society for the Study of Education.

Chaffee, S., McLeod, M., & Atkin, C. (1971). Parental influences on adolescent media use. *American Behavioral Scientist, 14,* 323–340.

Chamberlin, L.J., & Chambers, N. (1976). How television is changing our children. *The Clearing House, 50,* 53–57.

Char, C., & Meringoff, L.K. (1982). *Stories through sound: Children's comprehension of radio stories and the role of sound effects and music in story comprehension* (Tech. Rep., Harvard Project Zero). Cambridge, MA: Harvard University.

Childers, P., & Ross, J. (1973). The relationship between viewing television and student achievement. *Journal of Educational Research, 66* (7), 317–319.

Clark, R. (1983). Reconsidering research on learning from media. *Review of Educational Research, 53,* 445–459.

Clark, R., & Salomon, G. (1986). Media in teaching. In M.C. Wittrock (Ed.), *Handbook of research on teaching* (3rd ed., pp. 464–478). New York: Macmillan.

Clark, W. (1951). *Of children and television.* Cincinatti, OH: Xavier University Press.

Clemens, M.S. (1983). *The relationship between television viewing, selected student characteristics and academic achievement.* Doctoral dissertation, The Pennsylvania State University. (*Dissertations Abstracts International, 43,* 2216A.)

Cohen, D., & Rudolph, M. (1977). *Kindergarten and early schooling.* Englewood Cliffs, NJ: Prentice-Hall.

Collins, A., Brown, J.S., & Larkin, K.M. (1980). Inference in text understanding. In R.J. Spiro, B.C. Bruce, & W.F. Brewer (Eds.), *Theoretical issues in reading comprehension* (pp. 385–407). Hillsdale, NJ: Lawrence Erlbaum Associates.

Collins, W.A. (1979). Children's comprehension of television content. In E. Wartella (Ed.), *Children's communicating; Media and development of thought, speech, understanding* (pp. 21–52). Beverly Hills, CA: Sage.

Collins, W.A. (1983). Interpretation and inference in children's television viewing. In J. Bryant & D.R. Anderson (Eds.), *Children's understanding of television: Research on attention and comprehension* (pp. 125–150). New York: Academic Press.

Collins, W.A., & Wellman, H. (1982). Social scripts and developmental patterns in comprehension of televised narratives. *Communication Research, 9,* 380–398.

Columbia Broadcast System (CBS). (1974). *Television and the classroom: A special relationship.* New York: CBS Television.

Compaine, B. (1980). The magazine industry: Developing the special interest audience. *Journal of Communication, 30,* 98–103.

Comstock, G. (1980). *Television in America.* Beverly Hills, CA: Sage.

Comstock, G. (1978). *Trends in the study of incidental learning from television viewing.* Syracuse, NY: Syracuse University. (ERIC Document Reproduction Service No. ED 168 605).

Comstock, G., Chaffee, S., Katzman, N., McCombs, M., & Roberts, D. (1978). *Television and human behavior.* New York: Columbia University Press.

Cook, T., Appleton, H., Conner, R., Shaffer, A., Tamkin, G., & Weber, S. (1975). *"Sesame Street" revisited.* New York: Russell Sage Foundation.

Cook, T., Curtin, T., Ettema, J., Miller, P., & Van Camp, K. (1986). *Television in the life of schools.* Paper presented at the Conference on Assessing Television's Impact on Children's Education, Washington, DC.

Cooper, M. (1984). Televised books and their effects on children's reading. *Uses of English, 35,* 41–49.

Corder-Bolz, C.R. (1980). Mediation. The role of significant others. *Journal of Communication, 30,* 106–118.

Corder-Bolz, C.R., & O'Bryant, S. (1978). Can people affect television? Teacher vs. program. *Journal of Communication, 28,* 97–103.

Corteen, R., & Williams, T. (1986). Television and reading skills. In T.M. Williams (Ed.), *The impact of television: A natural experiment in three communities* (pp. 39–86). New York: Academic Press.

Dave, R.H. (1963). *The identification and measurement of environmental process variables that are related to educational achievement.* Unpublished doctoral dissertation, University of Chicago, Chicago, IL.

Doerken, M. (1983). *Classroom combat: Teaching and television.* Englewood Cliffs, NJ: Educational Technology Publications.

Dorr, A. (1986). *Television and children.* Beverly Hills, CA: Sage Press.

Dorr, A., Graves, S.B., & Phelps, E. (1980). Television literacy for young children. *Journal of Communication, 30,* 71–83.

Drew, D., & Reeves, B. (1980). Learning from a television news story. *Communication Research, 7,* 121–135.

Dweck, C.S., & Bempechat, J. (1983). Children's theories of intelligence: Consequences for learning. In S.G. Paris, G.M. Olson, & H.W. Stevenson (Eds.), *Learning and motivation in the classroom.* Hillsdale, NJ: Lawrence Erlbaum Associates.

Elkind, D. (1981). *The hurried child.* Reading, MA: Addison-Wesley.

English, D. (1981). Bait. *English Journal, 70,* 70.

Emery, F., & Emery, M. (1976). *A choice of futures.* Leiden: Martinus Nijhoff Social Sciences Division.

Fader, D. (1983). Literacy and family. In R. Bailey & R. Fosheim (Eds.), *Literacy for life* (pp. 236–247). New York: Modern Language Association.

Fairchild, H.H., Stockard, R., & Bowman, P. (1986). Impact of Roots: Evidence from the National Survey of Black Americans. *Journal of Black Studies, 16,* 307–318.

Feeley, J. (1974). Interest patterns and media preferences of middle-grade children. *Reading World, 13,* 224–237.

Fetler, M. (1984). Television viewing and school achievement. *Journal of Communication, 34* (2), 104–118.

Field, D. (1988). *Child and parent coviewing of television: Relationships to cognitive performance.* Doctoral dissertation, University of Massachusetts, Amherst, MA. (*Dissertation Abstracts International, 48,* 2799B.)

Field, D., & Anderson, D. (1985). Instruction and modality effects on children's television attention and comprehension. *Journal of Educational Psychology, 77,* 91–100.

Furu, T. (1971). *The functions of television for children and adolescents.* Toyoko: Sophia University.

Gadberry, S. (1974). Television as a babysitter: A field comparison of pre-schoolers' behavior during playtime and during television viewing. *Child Development, 45,* 1132–1136.

Gadberry, S. (1980). Effects of restricting first graders' TV viewing on leisure time use, IQ change, and cognitive style. *Journal of Applied Developmental Psychology, 1,* 45–57.

Gaddy, G. (1986). Television's impact on high school achievement. *Public Opinion Quarterly, 50,* 340–359.

Geiger, K., & Sokol, R. (1959). Social norms in television watching. *American Journal of Sociology, 65,* 174–181.

Gerbner, G., Gross, L., Morgan, M., & Signorielli, N. (1980). The "mainstreaming" of America: Violence profile No. 11. *Journal of Communication, 30,* 10–29.

Gerbner, G., Gross, L., Morgan, M., & Signorielli, N. (1982). Charting the mainstream: Television's contributions to political orientations. *Journal of Communication, 32,* 100–127.

Gerbner, G., Gross, L., Morgan, M., & Signorielli, N. (1984). Facts, fantasies, and schools. *Society, 21* (6), 9–14.

Gibbons, J., Anderson, D., Smith, R., Field, D., & Fischer, C. (1986). Young children's recall and reconstruction of audio and audiovisual narratives. *Child Development, 57,* 1014–1023.

Goldsen, R. (1977). *The show and tell machine.* New York: Dial Press.

Goodwin, E.E. (1983). The relationship of school achievement to time spent watching television among 10th and 12th grade pupils in United States High Schools; An analysis of high school and beyond data (University of Akron, 1983). *Dissertation Abstracts International, 43,* 2835A.

Gray, W.F., & Rogers, B. (1954). *Maturity in reading.* Chicago: University of Chicago Press.

Greaney, V. (1980). Factors related to amount and type of leisure reading. *Reading Research Quarterly, 15,* 337–357.

Greaney, V., & Hegarty, M. (1987). Correlates of leisure-time reading. *Journal of Research in Reading, 10,* 3–32.

Greaney, V., & Neuman, S.B. (1983). Young people's views of reading: A cross-cultural perspective. *The Reading Teacher, 37,* 158–163.

Greaney, V., & Neuman, S.B. (1990). The functions of reading: A cross-cultural perspective. *Reading Research Quarterly, 25,* 172–195.

Greenfield, P. (1984). *Mind and media: The effects of television, video games, and computers.* Cambridge, MA: Harvard University Press.

Greenfield, P., & Beagles-Roos, J. (1988). Radio vs. Television: Their cognitive impact on children of different socioeconomic and ethnic groups. *Journal of Communication, 38* (2), 71–92.

Greenstein, J. (1954). Effect of television upon elementary school grades. *Journal of Educational Research, 48,* 161–176.

Halpern, W. (1975). Turned-on toddlers. *Journal of Communication, 25,* 66–70.

Hamilton, H. (1976). TV tie-ins as a bridge to books. *Language Arts, 33,* 129–130.

Hardt, U. (1979). Appropriating television for teaching. *Oregon English, 1,* 8-13.

Hayes, D.S., Kelly, S.B., & Mandel, M. (1986). Media differences in children's story synopses: Radio and television contrasted. *Journal of Educational Psychology, 78*, 341–346.

Heath, S.B. (1983). *Ways with words*. New York: Cambridge University Press.

Help! Teacher can't teach! (1980, June). *Time*, pp. 54–63.

Himmelweit, H., Oppenheim, A., & Vince, P. (1958). *Television and the child*. London: Oxford.

Himmelweit, H.T., & Swift, B. (1976). Continuities and discontinuities in media usage and taste: A longitudinal study. *Journal of Social Issues, 32*, 133–156.

Hirsch, P. (1980). The "scary world" of the nonviewer and other anomalies: A reanalysis of Gerbner et al.'s findings on cultivation analysis, part 1. *Communication Research, 7*, 403–456.

Hirsch, P. (1981). On not learning from one's own mistakes: A reanalysis of Gerbner et al.'s findings on cultivation analysis and a critique of "mainstreaming," part 2. *Communication Research, 8*, 3–37.

Hirsch, P., & Carey, J. (Eds.). (1978). Communication and culture: Humanistic models in research [Special issue]. *Communication Research, 5*, 235–339.

Hoffner, C., Cantor, J., & Thorson, E. (1988). Children's understanding of a televised narrative. *Communication Research, 15*, 227–245.

Hoggart, R. (1957). *The use of literacy*. Fairlawn, NJ: Essential Books.

Holland, N. (1975). *Five readers reading*. New Haven, CT: Yale University Press.

It's at home where our language is in distress. (1985, February). *U.S. News & World Report*, pp. 54–57.

Hornik, R. (1978). Television access and the slowing of cognitive growth. *American Educational Research Journal, 15*, 1–15.

Hornik, R. (1981). Out-of-school television and schooling: Hypotheses and methods. *Review of Educational Research, 51*, 193–214.

Hughes, M. (1980). The fruits of cultivation analysis: A reexamination of some effects of television watching. *Public Opinion Quarterly, 44*, 287–302.

Huston-Stein, A., & Wright, J.C. (1979). Children and television: Effects of the medium, its contents, and its form. *Journal of Research and Development in Education, 13*, 20–31.

Huston, A., & Wright, J. (1983). Children's processing of television: The informative functions of formal features. In J. Bryant & D.R. Anderson (Eds), *Children's understanding of television: Research on attention and comprehension* (pp. 35–68). New York: Academic Press.

Iser, W. (1974). *The implied reader*. Baltimore: Johns Hopkins University Press.

James, N., & McCain, T. (1982). Television games preschool children play: Patterns, themes and uses. *Journal of Broadcasting, 26*, 783–800.

Jankowski, G. (1986). *Television and teachers: Educating each other*. (ERIC Document Reproduction Service, No. ED 268 600).

Jonsson, A. (1986). TV: A threat or a complement to school? *Journal of Educational Television, 12*, 29–38.

Katz, E., Gurevitch, M., & Haas, H. (1973). On the use of mass media for important things. *American Sociological Review, 38*, 164–181.

Keith, T.Z., Reimers, T.M., Fehrmann, P.G., Pottebaum, S.M., & Aubey, L.W. (1986). Parental involvement, homework, and TV time: Direct and indirect effects on high school achievement. *Journal of Educational Psychology, 78,* 373–380.

Klapper, J.T. (1960). *The effects of mass communication.* New York: Free Press.

Krugman, H. (1971). Brain wave measures of media involvement. *Journal of Advertising Research, 11,* 3–9.

Krull, R. (1983). Children learning to watch television. In J. Bryant & D.R. Anderson (Eds.), *Children's understanding of television: Research on attention and comprehension* (pp. 103–123). New York: Academic Press.

LaBlonde, J. (1967). *A study of the relationship between television viewing habits and scholastic achievement of fifth grade children.* Unpublished doctoral dissertation, University of Minnesota, Minneapolis, MI.

Larrick, N. (1975). *A parent's guide to children's reading* (4th ed.). New York: Bantam Books.

Leichter, H.J., Ahmed, D., Barrios, L., Bryce, J., Larsen, E., & Moe, L. (1985). Family contexts of television. *Educational Communication and Technology Journal, 33,* 26–40.

Lemish, D., & Rice, M. (1986). Television as a talking picture book: A prop for language acquisition. *Journal of Child Language, 13,* 251–274.

Lesser, G. (1974). *Children and television: Lessons from Sesame Street.* New York: Vantage Press.

Lesser, G. (1979, March). Stop picking on Big Bird. *Psychology Today,* pp. 57, 60.

Lesser, H. (1977). *Television and the preschool child.* New York: Academic Press.

Liebert, R.M., & Sprafkin, J. (1988). *The early window* (3rd ed.). New York: Pergamon Press.

Long, B., & Henderson, E. (1973). Children's use of time: Some personal and social correlates. *Elementary School Journal, 73,* 193–199.

Lorch, E., Bellack, D., & Augsbach, L. (1987). Young children's memory for televised stories: Effects of importance. *Child Development, 58,* 453–463.

Lu, Y., & Tweeten, L. (1973). The impact of busing on student achievement. *Growth and Change, 4,* 44–46.

Lull, J. (1980). The social uses of television. *Human Communication Research, 6,* 198–209.

Lyle, J., & Hoffman, H.R. (1972). Explorations in patterns of television viewing by preschool-age children. In E.A. Rubinstein, G.A. Comstock, & J.P. Murray (Eds.), *Television and social behavior. Vol. 4. Television in day-to-day life: Patterns of use* (pp. 275–273). Washington, DC: Government Printing Office.

Lyness, P. (1952). The place of the mass media in the lives of boys and girls. *Journalism Quarterly, 29,* 43–54.

Maccoby, E. (1954). Why do children watch television? *Public Opinion Quarterly, 18,* 239–244.

Mander, J. (1978). *Four arguments for the elimination of television.* New York: Willam Morrow.

Mankiewicz, F., & Swerdlow, J. (1978). *Remote control*. New York: Ballantine Books.

Mason, J., & Au, K. (1986). *Reading instruction for today*. Glenview, IL: Scott, Foresman and Company.

Mates, B.F. (1980). Current emphases and issues in planned programming for children. In E. Palmer & A. Dorr (Eds.), *Children and the faces of television* (pp. 19–31). New York: Academic Press.

McDonagh, E.C. (1950). Television and the family. *Sociology and Sociology Research, 35*, 113–122.

McLuhan, M. (1962). *The Gutenberg galaxy*. Toronto: University of Toronto Press.

McLuhan, M. (1964). *Understanding media*. New York: Signet Books.

McLuhan, M. (1967). Preface. In G.E. Stearn (Ed.), *McLuhan: Hot and Cool*. New York: New American Library.

Meadowcroft, J., & Reeves, B. (1985). *The development of schema-based strategies for attending to television stories*. Paper presented at the Speech Communication Association, Denver, CO.

Meringoff, L. (1980). A story a story: The influence of the medium on children's comprehension of stories. *Journal of Educational Psychology, 72*, 240–244.

Meringoff, L., Vibbert, M., Char, C., Fernie, D., Banker, G., & Gardner, H. (1983). How is children's learning from television distinctive?: Exploiting the medium methodologically. In J. Bryant & D.R. Anderson (Eds.), *Children's understanding of television: Research on attention and comprehension* (pp. 151–180). New York: Academic Press.

Messaris, P. (1983). Family conversations about television. *Journal of Family Issues, 4*, 293–308.

Messaris, P., & Kerr, D. (1983). Mothers' comments about TV: Relation to family communication patterns. *Communication Research, 10*, 175–194.

Minton, J.H. (1972). *The impact of "Sesame Street" on reading readiness of kindergarten children*. Unpublished doctoral dissertation, Fordham University, New York.

Moldenhauer, D.L., & Miller, W.H. (1980). Television and reading achievement. *Journal of Reading, 23*, 615–619.

Moody, K. (1980). *Growing up on television: The TV effect*. New York: Times Books.

Morgan, M. (1980). Television viewing and reading: Does more equal better? *Journal of Communication, 32*, 159–165.

Morgan, M. (1982, March). *More than a simple association: Conditional patterns of television and achievement*. Paper presented at the American Educational Research Association, New York, NY.

Morgan, M., & Gross, L. (1980). Television viewing, IQ, and academic achievement. *Journal of Broadcasting, 24*(2), 117–132.

Morrow, L.M. (1983). Home and school correlates of early interest in literature. *Journal of Educational Research, 76*, 221–230.

Murray, J., & Kippax, S. (1978). Children's social behavior in three towns with differing television experience. *Journal of Communication, 28*, 19–29.

Nagy, W.E., Anderson, R.C., & Herman, P. (1987). Learning word meanings from context during normal reading. *American Educational Research Journal, 24*, 237–270.

National Assessment of Educational Progress. (1986). *The reading report card.* Princeton, NJ: Educational Testing Service.

National Commission on Excellence in Education. (1983). *A nation at risk: The imperative for educational reform.* Washington, DC: U.S. Government Printing Office.

National Institute of Mental Health. (1982). *Television and behavior: Ten years of scientific progress and implications for the eighties* (DHHS Publication No. ADM 82-1195). Washington, DC: U.S. Printing Office.

Neuman, S.B. (1980a). Listening behavior and television viewing. *Journal of Educational Research, 73*, 15–18.

Neuman, S.B. (1980b). Why children read: A functional approach. *Journal of Reading Behavior, 12*, 333–336.

Neuman, S.B. (1981). *The effects of television on reading behavior.* Willimantic: Eastern Connecticut State College. (ERIC Document Reproduction Service No. ED 205 941).

Neuman, S.B. (1982). Television viewing and leisure reading: A qualitative analysis. *Journal of Educational Research, 75*, 299–304.

Neuman, S.B. (1986a). The home environment and fifth-grade students' leisure reading. *The Elementary School Journal, 86*, 335–343.

Neuman, S.B. (1986b). Television, reading and the home environment. *Reading Research and Instruction, 25*, 173–183.

Neuman, S.B. (1988). The displacement effect: Assessing the relation between television viewing and reading performance. *Reading Research Quarterly, 23*, 414–440.

Neuman, S.B. (1989). The impact of different media on children's story comprehension. *Reading Research and Instruction, 28*, 38–47.

Neuman, S.B., Burden, D., & Holden, E. (1990). Enhancing children's understanding of a televised story through previewing. *Journal of Educational Research, 83*, 258–265.

Neuman, S.B., & Prowda, P. (1982). Television viewing and reading achievement. *Journal of Reading, 25*, 666–671.

A.C. Nielsen Company. (1987). *1987 Nielsen report on television.* Northbrook, IL: Author.

Nye, R. (1970). *The unembarrassed muse.* New York: Dial Press.

Olson, D.R. (1976). Towards a theory of instructional means. *Educational Psychologist, 12*, 14–35.

Olson, D.R., & Bruner, J.S. (1974). Learning through experience and learning through media. In D.R. Olson (Ed.), *Media and symbols: The forms of expression, communication, and education* (pp. 125–150). Chicago, IL: The National Society for the Study of Education.

Omanson, R.C., Warren, W.H., & Trabasso, T. (1978). Goals, themes, inferences and memory: A developmental study. *Discourse Processes, 1*, 337–354.

Parker, E.B. (1963). The effects of television on public library circulation. *Public Opinion Quarterly, 27*, 578–589.

Parker, H. (1974). The beholders' share and the problem of literacy. In D.

Olson (Ed.), *Media and symbols: The forms of expression, communication, and education* (pp. 81–98). Chicago, IL: National Society for the Study of Education.

Paris, S. (1986). Teaching children to guide their reading and learning. In T. Raphael (Ed.), *The contexts of school-based literacy* (pp. 115–130). New York: Random House.

Paris, S., & Upton, L.R. (1976). Children's memory for inferential relationships in prose. *Child Development, 47*, 660–668.

Patton, J.E., Stinard, T.A., & Routh, D.K. (1983). Where do children study? *Journal of Educational Research, 76*, 280–286.

Paivio, A. (1978). A dual coding approach to perception and cognition. In H.L. Pick, Jr. & E. Saltzman (Eds.), *Modes of perceiving and processing information* (pp. 39–51). Hillsdale, NJ: Erlbaum.

Paivio, A. (1983). The empirical case for dual coding. In J.C. Yuille (Ed.), *Imagery, memory and cognition* (pp. 307–332). Hillsdale, NJ: Erlbaum.

Paivio, A., & I. Begg. (1981). *Psychology of language*. Englewood Cliffs, NJ: Prentice-Hall.

Pearson, P.D., Hansen, J., & Gordon, C. (1979). The effect of background knowledge on young children's comprehension of explicit and implicit information. *Journal of Reading Behavior, 11*, 201–209.

Peirce, K. (1983). Relation between time spent viewing television and children's writing skills. *Journalism Quarterly, 60*, 445–448.

Pellegrini, A.D. (1985). Relations between preschool children's symbolic play and literate behavior. In L. Galda & A. Pellegrini (Eds.), *Play, language, and stories* (pp. 79–97). Norwood, NJ: Ablex.

Pezdek, K., & Hartman, E. (1983). Children's television viewing: Attention and comprehension of auditory versus visual information. *Child Development, 54*, 1015–1023.

Pezdek, K., Lehrer, A., & Simon, S. (1984). The relationship between reading and cognitive processing of television and radio. *Child Development, 55*, 2072–2082.

Pichert, J.W., & Anderson, R.C. (1977). Taking different perspectives on a story. *Journal of Educational Psychology, 69*, 309–315.

Pingree, S. (1986). Children's activity and television comprehensibility. *Communication Research, 13*, 239–256.

Pingree, S., Hawkins, R., Rouner, D., Burns, J., Gikono, W., & Neuwirth, C. (1984). Another look at children's comprehension of television. *Communication Research, 11*, 477–496.

Postman, N. (1979). *Teaching as a conserving activity*. New York: Delacorte Press.

Postman, N. (1982). *The disappearance of childhood*. New York: Delacorte Press.

Postman, N. (1985). *Amusing ourselves to death*. New York: Viking.

Potter, R.L. (1976). *New season: The positive use of commercial television with children*. Columbus, OH: Charles E. Merrill.

Potter, W.J. (1987). Does television viewing hinder academic achievement among adolescents? *Human Communication Research, 14*, 27–46.

Price, K. (1983). Close-captioned TV: An untapped resource. *Matsol Newsletter, 12*, 1–2.

A public trust: The report of the Carnegie Commission on the future of public broadcasting. (1979). New York: Bantam.

Pylshyn, Z.W. (1981). The imagery debate: Analogue media versus tacit knowledge. *Psychological Review, 88*, 16–45.

Quisenberry, N., & Kasek, C. (1976). *The relationship of children's television viewing to achievement at the intermediate level.* Carbondale, IL: Southern Illinois University. (ERIC Document Reproduction Service No. ED 143 336.)

Rankin, P.M., & Roberts, C.W. (1981). Television and teaching. *The Reading Teacher, 35*, 30–33.

Reynolds, R.E., Taylor, M.A., Steffensen, M.S., Shirey, L.L., & Anderson, R.C. (1982). Cultural schemata and reading comprehension. *Reading Research Quarterly, 17*, 353–366.

Rice, M., & Woodsmall, L. (1988). Lessons from television: Children's word learning when viewing. *Child Development, 59*, 420–429.

Ridder, J.M. (1963). Pupil opinions and the relationship of television viewing to academic achievement. *Journal of Educational Research, 57*, 204–206.

Ridley-Johnson, R., Cooper, H., & Chance, J. (1983). The relationship of children's television viewing to school achievement and IQ. *Journal of Educational Research, 76*, 294–297.

Ritchie, D., Price, V., & Roberts, D.E. (1987). Television, reading and reading achievement: A reappraisal. *Communication Research, 14*, 292–315.

Roberts, D., Bachen, C., Hornby, M., & Hernandez-Ramos, P. (1984). Reading and television: Predictors of reading achievement at different age levels. *Communications Research, 11*, 9–49.

Roberts, D., & Rockman, S. (1986). *An approach to the study of television's influence on schooling: Teacher theories and the classroom environment.* Paper presented at the Conference on Assessing Television's Impact on Children's Education, Washington, DC.

Rosenblatt, L. (1978). *The reader the text the poem.* Carbondale: Southern Illinois University Press.

Rousseau, J. (1962). *Emile: Selections* (W. Boyd, Trans.). New York: The Bureau of Publications, Teachers College Press. (Original work published 1773)

Royko, M. (1982, February 7). *Chicago Sun-Times*, p. 32.

Rumulhart, D.R. (1980). Schemata: The building blocks of cognition. In R. Spiro, B.C. Bruce, & W.F. Brewer (Eds.), *Theoretical issues in reading comprehension* (pp. 33–58). Hillsdale, NJ: Lawrence Erlbaum Associates.

Salomon, G. (1974). Internalization of filmic schematic operations in interactions with learner's aptitudes. *Journal of Educational Psychology, 66*, 499–511.

Salomon, G. (1979). *Interaction of media, cognition and learning.* San Francisco: Jossey-Bass.

Salomon, G. (1983). The differential investment of mental effort in learning from different sources. *Educational Psychologist, 18*, 42–50.

Salomon, G. (1984). Television is "easy" and print is "tough": The differential investment of mental effort as a function of perceptions and attributions. *Journal of Educational Psychology, 76,* 647–658.

Salomon, G. (1986). The computer as educator: Lessons from television research. *Educational Researcher, 15,* 13–19.

Salomon, G. (1987). *AI in reverse: Computer tools that turn cognitive.* Paper presented at the Communications Forum, Massachusetts Institute of Technology, Cambridge, MA.

Samuels, S.J. (1970). Effects of pictures on learning to read, comprehension and attitudes. *Review of Educational Research, 40,* 397–407.

Schneider, L., & Lysgaard, S. (1953). The deferred gratification pattern. *American Sociological Review, 18,* 142–149.

Schramm, W., Lyle, J., & Parker, E. (1961). *Television in the lives of our children.* Stanford, CA: Stanford University Press.

Scribner, S., & Cole, M. (1981). *The psychology of literacy.* Cambridge, MA: Harvard University Press.

Scott, L.F. (1958). Relationships between elementary school children and television. *Journal of Educational Research, 52,* 134–137.

Searls, D.T., Mead, N.A., & Ward, B. (1985). The relationship of students' reading skills to TV watching, leisure time reading, and homework. *Journal of Reading, 29,* 158–162.

Signorielli, N. (1979, April). *Television's contribution to sex role socialization.* Paper presented at the Seventh Annual Telecommunications Policy Research Conference, Skytop, PA.

Singer, J.L. (1980). The power and limitations of television: A cognitive-affective analysis. In P.H. Tannenbaum (Ed.), *The entertainment function of television* (pp. 31–65). Hillsdale, NJ: Erlbaum.

Singer, J.L., & Singer, D. (1980). *Television, imagination and aggression: A study of preschoolers' play and television viewing patterns.* Hillsdale, NJ: Erlbaum.

Singer, J.L., & Singer, D. (1983). Implications of childhood television viewing for cognition, imagination and emotion. In J. Bryant & D.R. Anderson (Eds.), *Children's understanding of television: Research on attention and comprehension* (pp. 265–296). New York: Academic Press.

Singer, J.L., Singer, D., & Rapaczynski, W. (1984). Family patterns and television viewing as predictors of children's beliefs and aggression. *Journal of Communication, 34,* 73–89.

Slater, B. (1965). An analysis and appraisal of the amount of televiewing, general school achievement and socioeconomic status of third grade students in selected public schools of Erie County, N.Y. *Dissertation Abstracts, 25,* 5651A.

Smyser, S.L. (1981). A study of the relationship between television viewing habits and early reading achievement. *Dissertation Abstracts International, 41,* 4972A.

Solomon, B. (1976). The television reading program. *Language Arts, 53,* 135.

Spiro, R.J. (1980). Constructive processes in prose comprehension and recall. In R.J. Spiro, B.C. Bruce, & W.F. Brewer (Eds.), *Theoretical issues in reading comprehension* (pp. 245–278). Hillsdale, NJ: Lawrence Erlbaum Associates.

Stanovich, K.E. (1986). Matthew effects in reading: Some consequences of individual differences in the acquisition of literacy. *Reading Research Quarterly, 21*, 360–407.

Starkey, J., & Swinford, H. (1974). *Reading? Does television viewing time affect it?* DeKalb: Northern Illinois University. (ERIC Document Reproduction Service No. ED 090 966.)

Stein, N., & Glenn, C.G. (1979). An analysis of story comprehension in elementary school children. In R. Freedle (Ed.), *New directions in discourse processing* (pp. 53–120). Norwood, NJ: Ablex.

Streicher, L.H., & Bonney, N.L. (1974, Summer). Children talk about television. *Journal of Communication*, pp. 54–61.

Szabo, M., & Lamiell-Landy, A. (1981). Television-based reading instruction, reading achievement, and task involvement. *Journal of Educational Research, 74*, 239–244.

Taylor, D. (1983). *Family literacy.* Exeter, NH: Heinemann Educational Books.

Television and growing up: The impact of televised violence. (1971). Report to the Surgeon General, United States Public Health Service. Washington, DC: U.S. Government Printing Office.

Telfer, R.J., & Kann, R.S. (1984). Reading achievement, free reading, watching TV, and listening to music. *Journal of Reading, 27*, 536–539.

Thompson, G. (1964). Children's acceptance of television advertising and the relationship of televiewing to school achievement. *Journal of Educational Research, 58*, 171–174.

Timmer, S.G., Eccles, J., & O'Brien. (1985). How children use time. In F.T. Juster & F. Stafford (Eds.), *Time, goods, and well being* (pp. 353–382). Ann Arbor, MI: Survey Research Center.

Torgesen, J.K. (1986). Learning disabilities theory: Its current state and future prospects. *Journal of Learning Disabilities, 19*, 399–407.

Tower, R., Singer, D., Singer, J., & Biggs, A. (1979). Differential effects of television programming on preschooler's cognition, imagination and social play. *American Journal of Orthopsychiatry, 49*, 265–281.

Trabasso, T., & Sperry, L. (1985). Causal relatedness and importance of story events. *Journal of Memory and Language, 24*, 595–611.

Trelease, J. (1982). *The read-aloud handbook.* New York: Penguin.

TV's "disastrous" impact on children. (1981, January). *U.S. News & World Report*, pp. 43–45.

van den Broek, P., & Trabasso, T. (1986). Causal networks versus goal hierarchies in summarizing text. *Discourse Processes, 9*, 1–15.

von Feilitzen, C. (1976). The functions served by the media. In R. Brown (Ed.), *Children and Television* (pp. 90–115). Beverly Hills, CA: Sage Publications.

Walberg, H. (1984a). Families as partners in educational productivity. *Phi Delta Kappan, 65*, 397–400.

Walberg, H. (1984b). Improving the productivity of America's schools. *Educational Leadership, 41*, 19–30.

Walberg, H., & Shanahan, T. (1983). High school effects on individual students. *Educational Researcher*, pp. 4–9.

Walberg, H., & Tsai, S. (1983). Matthew effects in education. *American Educational Research Journal, 20*, 359–373.

Walters, J., & Stone, V. (1971). Television and family communication. *Journal of Broadcasting, 15*, 409–414.

Watkins, B., Huston-Stein, A., & Wright, J. (1981). Effects of planned television programming. In E. Palmer & A. Dorr, *Children and the faces of television: Teaching, violence, selling* (pp. 49–69). New York: Academic Press.

Watt, J., & Welch, A. (1983). Effects of static and dynamic complexity on children's attention and recall of televised instruction. In J. Bryant & D.R. Anderson (Eds.), *Children's understanding of television: Research on attention and comprehension* (pp. 69–102). New York: Academic Press.

Wertham, R. (1954). *Seduction of the innocent*. New York: Kennikat Press.

What TV does to kids. (1977, February 21). *Newsweek*, pp. 63–70.

Whitehead, F., Capey, A.C., Maddren, W., & Wellings, A. (1977). *Children and their books*. London: Macmillan Education.

Why children's TV turns off so many parents. (1985, February 18). *U.S. News and World Report*, p. 65.

Williams, P.A., Haertel, E.H. Haertel, G.D., & Walberg, H.J. (1982). The impact of leisure-time television on school learning: A research synthesis. *American Educational Research Journal, 19*, 19–50.

Williams, T.M. (1986). Background and overview. In T.M. Williams (Ed.), *The impact of television* (pp. 1–36). Orlando, FL: Academic Press.

Winn, M. (1977). *The plug-in drug*. New York: Viking Press.

Witty, P. (1966). Studies of mass media, 1949-1965. *Science Education, 50*, 119–126.

Witty, P. (1967). Children of the television era. *Elementary English, 44*, 528–535.

WNET, Thirteen Project. (1980). *Critical television viewing*. New York: Cambridge Publishers.

Wolf, R. (1964). *The identification and measurement of environmental process variables related to intelligence*. Unpublished doctoral dissertation, University of Chicago, Chicago, IL.

Zuckerman, D.M., Singer, D.G., & Singer, J.L. (1980). Television viewing, children's reading, and related classroom behavior. *Journal of Communication, 30*, 166–174.

Author Index

219

Subject Index